The 8 Biggest Mistakes People Make With Their Finances Before and After Retirement

Terence L. Reed, CFP

Dearborn™
Trade Publishing
A **Kaplan Professional** Company

This publication is designed to provide accurate and authoritative information in regard to the subject matter covered. It is sold with the understanding that the publisher is not engaged in rendering legal, accounting, or other professional service. If legal advice or other expert assistance is required, the services of a competent professional should be sought.

Vice President and Publisher: Cynthia A. Zigmund
Editorial Director: Donald J. Hull
Senior Project Editor: Trey Thoelcke
Interior Design: Lucy Jenkins
Cover Design: DePinto Studios
Typesetting: Elizabeth Pitts

Library of Congress Cataloging-in-Publication Data

Reed, Terence L.
  The 8 biggest mistakes people make with their finances before and after retirement / Terence L. Reed.
      p.   cm.
   Includes index.
   ISBN 0-7931-4906-1 (7.25 × 9 pbk)
   1. Retirement income—United States—Planning. 2. Finance, Personal—United States. 3. Investments.   I. Title: Eight biggest mistakes people make with their finances before and after retirement. II. Title.
   HG179 .R365   2001
332.024′01—dc21

                                        2001003647

Dearborn Trade books are available at special quantity discounts to use for sales promotions, employee premiums, or educational purposes. Please call our special sales department to order, or for more information, at 800-621-9621, ext. 4364, or write to Dearborn Financial Publishing, 155 North Wacker Drive, Chicago, IL 60606-1719.

Contents

Foreword vii

Preface ix

Acknowledgments xi

1. Not Investing for the Long Term 1

Past Investment Advice 3
What to Use for Your Fixed Investments 5
The Dividend-and-Interest Method 9
Systematic Withdrawal 11
Failure to Accumulate 14
Stretching Her Resources 15

2. Taking on Financial Risk 21

Financial Risk 21
Diversification Matters 22
Put It in Writing Please 23
Political Risk 23
Look at Risk before You Invest 23
Key Points on Financial Risk 29
Key Points on Market Risk 30
Key Points on Inflation Risk 30
Key Points on Interest Rate Risk 31

3. Failure to Do Dignity Planning 33

Our Sense of Self 33
Dignity Planning 34
Your Medical Decisions 35
Your Financial Affairs 37
Durable Power of Attorney 44
Disability Insurance 53
Plan for the Best, Prepare for the Worst 53
Important Policy Benefits 54

4. Not Having Good Long-Term Care Coverage 55

A Case in Point: Without Resources 55
If Medicare Doesn't Pay, Who Does? 57
Long-Term Care Insurance 59
Indemnity Plans 61
Don't Overinsure 62
Would You Like Your Policy Tax Qualified or Nonqualified? 64
Who Should Consider Purchasing Long-Term Care Insurance or Home Care Coverage? 66
Another Way to Reduce Premium Costs 73
How to Check on the Financial Status of an Insurance Company 74

5. Not Planning Properly for the Transfer of Your Estate 75

Put It in Writing 75
A Matter of Will 77
Loss of Some Tax Advantages 83
Typically Married Couples 84
Gift to Minors 85
Using Living Trusts 86
A Brief History of Certain Tax Laws 91
How Much Is a Tax Credit Worth? 93
Key Points to Remember about the Federal Estate Tax 95
A Case in Point: Harry and Sharon Make a Mistake 96
How to Preserve Your Unified Credit Amount 98
Other Major Mistakes People Make 100
Skipping Generations 101
Gifting Assets at the Wrong Time 102
Owning Life Insurance in Your Own Name 103
Other Irrevocable Trusts That Can Dramatically Reduce Taxes or Replace Wealth 106
Charitable Remainder Trusts 107
Using the Wrong Beneficiary on Your IRA 109
Common Disasters and IRA Plans 110

Naming Children as Beneficiaries 111
Seven Key Points to Keep in Mind 115

6. Paying Too Much in Taxes 117

Tax Awareness 118
The Power of Deferring Capital Gains 122
Mutual Funds—The Hidden Tax 125
Tax-Free Investments 127
Tax-Deferred Annuities 131
Taxation of Social Security Benefits 135
What Is So Wrong with Congress Taxing Our Social Security Benefits? 136
Eight Major Tax Traps That You Should Be Aware Of 138

7. Using the Wrong Investment Strategies 147

Accumulation versus Investment 147
Taking the Next Step 148
An Investment Is 148
Mutual Funds 148
Unit Investment Trusts 157
Individual Stocks 164
Individual Bonds 169
Variable Annuities 173
Rules for Being a Successful Investor 182
Other Books to Assist You in Becoming a Better Investor 195

8. Having the Wrong Type of Life Insurance 197

There Are Many Choices 199
Financial Leverage 201
Newer Types of Coverage 203
The Benefits of Having a Tax-Free Spigot 204
The Purpose of Life Insurance 206
How to Pay Estate Taxes Economically 207
Collecting before Your Time 210
Viatical Settlements 211
Insurance Company Rating Systems 212

Glossary 215

Index 221

Foreword

Money and its accumulation is a fascinating and important subject, yet it remains confusing to many retirees. This stems from the fact that there are too many sources of financial information, each with its own agenda. In fact, successful people share two important personality traits: They are accumulators and they are investors. Seldom are people good at doing both of these jobs. It simply requires a different mindset to do each.

Terence's book should help every retiree do much better at both of these tasks. He has included strategies and techniques used by financial professionals, yet Terence has conveyed these thoughts in a manner that can be utilized by the average retiree.

Over the years, Terence has taught and lectured on various financial topics. He has consistently brought up the important issues that retirees are actually facing, and given workable solutions. For years on his radio show, Terence has offered practical and realistic solutions for retirees faced with real financial problems. This book is the result of Terence having listened to his audience and actual clients. This book should serve as a valuable road map toward being a better investor and for giving your family more security.

The information that follows in this book, *The 8 Biggest Mistakes People Make with Their Finances Before and After Retirement,* will clearly communicate the primary mistakes people are making in their retirement planning. Use this book both as an information source and as a guide to financial situations as they arise. You will find a multitude of tips and suggestions. There is no question that you will benefit from reading this book.

Richard W. Paul, CFP, RFC, CEP

Preface

Most of us only retire once. Wouldn't it be nice to be able to practice this event before we actually have to do it? Over the past 20 years, I've assisted hundreds of clients through the retirement process and, more importantly, I have allowed them to stay retired with less stress, less anxiety, and with the knowledge that they can focus on the important issues such as their health, family, and, perhaps, travel. In this book, important strategies, tactics, and information are given that you can access in a timely fashion.

I encourage you to use this book both as a knowledge builder and as a valuable resource tool to be used over time. Read over the information casually to note the areas you may be weak in and then go back to do a more detailed study. Keep in mind that this book was designed to be used. Don't hesitate to mark various pages that you feel require the urgent attention of either yourself or a loved one!

Consider using this book as a bridge between yourself and the financial professionals in your life. If you find that your personal financial plan does not include the strategies written about in this book, find out why not. Listen and interact intelligently with your advisors. Keep in mind that tax laws are constantly changing. The tax and estate rules illustrated in this book are current as of May 15, 2001. Many new changes are proposed and may be phased in over the next ten years. This makes it imperative that you seek out a competent tax advisor before implementing any of the strategies discussed in this book.

After reading this book, many people will realize they have some major potholes on their road to retirement. This book can serve as a wake up call to help you greatly improve your financial picture. Still other readers will find this book a valuable resource for confirming if they are on the right track or if their advisors have given them the full attention they deserve. Remember, it's never too late to apply good financial advice! Above all, remember this is your life. Make it as secure, enjoyable, and filled with as much bliss as God intended!

Acknowledgments

First and foremost, I would like to give special thanks to my parents Howard and Edith Reed for teaching me the meaning of hard work and prudent money management. They also gave me complete independence at a very early age and allowed me to make mistakes when the consequences were low. They spoke up only when a course correction was necessary. Their philosophy of creating an independent thinker and, therefore, an independent person was priceless. The foundation of such an upbringing has served me well as an investment counselor and as an independent financial consultant over these past 20 years.

Warmest sincere appreciation goes to Captain Bud Gottesman and his first mate Elaine Gottesman for the wonderful friendship and encouragement they have shown over the years. They have shown me how the good life can be achieved, while maintaining and upholding all the values we hold dear as a society. They have helped countless people, while maintaining a humble profile. Listed in the dictionary under *good* and *considerate* you will find their names.

My sincere thanks to Joseph M. Maria, president of Wall Colmonoy Corporation, for the consistency he has shown as a business leader and as a person. Much can be learned by observing how people should be treated and giving them room to grow. I can only guess how many people he has enabled to grow and reach their full potential as ethical and successful businesspeople.

Thanks to the countless friends I have gathered over the years including Captain Larry Wynne, attorney Don Tuttle, attorney John S. Davidson, and attorney William Drollinger. For technical and spiritual support my warmest and sincere thoughts go out to Doug Tessler and Simm Gottesman. Sincere thanks to my financial associates Sandra Park; Richard W. Paul, CFP; Mark Wojcik, CPA; Gregg Dolinski; Jeff Davis; and attorney Michael Marsalese.

Family members matter a lot and my warmest thanks go to my family for being always available for consultation and support. Special thanks go to Gary Reed and Jim Reed for the hours upon hours we have spent in discussions on world events. To all the women in my family who bring sunshine into my life and keep things interesting, warmest thoughts and fondest wishes go out to Margaret Fernandez, Daina Reed, Dakota Fernandez, and Veronica Reed.

And finally, special thanks are given to Nancy Durand, Michael Park, and Nathan Pride for their combined assistance in bringing this book to life.

Not Investing for the Long Term

According to a recent study, the average 60-year-old has a 25 percent chance of living 30 or more years. In 1940, statistics showed only 7 percent of the population reaching age 90. With the great strides being made in biotechnology, drug therapy, and immunizations against dreaded ailments such as flu and pneumonia, today's retirees can be expected to live even longer. This trend is expected to continue and even grow in the future.

Many insurance actuaries who track life expectancy believe that the average newborn in a developed country should reach an age of 93! That is the forecasted average, which means some will live less and others, of course, will live longer! If infant mortality were taken out of the equation, life expectancy would be even greater. The ironic fact of life is that the longer you live, the longer you will continue to live. The Internal Revenue Service has a table for mortality in Publication 590. This table is used to calculate the approximate life expectancy of an individual. Their mortality table illustrates this point as shown in Figures 1.1 and 1.2.

As you can see, at age 60 life expectancy is 24.2 years. That being the case, you would suppose that 10 years later, life expectancy would have dropped to 14.2 years (24.2 − 10 = 14.2 years).

However, in 10 years, Publication 590 shows life expectancy to be 16.2 years. That, of course, is 2 years longer than originally forecasted. At age 80, based on the age 60 calculations, there would be 4.2 years remaining. However, when we look at IRS Publication 590 again, we discover that they expect an average 80-year-old to live another 9.5 years!

The reason, of course, is that by reaching an older age, you most likely have been doing something right. Reckless behavior, such as accidents or harmful life-

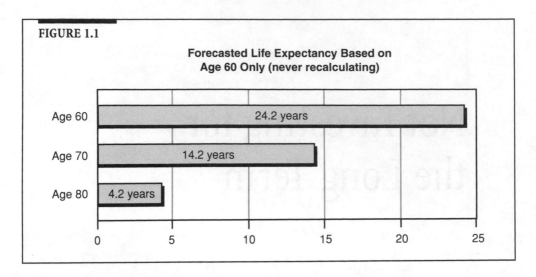

FIGURE 1.1

**Forecasted Life Expectancy Based on
Age 60 Only (never recalculating)**

style habits, will take many people before their time. Heavy drinking or habitual smoking will usually impact people by the time they hit their 50s and 60s. Those that avoid such bad habits, eat correctly, and exercise regularly may find themselves living far longer than anticipated. This confirms what most retirees already know—it pays to take care of yourself.

A recent article on life expectancy appearing in the University of California's *Berkeley's Wellness Newsletter* states that the United States appears to have the highest proportion of centenarians in the world. It's anticipated that the next census will confirm that the number of American 100-year-olds will have doubled during the 1990s from 37,000 to over 72,000 (more than 80 percent of them women). Conservative estimates target the number to double every decade, reaching over one million centenarians by 2050. Therefore, it seems prudent to not only hope for a long life, but also to financially plan for one!

While this extra time may allow for more leisure activity and community involvement, there is a major pitfall. Will your retirement income increase with inflation rates to provide enough income to live on? To view the effects of inflation firsthand, all you have to do is travel to the local movie house. Ticket prices and the cost of refreshments will make a believer out of you.

Thirty years ago, a first class postage stamp sold for 6¢. Today, that price has increased more than fivefold. Twenty dollars of groceries used to fill a few large bags and now barely fills a single bag. Almost every retiree in need of prescription medication has felt the sting of rising inflation. The items that we require the most (the necessities of life) have gone up tremendously in price. Figures 1.3 and 1.4 illustrate the rising price index and declining purchasing power of a dollar.

Those retirees who fail to plan for inflation will most certainly find themselves wanting later. Only the very wealthy or the very foolish can ignore the constant ero-

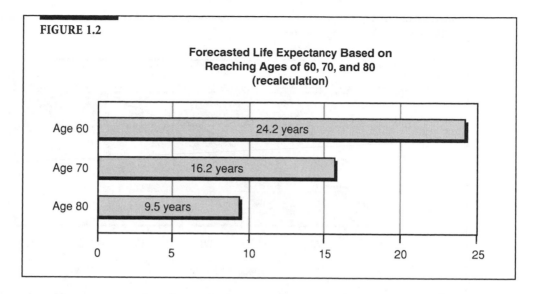

FIGURE 1.2

**Forecasted Life Expectancy Based on
Reaching Ages of 60, 70, and 80
(recalculation)**

sion power of inflation. Figure 1.5 details the effect of inflation on the dollar over the past 30 years.

Past Investment Advice

In the past, advice for those heading into retirement was extremely conservative. The recommendation was to get out of equities (stocks) and equity mutual funds and to purchase stable income-producing debt instruments (bonds) and certificates of deposit. While these debt instruments provide current income, they produce little, if any, growth of your original investment.

Many investors who followed this advice are finding it difficult to maintain their standard of living. Imagine yourself retired for 20, 30, maybe 40 years. Will fixed investments such as bonds and certificates of deposit allow you to keep up with inflation? Will you be able to maintain the lifestyle that you're accustomed to? Past methods of handling your retirement dollars simply won't keep up with expenses and future needs. As you well know, the cost of replacing your roof or furnace will only increase in the years to come.

Many seniors are also feeling the impact of the lower interest rates that fixed investments are providing. They find themselves cutting back on major expenses such as vacations and automobile purchases. Some may find themselves cutting back on gifts to grandchildren or, worse, their groceries.

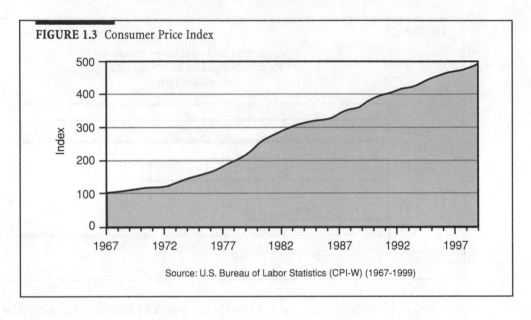

FIGURE 1.3 Consumer Price Index

Source: U.S. Bureau of Labor Statistics (CPI-W) (1967-1999)

Know Your Time Horizon

The lesson is clear: look at a longer time horizon for your investment dollars. Realize that you or your spouse may live many more years. Make sure there are adequate funds to support you. Chapter 6 reveals why you want to avoid taxes and allow your funds to grow as quickly as possible in tax-favored vehicles.

An old rule of thumb was to take your current age and make that the percentage amount of your portfolio invested in fixed investments. Thus, a 60-year-old would place 60 percent of his portfolio into bonds or money market instruments and keep the remaining 40 percent in equities. As this person grew older, he would constantly shift more of his investment dollars toward fixed investments. When reaching age 70, he would have 70 percent invested into fixed vehicles and 30 percent in equities.

This rule served generations well in past years as inflation rates were generally lower. However, with longer lives and constant inflation, this may not serve future needs. Consider taking your current age minus 20 and using that portion for fixed investments. For example, an 80-year-old retiree would take her age minus 20 and place that number (60) as a percentage into a fixed portfolio with the 40 percent balance placed in equities. This will give slightly more exposure to equities, which historically work better as a hedge against inflation. Figures 1.6 and 1.7 illustrate the differences between this new rule and the old standard.

Old Rule: Your age equals the amount you place into fixed investments. An 80-year-old would have 80 percent invested in fixed investments (bonds) with the remaining 20 percent invested into equities. This rule is unsuitable for today's seniors.

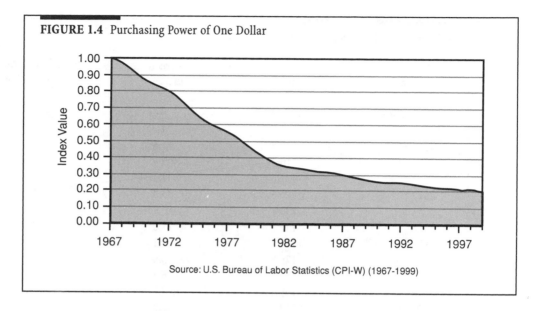

FIGURE 1.4 Purchasing Power of One Dollar

Index Value

Source: U.S. Bureau of Labor Statistics (CPI-W) (1967-1999)

New Rule: Your age minus 20 equals the amount you place into fixed investments. An 80-year-old would subtract 20 from his age, thereby investing 60 percent into fixed investments, with a larger amount, 40 percent, going toward equity.

The additional percentage of investments allocated toward equities should be invested in more conservative equity positions. These include large dividend-yielding stocks, value stocks, utility stocks, or good equity income mutual funds. Remember, during an underperforming stock market, your dividends can provide incoming revenue. Many good dividend-paying stocks are yielding 3 percent or higher.

Past generations could afford to be more conservative in their investment approach because their life expectancy was not as long and inflation was not such a constant threat. Our monetary system used to be backed by precious metals, such as silver and gold. Today, the full faith and credit of the U.S. government and its ability to tax its citizens, is the only backing we have for our money. Unfortunately, when the government pays off debts or incurs additional expenses, it simply prints new money. This will invariably cause more inflation.

What to Use for Your Fixed Investments

When investment professionals talk of fixed investments, they generally are talking about bonds, notes, and bills. These are known as debt instruments. These fixed investments generally denote that you are not an equity owner of any issuer but, rather, lending these issuers funds. You are also in a lending position when you place your money into a money market fund or certificate of deposit. An annuity cer-

FIGURE 1.5 The Effect of Inflation on the Dollar

Year	Index	Percent Increase	Purchasing Power of the Dollar
1967 (Base)	100.0	—	$1.00
1068	104.2	4.2	.96
1068	109.8	5.4	.91
1970	116,3	5.9	.86
1971	121.3	4.3	.82
1972	125.3	33.3	.80
1973	133.1	6.2	.75
1974	147.7	11.0	.68
1975	161.2	9.1	.62
1976	170.5	5.8	.59
1977	181.5	6.5	.55
1978	195.4	7.7	.51
1979	217.4	11.3	.46
1980	246.8	13.5	.41
1981	272.4	10.4	.37
1982	290.6	6.7	.34
1983	301.5	3.8	.33
1984	312.2	3.5	.32
1985	323.4	3.6	.31
1986	325.7	0.7	.31
1987	340.2	4.4	.29
1988	357.9	5.2	.28
1989	371.1	3.7	.27
1990	399.4	7.6	.25
1991	404.7	1.3	.25
1992	416.3	2.9	.24
1993	423.1	1.6	.24
1994	438.6	3.7	.23
1995	449.5	2.5	.22
1996	464.3	3.3	.22
1997	471.3	1.5	.21
1998	478.6	1.6	.21
1999	491.8	2.8	.20
2000	503.1	2.2	.19
2001	514.0	2.1	.19

Source: U.S. Bureau of Labor Statistics. Inflation as measured by the CPI.

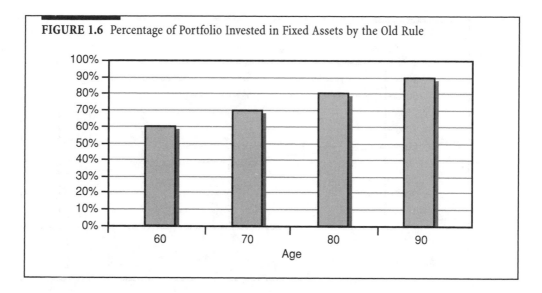

FIGURE 1.6 Percentage of Portfolio Invested in Fixed Assets by the Old Rule

tificate or contract with an insurance company is also generally considered a fixed investment.

While people talk about all the risks associated with equity investments, don't underestimate the ability to lose money in fixed investments. Many people fail to realize that you could be taking on enormous financial risk with fixed investments. Financial risk is the ability to lose some or all of your money.

When investing in fixed investments, you are relying on the character and ability of that issuer to pay you back. That is why countless senior citizens invest only with banks that offer Federal Deposit Insurance or with insurance companies that are governed by the legal reserve system.

This is why you must be careful when investing in corporate bonds, municipal bonds, mortgage notes, or other debt instruments. In fact, when investing in bonds the average investors would be better served by dealing with only government securities, thereby dramatically reducing their exposure to risk.

Investing with Your Government

For the fixed income portion of your portfolio, you may want to consider investing directly with the U.S. Government. The Department of Treasury offers Treasury bills for short-term savers as well as long-term instruments known as notes and bonds. You can purchase these directly through the government or through the services of a broker. Watch out for government agency offerings such as Federal Home Loan Mortgage Corporation (FHLMC, aka Freddie Mac) and others, as they may not carry quite the same safety of direct government offerings.

Because all bond investors face the risk of inflation eroding the buying power of their fixed instruments, you may wish to consider newer Treasury inflation-pro-

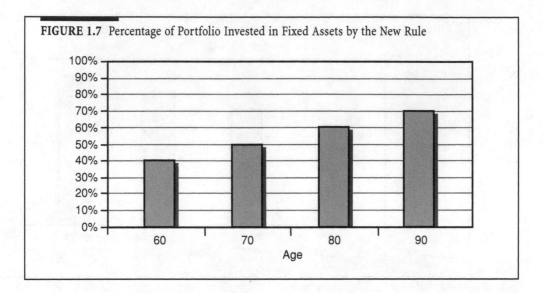

FIGURE 1.7 Percentage of Portfolio Invested in Fixed Assets by the New Rule

tection securities. These securities are issued by the United States Treasury in book entry form and are sold in minimum amounts of $1,000. They are issued at a fixed interest rate that is paid twice a year. Adjusting the principal amount of the securities each year based on changes in the inflation rate provides inflation protection.

How Inflation-Protection Bonds Work

An investor has a newly issued Treasury inflation-protection bond of $1,000. It is earning 4 percent in annual interest and the previous six months saw inflation rise by 1 percent. The principal bond amount of $1,000 would also increase by 1 percent, giving a value of $1,010. Not only has the principal increased, but the interest payable of 4 percent is based on the newer amount of $1,010. This would be very desirable if you were faced with rapid inflation such as that which occurred in the 1970s and early 1980s.

These inflation-protection bonds will probably serve better than traditional government securities in the years to come. A knowledgeable broker who deals primarily with bonds could prove helpful or contact the United States Treasury directly at 202-622-2000 or <www.ustreas.gov>.

When dealing with any broker or financial advisor, a word of caution is in order. Always obtain a second or third opinion. This is important for two major reasons. First, speaking with several advisors will bring your knowledge level up and allow you to make a better informed decision. Second, there is nothing like one professional critiquing another. Each may point out flaws or inadequate information provided by the other. Many times, other professionals will point out risk factors or expenses not considered before. Inadequate advice will be pointed out and may reveal inexperienced practitioners.

Past Methods

Why do so many investors stick with fixed investments? The answer is twofold. Investors feel comfortable with what they know. Also, the investment institutions giving the advice often benefit from fixed investments. A common misconception is that you need to invest mostly in income-producing investments.

The choices you have with income-producing assets are limited. Some common ones are bonds, notes, bills, certificates of deposit, and money market funds. Investing in these instruments may be momentarily comfortable. However, they may hurt you in the long run as they serve as poor inflation hedges.

The Dividend-and-Interest Method

Many retirees were brought up with the belief that they could only receive interest or dividends from their investments. Therefore, if they had a $100,000 certificate of deposit at the bank that was paying 5 percent per year, that was the income they would use for income expenses. Likewise, if they held a bond or stock that was paying 6 percent per year, they would live off of that income. This was known as the dividend-and-interest method.

For years, bankers, trust companies, and so-called prudent investors followed this method to calculate how much they would have to live off. This method works fine if you truly are living off a large fortune. It accomplishes two things very well. First, you know what you have coming in each year. And second, this method preserves your original principal amount.

During times of our country's history when our money was backed by gold or silver reserves, this method was probably prudent. Now, however, we are experiencing a constant stream of inflation. This requires a shift in our thinking. Why be limited to just the interest or dividends from an investment?

Using the dividend-and-interest method will usually limit you to just receiving moderate dividends and interest from your bonds and certificates of deposit. Taking more than this would mean invading your principal! This could prove disastrous to your financial well-being.

There Is a Newer Method

Enter a newer method of living off of your funds, the systematic withdrawal method. This method is meant to be used with stocks or stock funds only. This method may provide the needed additional income that so many retirees are seeking.

Because stocks (equities) have a propensity to rise with inflation, you can use them not only as a long-term inflation hedge, but also to receive more income during your retirement years. The systematic withdrawal method works really well with almost any type of equity mutual fund. This method can also be used for a stock-only portfolio.

For example, let's use a hypothetical portfolio of $10,000 that has been invested in a diversified stock mutual fund. Keep in mind that stocks have probably provided some of the best returns in the long term and have especially done well in keeping up with inflation over the years. You instruct your mutual fund company that you require 6 percent withdrawal per year.

Furthermore, you can request to have this 6 percent sent to you in equal monthly amounts that will total 6 percent per year. This income will flow to you as long as there are funds in your account. Now the average stock mutual fund will grow more than 6 percent over the years, so you will find yourself not only receiving the 6 percent each year but also experiencing excellent portfolio growth.

The chart in Figure 1.8 illustrates how stocks have performed over the long term compared to fixed investments such as bonds and Treasury bills. Remember that this chart uses average returns on stocks. It is based on a hypothetical portfolio of $10,000 that has been invested in a diversified stock mutual fund.

Why Not Just Use Dividends?

Because the average dividend yield on most stocks has fallen to an all-time low of around 2 percent, you would find yourself wanting if dividends were your sole source of income. The reason stock dividends currently are so low is that most companies and shareholders believe that dividends are a poor use of a corporation's earnings. Shareholders who usually are trying to accumulate wealth would rather have companies either reinvest the dividends into strengthening product lines or expansion.

In other words, why distribute dividends when the company could make more money with these funds? Add to this the negative tax aspects of corporate dividends (double taxation), and you can see why the trend favors companies not paying dividends.

Also, if you attempt to just invest in higher-yielding stocks, you may equal 6 percent per year in income that the systematic withdrawal method traditionally provides you, but overall, find very little growth in your portfolio. The reason for this is

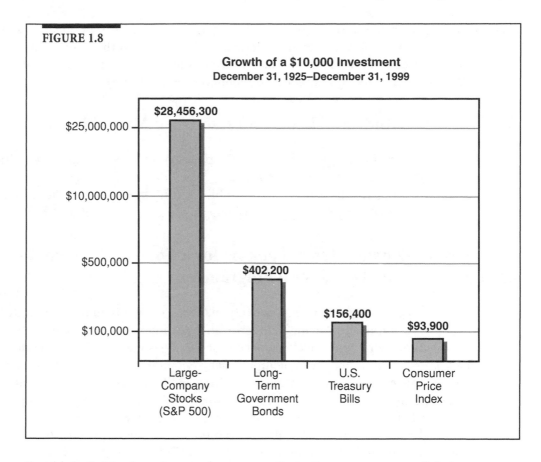

FIGURE 1.8

Growth of a $10,000 Investment
December 31, 1925–December 31, 1999

that high dividend-paying stocks are usually in the mature stage of their corporate life cycle or they are companies that stress income over growth.

Systematic Withdrawal

The systematic withdrawal method is a creative concept that could improve your standard of living now, while serving your heirs later. This concept states that you do not strictly look at what income or dividend yield an investment could provide. What you look at is the overall total return of that investment over prolonged time periods. This total return takes into account the income as well as the underlying growth of the investment. Regardless of market performance, you could generally take an estimated annual withdrawal of 6 to 7 percent.

This means that you will withdraw this amount each year based on the belief that the remaining assets will grow consistently in future years. It stands to reason that you should only use the systematic withdrawal method with large-company stocks and diversified mutual funds. Your accounts, of course, will fluctuate with the equity markets. Remember that the market has more up than down years. This method is extremely powerful. The following is an example of the systematic withdrawal method. Always obtain several opinions before proceeding.

A Systematic Withdrawal Using an Established Mutual Fund

The chart in Figure 1.9 illustrates the power of using a systematic withdrawal program within a stock mutual fund. Your results will vary and no guarantees can be made that your results will be as favorable. Taking systematic withdrawals that exceed 9 percent per year could prove damaging to your financial well-being.

Some Tips to Consider When Looking for a Good Mutual Fund to Use for Systematic Withdrawal Programs

To begin with, selecting an actively managed mutual fund over an index fund is highly recommended. In the short term, an index fund may have higher return figures, but long term, an actively managed fund that has managers at the helm would be your best bet. Economic conditions change quickly and having a fund manager who can take advantage of changing market conditions makes the most sense. An actively managed fund could shift into smaller company stocks or vary its percentage invested in various segments of the markets. Look for an experienced fund manager and management group with a proven fund track record. A fund that has seen down markets and survived those tough times could go a long way in keeping you on track to your financial goals.

Certain funds are managed by a single manager or by several portfolio managers. When investing with a single fund manager, check often to make sure that the manager that built the track record is still involved.

An example of this type of fund is the Davis New York Venture fund. The Davis family is very much involved in this fund. The sons manage the portfolio day to day with the father who built the majority of the track record in the background. They and their own employees invest side by side with you. Their own money is invested in their funds so you can rest easier knowing that they are watching the portfolio very closely. In other words, they eat their own cooking!

Likewise, the American Funds are good choices because several portfolio managers actively manage them. This method is called the multiple manager approach. They have an average of at least five investment managers per fund. They typically have very experienced managers with very low turnover compared to the typical mutual fund. The multiple manager approach can spare you the dilemma of what to do if a star performing manager were to leave.

FIGURE 1.9 Systematic Withdrawal over the Past 30 Years

Based on the Performance of an Actual Fund

Date	Initial Investment	Offering Price	Sales Charge Included	Shares Purchased	Net Asset Value per Share	Initial Net Asset Value
1/1/1970	$100,000	$6.845	3.50%	14,609.204	$6.605	$96,494

Annual Withdrawals of $6,000 (6.0% Annually) Beginning 12/15/70
Dividends and Capital Gains Reinvested

	AMOUNTS WITHDRAWN					VALUE OF REMAINING SHARES			
Date	From Income Dividends	From Principal	Annual Total	Cumulative Total	Annual Capital Gain Distribution	Remaining Original Shares	Capital Gain Shares	Total Value	Shares Held
12/31/1970	$ 2,978	$ 3,022	$ 6,000	$ 6,000	$ 4,237	$ 88,531	$ 4,285	$ 92,815	$14,814.871
12/31/1971	2,920	3,080	6,000	12,000	1,966	95,603	6,782	102,385	14,636.891
12/31/1972	2,882	3,118	6,000	18,000	3,506	101,586	10,996	112,582	14,707.002
12/31/1973	3,050	2,950	6,000	24,000	2,479	76,235	11,176	87,411	14,580.639
12/31/1974	4,455	1,545	6,000	30,000	0	56,995	8,632	65,587	14,165.612
12/31/1975	3,764	2,236	6,000	36,000	473	70,951	11,577	82,528	13,858.560
12/31/1976	3,320	2,680	6,000	42,000	1,541	84,971	15,861	100,831	13,727.895
12/31/1977	3,408	2,592	6,000	48,000	1,973	75,531	16,596	92,126	13,618.103
12/31/1978	3,590	2,410	6,000	54,000	0	81,242	18,374	99,616	13,299.884
12/31/1979	4,230	1,770	6,000	60,000	1,197	90,559	22,142	112,741	13,263.636
12/31/1980	5,243	757	6,000	66,000	2,653	102,360	28,033	130,393	13,512.226
12/31/1981	6,349	- 349	6,000	72,000	8,918	91,840	33,699	125,538	14,529.882
12/31/1982	7,639	- 1,639	6,000	78,000	7,991	111,425	50,265	161,690	15,867.544
12/31/1983	7,408	- 1,408	6,000	84,000	7,140	124,569	63,624	188,193	16,713.404

	AMOUNTS WITHDRAWN					VALUE OF REMAINING SHARES			
Date	From Income Dividends	From Principal	Annual Total	Cumulative Total	Annual Capital Gain Distribution	Remaining Original Shares	Capital Gain Shares	Total Value	Shares Held
12/31/1984	$ 7,823	-$ 1,823	$ 6,000	$ 90,000	$ 8,524	$123,809	$ 70,741	$194,550	$17,686.344
12/31/1985	8,264	- 2,264	6,000	96,000	8,666	155,441	97,991	253,432	18,758.868
12/31/1986	9,406	- 3,406	6,000	102,000	48,749	154,951	147,632	302,584	22,940.483
12/31/1987	12,106	- 6,106	6,000	108,000	17,596	152,967	159,957	312,925	24,815.595
12/31/1988	14,049	- 8,049	6,000	14,000	19,056	165,187	183,369	348,556	26,936.328
12/31/1989	16,179	- 10,179	6,000	120,000	23,472	205,036	239,936	444,972	29,197.614
12/31/1990	17,488	- 11,488	6,000	126,000	6,563	206,705	235,236	441,941	30,436.683
12/31/1991	13,565	- 7,565	6,000	132,000	11,694	257,089	295,737	552,827	31,626.232
12/31/1992	14,970	- 8,970	6,000	138,000	10,208	272,500	312,888	585,387	32,721.485
12/31/1993	15,509	- 9,509	6,000	144,000	24,787	294,943	352,355	647,298	34,577.905
12/31/1994	16,708	- 10,708	6,000	150,000	20,919	288,708	353,558	642,265	36,347.789
12/31/1995	18,351	- 12,351	6,000	156,000	33,685	366,707	466,234	832,942	38,544.264

FIGURE 1.9 Systematic Withdrawal over the Past 30 Years (Continued)

| | AMOUNTS WITHDRAWN | | | | VALUE OF REMAINING SHARES | | | | |
Date	From Income Dividends	From Principal	Annual Total	Cumulative Total	Annual Capital Gain Distribution	Remaining Original Shares	Capital Gain Shares	Total Value	Shares Held
12/31/1996	$ 19,398	-$ 13,398	$ 6,000	$162,000	$ 40,084	$425,578	$ 562,451	$ 988,029	$40,777.105
12/31/1997	20,502	- 14,502	6,000	168,000	106,891	511,517	764,938	1,276,455	45,184.258
12/31/1998	23,359	- 17,359	6,000	174,000	135,116	581,310	981,590	1,562,900	50,302.536
12/31/1999	25,991	- 19,991	6,000	180,000	155,750	627,162	1,188,197	1,815,359	55,926.033
Totals	314,903	- 134,903	$180,000	180,000	715,833	627,162	1,188,197	1,815,359	55,926.033

Average Annual Total Return for This Illustration: 12.49% (Annual Compounding)

Average Annual Total Returns for Periods Ending 12/31/99	1-Year	5-Year	10-Year
After Maximum 5.75% Sales Charge:	9.84%	22.27%	15.33%

Summary of the Systematic Withdrawal Plan

- This investor started with a deposit of $100,000.
- This investor received $6,000 per year for living expenses.
- The account fluctuated in value over the years.
- At the end of 30 years, the account grew to over $1,815,000.
- This account provided income and an inflation hedge.

This information is for example purposes only and no guarantees are made.

This approach also provides prudence in your financial affairs. It would be highly unlikely that multiple fund managers would commit all their funds to just one strategy. Add to this the American Funds' long track record and low fees and you will see why they would probably be a good choice for use with systematic withdrawal programs.

Other fund families that offer a margin of safety are the Fidelity Funds and the American Century Funds. Both of these fund groups look at master lists of stocks that have been thoroughly analyzed by their research staffs and computers. This should reduce risk to favor stronger and more consistent returns.

Failure to Accumulate

What happens if you have failed to accumulate a significant enough portfolio to draw upon during your retirement? If you are a homeowner, you may need to seriously check out a reverse mortgage. This is when you use your home as a source of retirement funds. The equity value of your home can serve as collateral for financial institutions, providing you with monthly income checks or a lump sum check.

Stretching Her Resources

Here's how one client was able to use a reverse mortgage to her advantage. After her husband Henry passed away, Agnes found herself alone in a large house that was paid off. She had very little savings as her husband's final medical expenses brought them to the brink of financial ruin. In other words, she was house rich and cash poor. When she consulted with a real estate agent, she found her house to be worth well over $250,000. The only problem was that she would have to sell her home to access those funds or take out a mortgage that would require monthly payments.

Many retirees find themselves in this situation. Their house is paid for and they are on a fixed income that just doesn't seem to be enough to maintain a viable standard of living.

What Is a Reverse Mortgage?

Under a traditional home mortgage, a borrower receives funds from a bank to purchase a home. Monthly payments of principal and interest are made to the lending institution each month. This payment represents mortgage debt and must be paid back in a timely fashion.

A reverse mortgage, as the name implies, is quite different. Instead of paying the bank or lending institution, they pay you. They take into account the value of your home and use that information to calculate how much they can provide to you in funds. You are, in essence, using your home as a private bank account to withdraw funds. You are not required to make monthly payments.

A reverse mortgage allows you to draw funds from your home on a monthly basis or in one lump sum. The lender is generally only entitled to receive back the loan amount plus loan interest when you sell the home or upon your demise. Therefore, the loan does not have to be paid until either of these events occur. This allows you to remain in control of your home and retain most of the advantages of home ownership such as home appreciation and security. This financial arrangement is the preferred method for assessing your home's value if the need should arise. Typically, this area of the mortgage market is well regulated and offers many commercial lenders with various programs for the consumer.

Similar to a reverse mortgage is a transaction called a private annuity. This type of transaction allows a retiree to receive income for life in exchange for the lender receiving the house upon the retiree's demise. While the potential income payments may be greater, you are taking on the risk that you will only receive some payments, because after your demise the lender will receive your home's complete value. This is not a good deal for your heirs. Of course, if longevity runs in your family, this program may be of value. Usually, private individuals transact this arrangement.

A well-known case occurred in France when 47-year-old Andre-Francois Raffray, an attorney, offered 90-year-old Jeanne Calment $500 per month payments for life. In exchange, Raffray would receive her home upon her demise. Little did Raffray expect that Jeanne Calment would go on to become the longest living woman in history! Calment reached the age of 120 in 1996, the year that Raffray died at age 77. The attorney had paid out over $184,000 for the home that he would never occupy and it was estimated that he had paid over twice the home's appraised value. In addition, Raffray's estate was required to continue the payments to Jeanne Calment after he passed away!

Is This Too Good to Be True?

Many people fear that they will lose control of their home with a reverse mortgage. While it is true that you are attaching debt to your home, you will be listed as sole owner of your house. If you try to sell your home, a lien will appear on the title work showing that there is a mortgage note, which must be paid off in order to have a clear title. Clearing the title is required if you wish to sell your home. Simply put, if you wish to sell your home, you must pay back the amount borrowed with interest.

You, as the owner, are still responsible for the maintenance and repair of the home as well as being responsible for the payment of property taxes and insurance. Unlike a conventional mortgage, you will not have to pay any current mortgage payments for the use of the reverse mortgage funds. These loans are typically paid back when you sell your home, refinance, or pass on. The lender takes only what they are owed and the difference flows to you or your estate. Some companies request the loan amount back at the end of a certain time period. Make sure you shop around for a lender that meets your needs.

Most reverse mortgages require that you be at least 62 years of age and that the home be owner-occupied. You are allowed to have existing first mortgages on your property, but the lender will usually insist that these mortgages be paid off with proceeds from the reverse mortgage upon closing.

Due to lending laws, the borrower cannot ever owe more than what the home is actually worth. Most reverse mortgage lenders use only the property as collateral and therefore, cannot seek other funds from you for the repayment of such loans. Always check to make sure that the lender is an approved government mortgage lender who follows government guidelines on such loans.

It should be stressed that a reverse mortgage should not be your first option for retirement income, but if you have failed to accumulate enough funds, it could prove a godsend. Luckily, mortgage lenders are offering these programs much more actively. Today, the government issues guidelines that you should look into before moving ahead. Reverse mortgages also are a good source of funds for funding an investment account that, in turn, could be used to fund lifetime needs such as long-term care.

How Much Can You Borrow?

The amount of equity you can access via a reverse mortgage will depend on the program you select and other major factors such as:

- Your age (and that of your spouse, if applicable)
- The value of your home
- Current interest rates

Typically, for the average homeowner, the federally insured Home Equity Conversion Mortgage or Fannie Mae's Home Keeper mortgage provides the most access to your home's value.

You must also determine how you wish to receive your funds. Your options are many and vary depending on the program you select. It pays to shop around to obtain several informed opinions before proceeding. Select the program that matches your needs. For instance, do you need an immediate lump sum amount upon closing to deal with current expenses, debts, and other financial needs? If so, consider the Home Keeper program from Fannie Mae. If you simply wish to have access via a credit line to your home's equity value during the life of your loan, your best bet might be the Home Equity Conversion Mortgage, also known as HECM.

You are given the option of either a lump sum amount or a credit line amount, not both. No loan repayments are due until your home is either sold or you pass away. Because the reverse mortgage area is a specialty area, rates are constantly changing and this dramatically influences what loan amount you may be able to obtain. The chart in Figure 1.10 is an example of a reverse mortgage and shows estimated numbers only.

For more detailed information, you may wish to contact the National Center for Home Equity Conversion (NCHEC), a nonprofit organization, at their informative Web site <www.reverse.org> or write or phone them at:

NCHEC
360 N. Robert, Suite 403
St. Paul, MN 55101
651-222-6775

FIGURE 1.10 An Example of a Reverse Mortgage

**A Reverse Mortgage for Agnes, Age 70,
Based on a Home Appraised at $250,000**

	Home Equity Conversion Mortgage	Home Keeper Program
Lump Sum Available	$ 65,000	$101,000
Credit Line Available	65,000	101,000
Credit Line Growth	Increases each year (if not used initially)	Does not increase
Credit Line in 5 Years	$ 95,000	$101,000
Credit Line in 10 Years	142,000	101,000
Monthly Income Option	500	500

Maintaining Your Independence

Maintaining independence is a major reason people use reverse mortgages. These funds not only can be used to maintain your standard of living but also to fund long-term care insurance programs, which can go a long way in maintaining a customary lifestyle. Some people use reverse mortgages to pay off high-interest credit card debt, that may have accumulated over the years. In this instance, a reverse mortgage can give you a fresh start. A negative point associated with reverse mortgages is that you will leave less for your beneficiaries. Of course, you should not entertain the thought of a reverse mortgage if you do not need the funds.

How a Reverse Mortgage Works When Borrowing

Figure 1.11 illustrates the flow of funds in a reverse mortgage.

- You must own your own home.
- Generally, all owners must be at least age 62.
- Your home usually must be your principal residence.
- The federally insured Home Equity Conversion Mortgage generally allows your home to be a single-family property, a two- to four-unit building, or a federally approved condominium or planned unit development (PUD).
- You must own the home free and clear or be prepared to pay off any existing loan balances with proceeds from reverse mortgages.
- The borrower usually can receive funds via lump sum, a line of credit, or through periodic payments.

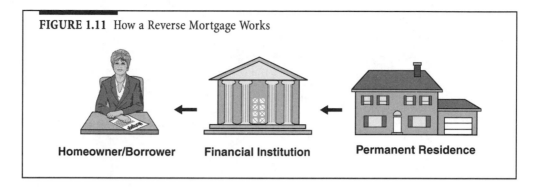

FIGURE 1.11 How a Reverse Mortgage Works

Homeowner/Borrower   Financial Institution   Permanent Residence

- The borrower remains owner of the home and must keep up on property taxes, repairs, and insurance.
- Your loan amount will vary depending on the lender and type of program selected.

How a Reverse Mortgage Handles Repayment

- No repayment is usually due until the last surviving borrower passes away, sells the home, or moves.
- No repayment is required as long as the home is the borrower's primary residence.
- If the loan ends due to the death of the last surviving borrower, the loan must be repaid before the home's title can be legally transferred to the borrower's heirs.
- The borrower can never owe more than the value of the home at the time the loan is repaid.
- Most traditional reverse mortgages are considered nonrecourse loans. As such, the lender does not have recourse to assets other than your home. This offers excellent protection for your other assets as well as for your heirs.

2

Taking on Financial Risk

Nothing is more disturbing to a financial professional than seeing people taking on risk factors so willingly. More money has been lost and lives diminished because of these risk factors than you might imagine. All of us know people who have suffered setbacks in their business ventures or personal investments. Sometimes it seems that people are gluttons for punishment or that they like to suffer. Of course, we know most don't. So what accounts for certain people losing constantly in one investment venture after another?

Why do some investors thrive and prosper while others languish? The answer, in most cases, can be found in certain risk factors. Most people have no problem seeing the good in most situations: the possibilities a new concept might generate, the potential of a new product, or the allure of a new company that is being offered to the public for the first time. Perhaps the vision of possibilities blinds investors to the downsides. These downsides are commonly known as *risk factors*. The greatest of all risk factors is financial risk.

Financial Risk

Financial risk is the ability to lose some or all of your principal. In short, you may get back less than you started with. This includes the possibility of not receiving any gains on your investment in addition to the loss of part or all of your original investment. Think of the quote attributed to Will Rogers, "I am not so concerned about the return *on* my money as I am of the return *of* my money."

Once Your Money Is Lost

Once your investment is lost, you lose not only that money but all of the future money those funds could have generated. Think of all the future wealth lost when you suffer a financial loss. Therefore, avoid this type of risk as much as possible. Financial risk comes in many forms. It can never be totally eliminated but, by using common sense and good business tactics, you can dramatically reduce it.

Think of lending money to a friend who has a reputation for never paying back what he borrows. Are you taking on financial risk? You'd better believe it! Now, if you choose only to lend money to friends who have the reputation of always paying their debts on time, you would reduce the risk of not being paid back. In a nutshell, this is a lot of what reducing financial risk is all about. Look to the integrity of the person or institution that you are dealing with. Are they reputable? Are they established? Do they have the ability to survive in their business venture or to pay you back?

Credit Risk

Some people refer to the aspects just mentioned as credit risk. To protect yourself from credit risk, check out the quality of the person or company with whom you are dealing and diversify among several companies or people with whom you are investing. Place your eggs in different baskets. Consider investing in different types of investments as well, in case the economy or business conditions negatively impact certain investments. Diversification can protect a major portion of your portfolio.

Diversification Matters

Imagine the investors who diversified only among several banks during the depression years of the 1930s. Many of these investors failed to fully diversify by investing in other business entities or vehicles such as bonds or insurance policies. Chances are, they lost nearly everything they had invested.

Pity the people that invested everything they owned in real estate partnerships during the early 1980s. Most of these programs were dramatically impacted by federal tax law changes. Many investors in these programs initially gained some tax benefits, only to lose nearly their entire original principal. Many investors were senior citizens unable to recover from these losses. These programs permanently damaged their finances. Protect yourself by diversifying not only among different institutions but also by diversifying into several different types of investments.

Put It in Writing Please

A surefire way to further reduce risk is by placing all agreements in writing. Make sure that the document is deemed legal and has been properly executed. The person or institution should be of such a nature that you could recover your investment. Are they financially strong? Are they located in a community, district, state, or country where you can easily bring action to recover your investments? Are they backed by any type of collateral? A loan backed by an asset is always preferable to one backed by a promise or good intentions.

Political Risk

Political risk is another form of financial risk. When you invest outside of the United States, there is a possibility that there may be a change in government. This is particularly true in underdeveloped countries. What about changes in their leaders or their laws? This is why informed investors usually invest in stable countries where political risk and, therefore, financial risk is reduced. Avoid investing in foreign countries with lesser known companies or individuals. Many investors can relate horror stories from trying to recover funds that are owed to them from international dealings. Often, the funds owed are due to misunderstandings or differences in the way various cultures do business. Sometimes, it is simply fraud on behalf of these foreigners. They know that it is nearly impossible for you to bring legal action, let alone recover any of your investment. Unfortunately, corruption is a common business practice in some of these countries.

Look at Risk before You Invest

Always look at an investment from the viewpoint of what could go wrong. Then, and only then, should you look at the potential profit streams that may be generated from the investment or business venture. Keep in mind: Every investment is a business venture as well.

A few examples of questions you should ask before investing:

- You are involved in a business transaction when purchasing a used car. You are offering cash for the vehicle. Do the sellers have a clear title to the car? Is the car in good running condition? Will a mechanic verify this? Will any and all warranties transfer with the car? Will you be able to resell the auto if necessary? Only after analyzing what can go wrong, should you look at positive factors such as price and condition.

- In setting up a bank account, you are offering your hard-earned dollars in exchange for the bank's promise to pay back your investment with interest. Are the accounts guaranteed by a legitimate source such as the FDIC?

- When investing in stocks, you are placing your dollars with a company with the premise that it will pursue a business plan and produce as much earnings on your contribution as possible. Hopefully, it will do well enough so that your stock share price will increase significantly in value. How well is the company managed? Does it have the required capital in place to carry out its business plans? Does it have too much debt? Also, does it have a proven product or service?

A few case histories may help to illustrate the different types of risk.

Case 1: An Example of Financial Risk

The teller at the bank referred Eleanor to a sharp looking professional lady sitting in a small glass cubicle. Eleanor assumed that this bank person was an assistant manager but found out after a brief conversation that this nice lady goes from bank branch to bank branch to help older people like Eleanor to make more interest on their money.

The lady explained how Eleanor could start receiving more income on her money almost immediately. There were mortgage investments that paid high monthly income checks. These mortgage investments were backed by the value of the real estate in the portfolio. The nice lady explained how all of these mortgage notes were based on real estate properties in her own home state. Eleanor was thrilled at the thought of receiving almost double the current income that she had been receiving from her passbook savings account. She promptly invested half of her funds into this investment.

Six months later, Eleanor received a phone call from the nice bank lady suggesting that Eleanor should add more to her accounts and she did. Eleanor enjoyed the higher monthly income checks for almost three years. Suddenly the amount of the checks started dropping.

When the story of a local real estate fraud hit the newspaper, her checks stopped completely. Court battles carried on month after month and Eleanor received very promising letters regarding the possible outcome of the litigation in addition to more subdued letters stringing her along. She was shocked to learn that the company involved was using the same real estate assets to back several different programs. In essence, borrowing on the same home twice.

Eleanor had placed several calls to the bank and was dismayed to learn that the bank backed none of these programs. They never had. The nice professional woman who had advised her to go into these investments had left the bank. Ironically, the lady had left for a more secure job selling real estate.

In the end, Eleanor had just a stack of papers to show for her lost investment. A lifetime of hard work and savings in exchange for a pound of useless papers. Her complete loss is a textbook example of financial risk—the loss of her money.

Case 2: An Example of Market Risk

Robert heard about everybody making money in the stock market. Friends at the local VFW hall were making a fortune (if stories can be believed). His wife told him that even members of her bowling league had doubled their money on a locally based computer company.

Robert, playing a hunch, drove down to his neighborhood discount brokerage firm and promptly invested $10,000 of his hard-earned money into this stock. He spent less time analyzing this stock than he spent comparing competing brands of paint at the hardware store the week before. That's right, he spent more time worrying about whether to purchase a well-known premium brand of paint versus a less expensive brand. A $15 decision took more of his time and energy than a $10,000 investment!

Robert received his first brokerage statement and was full of inner pride. His stock pick went up over 10 percent. At this rate, Robert felt he could be on his way toward a 120 percent annual return (10 percent a month, times 12). When his next statement arrived two months later, Robert started thinking that maybe he should make another purchase. After all, this investing business isn't so hard. His wife urged him to wait. "Let's see how this stock fares during the approaching holiday season," she said.

After receiving several more statements, Robert noticed that his stock shares had suddenly fallen by 50 percent. There was something stated in the annual report about a recession in Asia and some major accounting problems to account for this decline. Robert then noticed that his stock just sat at the depressed price. He checked with his friends and they made no mention of the stock. They talked about a new conquest, some medical company that he can't quite pronounce. Over a year passed and Robert had become increasingly uneasy. This investment business may seem easy, but it takes time and an ungodly amount of patience.

After the second year of holding the stock, Robert noticed the price rose. His most recent statement showed that the stock he had purchased was now close to the price that he originally paid for it. Robert quietly slipped into his car and drove back to the discount brokerage to place a sell order. After fees and some taxes that he owed, he figured to break even. The young clerk behind the counter mentioned a few stocks that can't miss. In fact, almost all of their customers were buying them. Robert remembered a sign from the day before when he was in the bank lobby. It was advertising a fixed account that was yielding over 6 percent. He silently chose that option as he headed out the door. The downturn that Robert experienced is what is known as *market risk*. He is not alone.

Case 3: How Market Risk Can Turn into Financial Risk

Jack and Alice, like many couples, have monies invested in individual stocks and mutual funds. They have been quite pleased with their performance over the past several years. In fact, they have been so pleased that they shifted monies that were invested into bonds and money market funds over to the better performing stocks and stock mutual funds. Unfortunately, they started shifting into these accounts toward the high point of the stock market's new heights. Suddenly, without warning, the stock market dipped down. Jack and Alice were not too nervous because this happened many times before.

This time, however, the market did not come roaring back. It decreased even further. Worst of all, after it decreased, it remained down. The economy weakened on this news and the market entered a protracted bear market. The price of stocks remained stagnant. Years passed and all that was reported was more bad news on corporate earnings while stocks continued to suffer.

Jack and Alice were left with a declining portfolio and very little income to live on. Due to rising inflation, Jack and Alice saw banks and credit unions offering high-yielding safe investments. These accounts were offering several times the income that their stock dividends were providing. Fearing that the stock market could go down further, they clenched their teeth and sold off a good portion of their portfolio at a loss to reinvest in higher-yielding and more reliable investments like certificates of deposit and bonds.

They took some huge losses, but at least they can sleep at night now, free of the gut-wrenching worry that they were experiencing. Ironically, the point at which they sold their stocks was the point in time when they turned market risk into financial risk. Market risk is the potential for your money to fluctuate up and down in value. If you are unable to tolerate these fluctuations, you may end up selling in these down markets and losing funds.

Never underestimate the impact of market risk as it often turns into financial risk when least expected. People are emotional creatures and they react typically in bad markets by shifting their concerns from greed (receiving higher returns) to security (protecting their assets).

Case 4: Inflation Risk Is Real Risk

Sally's husband had always done the investing and he had dabbled in all types of stocks. Many of these company's names were completely foreign to Sally. When her husband passed away suddenly, Sally immediately had the entire stock portfolio converted to money market instruments. She could understand these types of investments.

She knew which banks paid the highest interest rates and she was always on the lookout for an extra quarter of a percent in return. She was onto all the tricks and gimmicks banks played on their certificate of deposit holders. For instance, she knew that compound interest was much better than simple interest because it was important for your interest to earn interest as well. She also looked into how frequently the banks would credit her interest.

This strategy served her well during her sixties. She enjoyed nice vacations and always sent the grandchildren the nicest gifts. However, during her seventies, she noticed that her income wasn't keeping up with her living expenses. She had to cut back on luxury items. Suddenly, she realized that she might outlive her funds!

Not one to panic, she simply put off any major expenses. The carpet she had installed 20 years ago could last another 10 years. She realized that she really didn't need a new auto quite yet, even though her mechanic kept telling her to sell her vintage car because of the increasing rate of repair bills. She knew that those repair payments would not cost as much as a new auto; not yet, anyway.

Suddenly, Sally's social life slowed down as she realized that she would have to stop vacationing with her local travel group. Frankly, the most painful hurt was when she realized that she would not be able to send her grandchildren their customary birthday and Christmas presents. A simple card would have to do.

Sally's bank certificates were now running on vapors. They were only producing a small amount of interest while inflation kept doubling prices every 10 to 15 years. If the government would just stop taxing bank interest, maybe she would have enough to live on. She knew that that would never happen. Sally was suffering from the impact of rising prices. This is known as inflation risk.

Case 5: An Example of Interest Rate Risk

Mary and Bill always played it safe by splitting their investment assets between stocks and fixed investments such as bonds and certificates of deposit. They put a little into each basket so that they could rest easy. In fact, they felt lucky to have purchased some long-term corporate bonds for their portfolio years ago. They had invested in bonds maturing in 20 years that were recommended through a local stockbroker in their neighborhood. The interest rate paid on these securities was a healthy 6 percent per year. That was quite a bit more than bank certificates of deposit offering only 5 percent.

Mary and Bill wondered if they should have bought more at the time. Over the years, they started noticing that interest rates were on the rise. In fact, the cycle of inflation was active again and prices were moving quickly upwards. A gallon of gas increased by 40 percent and groceries were going up monthly.

When Mary called the local stockbroker, she was shocked to find out that newer corporate bonds were now yielding over 9 percent! Imagine earning 3 percent more per year on newer bonds than what she and Bill were currently earning? She inquired from the broker if she should sell her older bonds to buy the newer bonds. The stockbroker explained that she would have to sell at a loss.

It seemed no one wanted her older bonds. Buyers could just purchase the newer bonds that were readily available and were paying a higher interest rate. The broker did explain that because there were 15 years until her bonds matured, he could sell them at a 40 percent discount to entice a buyer. She wasn't about to sell at such a discount. She and Bill had to sit back and wait. Maybe interest rates would come back down.

They would often discuss how nice that extra 3 percent interest from the newer bonds would be and how much it would help with their increasing expenses. Not only were they experiencing market risk but also another risk factor known as interest rate risk.

Had they purchased various bonds with different maturity dates, they would have been more adaptable to changing interest rates. Spread your bond and fixed investment maturities over various time periods such as 3, 5, 10, and 20 years. This will allow you to have funds maturing at different times. These proceeds can then be placed into current offerings that are being made available. It will also allow you to have funds coming due that will be freely accessible without tremendous market penalties.

In summary, the four major risk factors are:

1. Financial risk
2. Market risk
3. Inflation risk
4. Interest rate risk

In addition to these four major risk factors, do not overlook the risk of tax law changes. Before investing, consider the following:

- Understand the tax ramifications of any investment transaction.
- Make sure all proper tax forms are filed for any investment.
- Look at current legislation being proposed and always seek sound tax planning advice.
- Do not buy an investment strictly for tax purposes unless you thoroughly understand the transactions and are comfortable with them.

Key Points on Financial Risk

- If an investment is unfamiliar, do not invest.
- If the investment sounds too good to be true, it probably is.
- Only deal with reputable people or institutions.
- Make sure they are who they say they are.
- Never buy over the phone unless you initiated the conversation and know the party on the other end.
- Be aware of the business entity with which you are doing business. Is it a corporation, partnership, sole proprietorship, or a government entity?
- Always look for additional strength backing the entity with which you are about to invest. Do special insurance funds or coverage, government guarantees, assets, or other larger and stronger entities back it?
- Is the investment firm you are dealing with registered or licensed? Are its representatives?
- Always put it in writing and keep copies.
- Make sure that all written agreements are proper, legal, and enforceable.
- If possible, make sure that legal agreements can be pursued in your own state under local jurisdiction.
- Avoid small businesses, start-up companies, and most partnerships unless you have really done your homework and feel comfortable investing with them.
- What is backing the investment? Know in detail if the company has the ability to pay you back or how it plans on performing.
- Seek an informed second and third opinion on any potential investments before investing, not afterward when it may be too late.
- Avoid investments that have too high of penalties for withdrawal or limit your right to obtain your funds.
- When investing in certain investments such as real estate, make sure either you, or the other party, have the proper property and liability insurance coverage in place.
- Regarding your own personal protection from financial risk, make sure that you have adequate liability coverage in place on your auto, home, boat, etc. Consider adding an umbrella policy that adds a blanket amount of additional coverage over and above your individual policy limits.
- Certain professionals and individuals need to seriously consider the use of proper offshore accounts that can act as a great defense from frivolous lawsuits.
- Seek sound financial and legal advice when structuring any financial venture. Different forms of business structures offer varying amounts of protection.

- Consider creditor-resistant vehicles such as qualified retirement plans, life insurance, annuities, and irrevocable trusts.
- If entering into marriage, consider proper prenuptial agreements or separate property agreements.

Key Points on Market Risk

- Avoid illiquid investments—investments that are not immediately redeemable for cash.
- Make sure there is a ready market for your securities; avoid issues that are thinly traded.
- Avoid investments that have high costs up front or high penalties associated for early withdrawals.
- Avoid investments that limit your right to obtain your funds.
- Avoid small businesses, start-up companies, and most partnerships unless you have really done your homework and feel comfortable.
- Select investments you understand and make sure they match your individual investment personality.
- Plan out your investment time horizon and select investments that match that time frame.
- Diversify among various investments and asset classes to ensure that you can maintain your investment portfolio without panicking during rough times.
- Consider transferring risk to others by investing with index annuities that offer minimum guarantees along with stock market participation.
- Consider adding dividend-paying stocks to your portfolio. These dividends can keep you company during the volatile times that will always present themselves.
- Invest for the long term.
- Know what you own, why you own it, and how it will react during various market scenarios.

Key Points on Inflation Risk

- Stay current with investment trends and invest accordingly.
- Consider placing enough of your portfolio into stocks to keep up with the trend of long-term inflation increases.

- Consider purchasing real estate in desirable and stable areas that will benefit from changing demographics and appreciate with inflation.
- Avoid assets that do not hold their value very well such as most autos, boats, and recreation vehicles.
- Consider adding inflation-indexed bonds to the fixed portion of your portfolio.
- Consider index annuities that offer a guarantee of principal plus a minimum interest rate, yet allow you to participate in the stock market's growth as well.
- Keep current with your estate plan as rising asset values could cause a dramatic increase in federal estate taxes.

Key Points on Interest Rate Risk

- Invest a portion of your fixed income program into inflation index bonds.
- Make sure your certificates of deposit and fixed annuities have various maturity dates, which will allow you to take advantage of changing interest rates.
- Stagger your individual bonds with various maturities. This is known as laddering your portfolio.
- Avoid most mutual fund bond accounts as you lose control of when the portfolio bonds are sold. Individual bonds can be held to maturity in most cases (unless callable); bond mutual funds almost are never carried to maturity as the fund managers usually trade out of the bond positions before the maturity dates. This can dramatically increase interest rate risk by causing normal market risk (fluctuation) to become financial risk (loss of money).

Figure 2.1 places various types of investments in a risk/return pyramid.

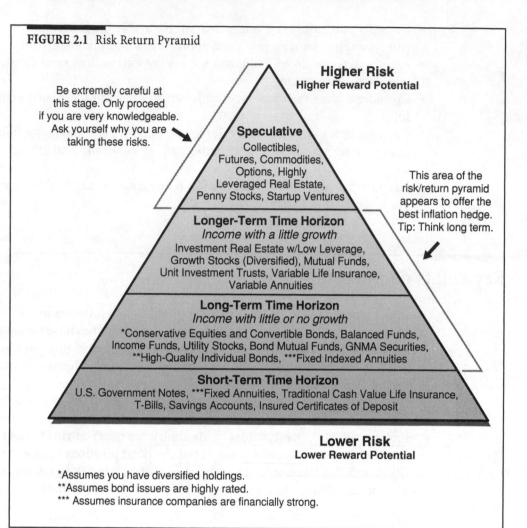

FIGURE 2.1 Risk Return Pyramid

Higher Risk
Higher Reward Potential

Be extremely careful at
this stage. Only proceed
if you are very knowledgeable.
Ask yourself why you are
taking these risks.

Speculative
Collectibles,
Futures, Commodities,
Options, Highly
Leveraged Real Estate,
Penny Stocks, Startup Ventures

This area of the
risk/return pyramid
appears to offer the
best inflation hedge.
Tip: Think long term.

Longer-Term Time Horizon
Income with a little growth
Investment Real Estate w/Low Leverage,
Growth Stocks (Diversified), Mutual Funds,
Unit Investment Trusts, Variable Life Insurance,
Variable Annuities

Long-Term Time Horizon
Income with little or no growth
*Conservative Equities and Convertible Bonds, Balanced Funds,
Income Funds, Utility Stocks, Bond Mutual Funds, GNMA Securities,
**High-Quality Individual Bonds, ***Fixed Indexed Annuities

Short-Term Time Horizon
U.S. Government Notes, ***Fixed Annuities, Traditional Cash Value Life Insurance,
T-Bills, Savings Accounts, Insured Certificates of Deposit

Lower Risk
Lower Reward Potential

*Assumes you have diversified holdings.
**Assumes bond issuers are highly rated.
*** Assumes insurance companies are financially strong.

3

Failure to Do Dignity Planning

When most people are asked to sum up what is really important to them, they mention family, crime rates in their community, world turmoil, etc. Upon closer introspection, however, when a person is left to contemplate important matters that impact just them as individuals, people tend to reflect about various personal and social matters. Key concerns include: How do others perceive them? Are they accepted by society at large or by smaller segments of people? Are they loved? Are they financially secure? Will they be able to age gracefully? A key question that flows under most people's consciousness is: Can they and will they maintain their dignity?

Much of what is learned in life and a great deal of what we hope to accomplish through work, hobbies, and deeds, pertains directly to establishing a persona and the subsequent maintenance of that image for ourselves and others. This plays an important role in life. Much of what we do ties directly in with how we are perceived by friends, neighbors, and acquaintances. The sense of self is probably the most important part of our personality. These concepts and images of self serve as an internal gyroscope for our very being.

Our Sense of Self

Ultimately, it is our sense of self that guides us in making almost all of our long-term decisions such as whom to marry, what career path to choose, which schools to attend, how we treat others, and how we expect others to treat us. We use these various thoughts to guide us through life's journey.

Can we really afford to ignore this force simply because we age? If you doubt the force of this presence—our aura of dignity and our feelings of self—just think of the many people you have known or encountered. How many people have perished because they refused to have some simple diagnostic medical tests performed? Perhaps they were embarrassed by the procedure or afraid to let others see them at a weak moment. Others we have known will give up great creature comforts to pursue a career in the military or a religious order. They will sacrifice much to pursue their sense of higher self, their sense of where they should be and how they should behave.

Failure to acknowledge this force, our sense of self coupled with our dignity, along with the failure to take constructive steps to ensure the success of this force, can lead to very undesirable consequences. We simply should not fail to do dignity planning.

Dignity Planning

Dignity planning is the building and maintenance of our self-image. Financially speaking, you should be prepared by having adequate financial resources available and proper documents drafted ahead of time. Adequate long-term care coverage as well as suitable medical coverage should be kept up to date.

Do you want to be beholden to others because you failed to adequately prepare for your retirement? Would you really want society to step in because you could not afford proper medical care? How would you feel if family and friends were forced to take care of you because you were seriously ill? What if you had no means of securing sound medical assistance?

Without proper planning, you could face one of the above scenarios or a similar situation. Benjamin Franklin said, "An ounce of prevention is worth a pound of cure." Taking simple financial planning steps today could prevent a lot of turmoil and aggravation later.

When contemplating dignity planning, focus on the here and now as well as the future. Taking responsibility for your actions will help you with dignity planning. You have worked hard over the years so that you would accumulate assets in order to have financial well-being. But are you failing to protect your future dignity?

Your Medical Decisions

What would happen if you had an auto accident today? Who would take care of you? Are you sure? Do they have the temperament, time, and resources that are necessary to tend to you?

Most people in the United States plan their vacations with more effort and forethought than their dignity planning. Over 90 percent of the adult population in this country does not have the necessary written documents in place; the documents that would give someone else the power to handle their medical decisions.

For medical situations, there are basically two kinds of documents that convey your health care directives. These documents will let others know of your medical wishes or desires. Because laws vary from state to state, you will need to check your state laws to see which health care directive is applicable for your situation.

The following details these two important documents:

- A *living will* is a legal document in which you state the kind of health care you would like (including no treatment) under dire medical circumstances. Living will documents should be recognized in all states.
- A *health care proxy* (or durable health care power of attorney) is a legal document in which you name someone to make decisions about health care and treatment in the event you are incapacitated. Health care proxies are more state specific. Greater power can typically be given by using your state's legal forms.

These documents can assist others in knowing what medical treatments you would want, as well as what medical procedures and treatments you are against. These health care directives specify whether or not you want to be revived if your condition proves to be terminal or even which hospital is your choice for treatment. Your medical concerns can be addressed and instructions given simply by having the proper documents drafted, signed, and in place ahead of time.

Use Caution

If you live in more than one state part of the year, by all means, make sure you have proper documents made up for each state. A small effort today could save your family or friends from making agonizing decisions later. Relieve them of these decisions by writing down your desires now.

How Long Will Your Funds Last?

Imagine a situation where you are in an irreversible coma and remain alive only because of sophisticated medical equipment. How long would it take with these types of procedures and intensive medical care to spend your personal wealth? Many urgent care wards and critical care centers far exceed the normal cost of a regular hospital bed. Add to this around-the-clock medical treatment and costly procedures and you realize that very few could afford this type of care on an extended basis.

Under a case that went all the way to the U.S. Supreme Court, *Cruzan v. Dir. MO Dept. of Health 1990,* the court held that a state may demand clear and convincing proof of a person's wish to die under certain conditions. Therefore, the person must make known his or her desire to have certain medical treatment or life support withdrawn under various circumstances. If you do not wish to be kept alive under various circumstances (e.g., if you are in an irreversible coma or persistent vegetative state) put it in writing.

When to Withhold Treatment

Do you really want all of your funds, which took you a lifetime to accumulate, to be spent on these types of medical efforts? If you are married, do you want all of your funds spent on high-tech devices and procedures that may prolong your discomfort while impoverishing your spouse? Under such treatment conditions, many people find the limits of their health insurance benefits being reached and then exceeded in no time at all.

What conditions might warrant having medical treatment withdrawn? Some medical advisors give four situations that might be considered "do not resuscitate" situations. The four "do not resuscitate" situations are:

1. In a coma with no hope of recovery
2. In a coma with a small likelihood of recovery with severe irreversible brain damage
3. Afflicted with permanent brain damage or disease, severe in nature and a terminal illness, such as cancer
4. Afflicted with severe brain damage or wasting disease, severe in nature but without terminal illness

These are guideline situations for people to consider if they want treatment withheld. Most medical experts will not recommend one way or the other. They just point out the situations. You must ask yourself the following question: Would I want treatment withheld under these circumstances?

These health care directive documents help others know your wishes and also allow to specifically appoint who should act on your behalf. Most people give this medical power to their spouse, followed by a grown child. Your situation may be different. Perhaps you wish to name a brother or sister as your patient advocate. Sometimes a close friend is named.

Couples living together without the benefit of marriage definitely need to execute health care directive documents. Otherwise, the power may fall to a family member by default. Imagine standing by helplessly while others make uninformed decisions for your loved one.

Lack of Authority

For married couples, don't assume that you have full, unrestricted powers of medical decisions for your spouse. In fact, in many situations, including a time of crisis, other relatives asserting their authority may surprise you. Consider the impact of your spouse's family stepping forward. They may assert justifiably their rights to have a say in medical matters.

Parents, brothers, or sisters of your loved one could step in with their opinions and prevent you from proceeding with the proper course of action that your loved one wanted. Children demand the authority to handle a parent's medical decisions all the time.

Stop your medical event from becoming a financial disaster that may cause family conflict. Write your wishes down, including who has the authority to handle your care. Remember, while you are competent and alert, you make all the decisions. Only if you are unable to communicate properly will your patient advocate or representative have authority.

You may find the following sample documents helpful. The documents are intended as reference material only. As always, consult with a knowledgeable attorney before proceeding with any legal document.

Figures 3.1 and 3.2 include the following documents:

- A sample living will and health care declaration document
- A sample durable power of attorney for health care document

Your Financial Affairs

Who will handle your financial matters if you are unable to? Most people have never given this a second thought. They assume their spouse or family members will automatically have the power to handle their financial affairs if they are unable to do so. Others believe a will document will allow someone to have control.

FIGURE 3.1 Sample Living Will and Health Care Declaration

LIVING WILL AND HEALTH CARE DECLARATION

Know all people by these presents that I, John Doe, residing at _____ hereby declare my will with respect to my medical care and treatment in the event I am unable for any reason to make known my will at the time medical decisions must be made.

Directive to forego or discontinue life-prolonging medical treatment when recovery is unlikely.

In the event I suffer from an injury, disease, illness or other physical or mental condition, including intractable pain, which renders me unable to communicate with others meaningfully, and from which there is no reasonable prospect of recovery to a cognitive and sentient life (even if my condition or illness is not deemed to be "terminal" and even if my death is not imminent), I direct that no medical treatments or procedures (except as provided in paragraph 3 below) be utilized in my care or, if begun, that they be discontinued.

Definitive of medical treatment.

By "medical treatments or procedures," I mean interventions by medical doctors, nurses, paramedics, hospitals, residential health care facilities or any other health care provider, in the care of my body and mind, including all medical and surgical procedures, mechanical or otherwise, treatments, therapies including drugs and hormones, which may substitute for, replace, supplant, enhance, or assist any bodily function. This specifically includes maintenance of respiration, nutrition, and hydration by artificial means. With respect to all medical treatments or procedures, I include both existing technology and any methods or techniques that may be hereafter developed and perfected.

Provision for pain control.

I ask that medical treatment to alleviate pain, to provide comfort, and to mitigate suffering be provided so that I may be as free of pain and suffering as possible.

Determination of prognosis.

My Health Care Agent acting pursuant to my duly executed Health Care Proxy shall follow my directions as set out in this Health Care Declaration whenever my Agent has ascertained by applying reasonable medical standards that my condition is as described in Section 1, above. In the absence of the instructions of my agent, any persons or institutions who are called upon to make decisions affecting my care shall comply with my directions contained herein. In the event of uncertainty or ambiguity as to how my wishes are to be interpreted or applied in any particular situation, any persons or institutions who are treating me shall comply with the interpretations and directions of my Health Care Agent.

Acknowledgment of effects of this Declaration.

I make and execute this Declaration knowing that, if complied with, my death may occur sooner than it would were all available and appropriate medical treatments considered and used. I accept this as a necessary result of a decision to avoid dependence and pain. And I make the decision now, for myself, after careful consideration, to ensure that I will have the level of medical care that I want, and to relieve others of the burden of decision.

Dated: _____, 20 ____

_____

Statement of Witness

I declare that the person who signed this document is personally known to me and appears to be of sound mind and acting of his or her own free will. He or she signed (or asked another to sign for him or her) this document in my presence.

_____ Address _____

_____ Address _____

FIGURE 3.2 Sample Durable Power of Attorney for Health Care

DURABLE POWER OF ATTORNEY FOR HEALTH CARE

1. Appointment of patient advocate(s). I, JOHN DOE, appoint JANE DOE as my agent (patient advocate).

I appoint the following person(s), in the order listed, as my successor patient advocate if my patient advocate is removed or is unable to serve. My successor patient advocate is to have the same powers and rights as my patient advocate.

JACK DOE

JILL DOE

My patient advocate or successor patient advocate may delegate his or her powers to the next successor patient advocate if he or she is unable to act.

2. Effective date and durability.

My patient advocate or successor patient advocate may only act if I am unable to participate in making decisions regarding my medical treatment. My attending physician and another physician or licensed psychologist shall determine, after examining me, when I am unable to participate in making my own medical decisions.

[Optional: My religious beliefs prohibit a medical examination to determine whether I am unable to participate in making medical treatment decisions; therefore, I want this determination to be made by _____ _____.]

This designation is suspended during any period in which I regain the ability to participate in my own medical treatment decisions.

I intend this document to be a durable power of attorney for health care, and it shall survive my disability or incapacity.

3. Patient advocate's powers. I grant my patient advocate authority to make all health care decisions for me. In making such decisions, she should follow my expressed wishes, either written or oral, regarding my medical treatment. If my patient advocate cannot determine the choice I would want based on my written or oral statements, she shall choose for me based on what she believes to be in my best interests regardless of whether the specific medical treatment or circumstance is addressed in this document.

Unless specifically limited by ¶4, my patient advocate is authorized as follows:

- to consent to, refuse, or withdraw consent from all types of medical care, treatment, and procedures
- to access my medical records, disclose the contents to others, and execute medical releases
- to authorize my admission to or discharge from (even against medical advice) any hospital, nursing home, or care facility
- to contract on my behalf for any health care–related service or facility, without my patient advocate incurring personal financial liability for such contracts
- to hire and fire medical and other support personnel responsible for my care on behalf of me and my estate, to release from liability all persons and entities who act in good-faith reliance on instructions given by my patient advocate and to execute any documents, such as a refusal of treatment form or a do-not-resuscitate order, that a physician or a facility may require to carry out my wishes regarding medical treatment

4. Life-sustaining treatment. I understand that I *do not* have to choose any of the instructions regarding life-sustaining treatment listed below. If I choose one, I will place a check mark by the choice and sign below my choice.

If I sign one of the choices listed below, I direct that reasonable measures be taken to keep me comfortable and to relieve pain.

[Choose only one.]

_____ **Choice 1:** I do not want life-sustaining treatment (including artificial delivery of food and water) if **any** of the following medical conditions exist:

I am in an irreversible coma or persistent vegetative state.

I am terminally ill, and life-sustaining procedures would only serve to artificially delay my death.

My medical condition is such that the burdens of treatment outweigh the expected benefits. In making this determination, I want my patient advocate to consider relief of my suffering, the expenses involved, and the quality of my life, if prolonged.

I expressly authorize my patient advocate to make decisions to withhold or withdraw treatment that would allow me to die, and I acknowledge such decisions could or would allow my death.

_____

_____ **Choice 2:** I want life-sustaining treatment (including artificial delivery of food or water) _unless_ I am in a coma or vegetative state that my doctor reasonably believes to be irreversible. Once my doctor has reasonably concluded that I will remain unconscious for the rest of my life, I do not want life-sustaining treatment to be provided or continued.

I expressly authorize my patient advocate to make decisions to withhold or withdraw treatment that would allow me to die, and I acknowledge such decisions could or would allow my death.

_____

_____ **Choice 3:** I want my life to be prolonged to the greatest extent possible consistent with sound medical practice without regard to my condition, the chances I have for recovery, or the cost of the procedures. I direct life-sustaining treatment to be provided to prolong my life.

_____

5. Differences of opinion among medical personnel. I understand that I do not have to choose any of the instructions regarding differences of opinion listed below. If I choose one, I will place a check mark by my choice and sign below my choice.

[Choose only one.]

_____ **Choice 1:** I grant broad discretion to my patient advocate if there is a difference of opinion among my treating physicians. If there is a difference of opinion about my medical treatment among the physicians treating me, my patient advocate shall consider the opinions of all the physicians and then choose the treatment to be administered to me.

_____

_____ **Choice 2:** I grant no discretion to my patient advocate if there is a difference of opinion about my medical treatment among my treating physicians. If there is a difference of opinion about my medical treatment among the physicians treating me, my patient advocate shall choose the treatment that the majority of the physicians recommends.

_____

6. Difference of opinion among family members. I understand that I do not have to choose any of the instructions listed below regarding differences of opinion my family members may have concerning my medical treatment. If I choose one, I will place a check mark by the choice and sign below my choice.

[Choose only one.]

_____ **Choice 1:** I grant broad discretion to my patient advocate if there is a difference of opinion among my family members with regard to my medical treatment. If there is a difference of opinion among my family members regarding my medical treatment, my patient advocate shall consider the opinion of each family member and then choose the medical treatment to be administered to me.

_____

_____ **Choice 2:** I grant no discretion to my patient advocate if there is a difference of opinion among my family members with regard to my medical treatment. If there is a difference of opinion among my family regarding my medical treatment, my patient advocate shall choose the medical treatment that the majority of my family members prefers.

7. Protection of third parties who rely on these instructions and those of my patient advocate. No person or entity that relies in good faith on the instructions of my patient advocate or successor patient advocate pursuant to this document, without actual notice that this power has been revoked or amended, shall incur any liability to me or to my estate. If I am unable to participate in making decisions for my care and there is no patient advocate or successor patient advocate to act for me, I request that the instructions I have given in this document be followed and be considered conclusive evidence of my wishes.

8. Administrative provisions. My patient advocate shall not be entitled to compensation for services performed under this power of attorney, but he or she shall be entitled to reimbursement for actual and necessary expenses incurred as a result of carrying out his or her responsibilities as my patient advocate.

I revoke any prior durable powers of attorney that I have executed to the extent that they grant powers and authority within the scope of the powers granted in this document.

This document shall be governed by Michigan law. However, I intend for this durable power of attorney for health care to be honored in any jurisdiction where it is presented and for other jurisdictions to refer to Michigan law to interpret and determine the validity and enforceability of this document.

Photocopies of this signed power of attorney shall be treated as original counterparts.

I am providing these instructions voluntarily and have not been required to give them to obtain treatment or to have care withheld or withdrawn. I am at least 18 years old and of sound mind.

Dated: _____

_____
JOHN DOE

WITNESS STATEMENT AND SIGNATURE

I declare that the person who signed this patient advocate designation did so in my presence and appears to be of sound mind and under no duress, fraud, or undue influence. I am not the husband, wife, parent, child, grandchild, brother, or sister of the person who signed this document. Further, I am not his presumptive heir and, to the best of my knowledge, I am not a beneficiary to his Will at the time of witnessing. I am not the patient advocate, the physician, or an employee of the life or health insurance provider for the person signing this document. I am not an employee of the health care facility or home for the aged where he resides or is being treated.

Witness 1

Dated: _____

_____
[Address and telephone]

Dated: _____

_____
[Address and telephone]

REAFFIRMATION OF PATIENT ADVOCATE DESIGNATION

Dated: _____   _____

Dated: _____   _____

Dated: _____   _____

ACCEPTANCE OF DESIGNATION AS PATIENT ADVOCATE

I accept the designation as the patient advocate for JOHN DOE (patient). I understand and agree to take reasonable steps to follow the instructions, both verbal and written, of the patient regarding his medical care, custody, and treatment.

I also understand and agree to the following:

This designation shall not become effective unless the patient is unable to participate in medical treatment decisions.

A patient advocate shall not exercise powers concerning the patient's care, custody, and medical treatment that the patient, if the patient were able to participate in the decision, could not have exercised on his or her own behalf.

This designation cannot be used to make a medical treatment decision to withhold or withdraw treatment that would result in the patient's death if the patient is pregnant.

A patient advocate may decide to withhold or withdraw treatment that would allow the patient to die only if the patient has expressed in a clear and convincing manner that the agent is authorized to make such a decision and that such a decision could or would allow the patient's death.

A patient advocate shall not receive compensation for the performance of his or her authority, rights, and responsibilities, but may be reimbursed for actual and necessary expenses incurred in the performance of his or her authority, rights, and responsibilities.

A patient advocate shall act in accordance with the standards of care applicable to fiduciaries when acting for the patient and shall act consistent with the patient's best interests. The known desires of the patient expressed or evidenced while the patient is able to participate in medical treatment decisions are presumed to be in the patient's best interests.

A patient may revoke his or her designation at any time and in any manner sufficient to communicate an intent to revoke.

A patient advocate may revoke his or her acceptance to the designation at any time and in any manner sufficient to communicate an intent to revoke.

A patient admitted to a health facility or agency has the rights enumerated in MCLA 333.20201, MSA 14.15 (20201).

If I am unavailable to act after reasonable effort to contact me, I delegate my authority to the persons the patient has designated as successor patient advocate in the order designated. The successor patient advocate is authorized to act until I become available.

Patient advocate

Dated: _____
_____

JANE DOE
[Address and telephone]

Successor patient advocate

Dated: _____
_____

JACK DOE
[Address and telephone]

Successor patient advocate

Dated: _____
_____

JILL DOE
[Address and telephone]

Sorry, but a will document appoints a personal representative to manage your financial affairs only upon your demise. If you are still living, yet unable to make financial decisions, you need to have special documents giving that legal power to someone.

Major Reasons to Have Documents

Keep in mind that, if you do not have legal documents to give instructions and appoint agents on your behalf in the event of your disability, your family or friends will be forced to get the court involved.

The procedures vary from state to state and even county to county within states. Generally, a public hearing will be posted and held to determine your mental capacity to govern yourself. This will allow the court to appoint someone to watch over you and your financial affairs in the event they find you incompetent.

A person will serve as a guardian or conservator over you. They must report to the court periodically to keep the court informed on your well-being. This is done for your protection. You may not approve of whom the court selects as your guardian or conservator. The scary part of all this is that the court can appoint anybody, including someone from a professional guardian service.

Even if you have a close friend or favorite relative in mind, they may be powerless to take care of you. Imagine the high fees and time wasted on such hearings? This process is sometimes referred to as a living probate situation. Others call it "hell on earth."

To add insult to injury, not only are your loved ones subjected to lengthy court proceedings, but whoever is appointed to take care of you must report to the court and keep accurate records of income and expenses.

There Have Been Cases

There have been numerous examples of greedy relatives being appointed as guardians or custodians just to have access to your funds. They have been known to pilfer funds and then disappear with no trace. While the courts try their best, many times they are faced with incredibly difficult situations. It simply is impossible to hand out proper justice in every situation. Protect yourself by taking time now to outline your needs, concerns, and wishes. Have the proper legal documents drafted ahead of time. Name the people you trust to serve as your power of attorney.

As a footnote, just because you go through a living probate in a guardianship or custodianship proceeding doesn't mean your estate is really probated. The term *living probate* is used because the probate court is usually involved in such hearings. Upon your demise, your family will be required to go through real probate proceedings where your will document will be reviewed and your estate settled. Hopefully, you have a will, which lets the court know your final wishes.

Your Legal Rights

It is an incorrect assumption that others can manage your affairs with very little difficulty. Sometimes, it is worth remembering all the duties and responsibilities we have as individuals. Everyone will, at times, become flustered in life because of the weight of responsibility that must be carried each day. Stop to ponder these responsibilities and you may be surprised.

In this country, when you come of age, you are given more legal rights than in almost any other country. You have the right to borrow funds, to acquire property, to lease, to purchase a home or business, etc. The rights to enter into contracts, to bargain, to invest, and to bring legal action are a few more powers you should not overlook.

Most people forget the total scope of powers they have as responsible citizens. Even though these responsibilities may not occupy everyday thinking, the powers still exist. If you are unable to act on these powers, you want to make sure someone else can.

These powers can be given to another via a power of attorney document. You will want to work with a knowledgeable advisor because your power of attorney document should be durable. This means that the document will last even if you are disabled.

Many times a normal power of attorney document will end if you become disabled. Care must be taken to include the wording within the document making it durable to ensure that someone can be appointed ahead of time to manage affairs throughout your incapacity.

Durable Power of Attorney

In a durable power of attorney, *the principal* is the person who is giving the power of attorney. This person must be a legal adult. *The holder* is the adult (or adults) who is acting on behalf of the principal.

General Durable Power of Attorney

Two major durable power of attorney documents are used. One type is known as the general durable power of attorney document. This legal document gives various powers to someone to act on your behalf as your attorney-in-fact, which is usually referred to as your agent. This is a very substantial power to give to someone. This person could use this document at any time to manage your affairs whether you are disabled or not. People rely on this document and follow the agent's instructions without question. Only your appearance or written revocation would negate this document.

Typically, this document is used by married couples that have been married for many years and have absolute trust in each other. Other times, this document is used when a spouse or family member is out of the country for an extended period of time.

Keep in mind that this is a lot of power to place in someone's hands. Many attorneys who draft these documents do so only after meeting with family members and analyzing their moral character and business sense. Some advisors recommend that these documents not be widely disseminated. They instead recommend that people having such documents keep them with their personal records.

In effect, the powers that these documents convey should only be used if the family member is sick, unable to respond, or disappears. At that point, the family can look into the person's files to utilize a durable power of attorney document. Children taking care of aging parents often use these types of documents. Such parents are still able to understand what they are doing, but perhaps have lost the initiative to handle their own finances.

Springing Durable Power

A safer and sounder alternative is to have a springing durable power of attorney document. This is similar in every respect to a regular general durable power of attorney document, yet has language within the document stating that the power of attorney takes place only if you are deemed incompetent or unable to conduct your own affairs.

Typically, two doctors will have to sign affidavits testifying to your incapacity. With this language placed into the durable power of attorney documents, you can feel a lot more comfortable in providing your family members with a signed copy. This will allow them to know more about your affairs and will prepare them to take action should the need arise.

What Powers Are Given

What powers are typically given in power of attorney documents? Usually, they are split into two categories: tax-related powers and nontax powers.

Powers that are typically included in a durable power of attorney are:

Tax-related powers

- The power to sign income tax and gift tax returns
- The power to complete transfers to a living trust if the principal is incompetent
- The power to make disclaimers
- The power to exercise special powers of appointment
- Powers may also be given allowing the holder to make gifts to a spouse (if required to equalize the estates), and to even create certain living trusts if need be.

Nontax powers

- The power to collect from creditors
- The power to have the right to sue for the benefit of the principal
- The power to sell, buy, or lease the principal's property
- The power to handle the principal's business operations

The tax-related powers usually assign the power to your agent to handle tax matters. This could include the power to prepare, execute, and file reports, returns, declarations, forms, and statements for any and all tax returns. These include income tax returns, gift tax returns, real estate, personal property, intangible or tangible tax returns, single business tax returns, etc.

You can give the power to have your agent pay such taxes and any interest or penalties involved. You are also able to give your agent the power to make and file any needed objections, protests, and claims for abatements, refund, or credit in relationship to any such tax proposal, etc.

The agent given the power to represent you can institute any proceedings on your behalf regarding your tax matters. A good document usually specifies that your agent has the right to hire good legal and tax counsel as well. These are not all the tax powers that could be included. Documents can vary from state to state because of different laws. Good legal counsel is crucial in assisting you with the proper powers to convey within your documents.

Nontax powers are even more numerous. They can include collection powers, real property powers, personal property powers, contract powers, banking powers, safe-deposit box access, power to employ agents on your behalf, settlement powers, power to deal with legal matters, power to handle dividends, power to transfer stocks, and the power to handle insurance and employee benefit plans to name a few.

This document should also address the power to handle Social Security and government benefits on your behalf. Think about the following situation. What if you are in a coma or suffering from a stroke? Who has the power to cash your Social Security check then? Act now by having the proper documents drafted.

Special Powers

Believe it or not, a well written power of attorney document gives your agent the right to borrow, from time to time, such sums of money and at such terms that the agent may find to be beneficial to your situation. If you are incapacitated and have a high interest rate house payment, large credit card debt, or the like, wouldn't it be nice for your agent to refinance your mortgage at a lower rate, saving you thousands of dollars in interest payments.

In other situations, an agent may need to borrow from some investments such as a brokerage account to preserve other assets such as real estate property when taxes are due. Sometimes an agent may need this power to hold onto rental properties, land, or business interests. Your agent may need funds to relocate you from one care facility to another. You will most certainly be faced with debts and expenses. Your agent needs to have the ability to deal with these issues.

Investment powers are usually included in this document because funds will be required for your support and maintenance. These powers can be very broad, so make sure that you select someone whom you trust as your agent to be named in your document. Consideration should be given to naming a contingent person to serve as your power of attorney agent in the event your primary choice is unable to serve.

Note that your power of attorney documents should take into account if you have a trust. Your agent may need the power to transfer assets to your trust. A revocable living trust typically contains many of the powers mentioned in the durable power of attorney documents. However, those powers within a living trust can only be exercised over assets titled under the trust.

Do not underestimate the value of a good advisor assisting you in this endeavor. Take advantage of all your options. This is not a document to skimp on nor is this a do-it-yourself document. The reasons are obvious. With so much depending on proper documents, don't take unnecessary risks that a poorly drafted document could create. You want your wishes known and your agent to be able to perform them. A poorly drafted document could cause anguish when there is no reason to incur such grief. Work with an attorney in deciding if you want your durable power of attorney to have a wide array of powers, known as general powers, or a document that is more limited.

You may find the following sample documents helpful. The documents are intended as reference material only. As always, consult with a knowledgeable attorney before proceeding with any legal document.

Figures 3.3 and 3.4 include the following documents:

- A sample durable power of attorney effective on execution
- A sample durable power of attorney effective on disability

FIGURE 3.3 Sample Durable Power of Attorney Effective on Execution

DURABLE POWER OF ATTORNEY EFFECTIVE ON EXECUTION

I, JOHN DOE, a resident of Wayne County, Michigan, designate MARY DOE as my attorney in fact (the agent) on the following terms and conditions:

Authority to act. The agent is authorized to act for me under this power of attorney and shall exercise all powers in my best interests and for my welfare.

Powers of the agent. The agent may perform any act and exercise any power with regard to my property and affairs that I could do personally, including exercising all of the specific powers set forth below:

Collect and manage. Collect, hold, maintain, improve, invest, lease, or otherwise manage any or all of my real or personal property or any interest in it.

Buy and sell. Purchase, sell, mortgage, grant options, or otherwise deal in any way with any real property, including real property described on the attached schedule; personal property, tangible or intangible; or any interest in it, on whatever terms the agent considers to be proper, including the power to buy U.S. Treasury bonds that may be redeemed at par; pay federal estate tax; and sell or transfer treasury securities.

Borrow. Borrow money, execute promissory notes, and secure any obligation by mortgage or pledge.

Business. Conduct and participate in any kind of lawful business of any nature, including the right to sign partnership agreements; continue, reorganize, merge, consolidate, recapitalize, close, liquidate, sell, or dissolve any business; and vote stock, including the exercise of any stock options and the carrying out of any buy-sell agreement.

Banking. Receive and endorse checks and other negotiable paper and deposit and withdraw funds (by check or withdrawal slip) that I now have on deposit or to which I may be entitled in the future, in or from any bank, savings and loan, or other institution.

Tax returns and reports. Prepare, sign, and file separate or joint income, gift, and other tax returns and other governmental reports and documents; consent to any gift; file any claim for a tax refund; and represent me in all matters before the Internal Revenue Service.

Safe-deposit boxes. Have access to and remove any property or papers from any safe-deposit box registered in my name alone or jointly with others.

Proxy rights. Act as my agent or proxy for any stocks, bonds, shares, or other investments, rights, or interests I may hold now or in the future.

Government benefits. Apply to any governmental agency for any benefit or government obligation to which I may be entitled.

Legal and administrative proceedings. Engage in any administrative or legal proceedings or lawsuits in connection with any matter under this power.

Life insurance. Exercise any incidents of ownership I may possess with respect to policies of insurance, except policies insuring the life of my agent.

Transfers in trust. Transfer any interest I may have in property, whether real or personal, tangible or intangible, to the trustee of any trust that I have created for my benefit.

Delegation of authority. Engage and dismiss agents, counsel, and employees, in connection with any matter, on whatever terms my agent determines.

Restrictions on the agent's powers. Regardless of the above statements, my agent (1) may not execute a Will, a codicil, or any Will substitute on my behalf; (2) may not change the beneficiary on any life insurance policy that I own; (3) may not make gifts on my behalf; and (4) may not exercise any powers that would cause assets of mine to be considered taxable to my agent or to my agent's estate for purposes of any income, estate, or inheritance tax.

Durability. This durable power of attorney shall not be affected by my disability and shall continue in effect until my death or until I revoke it in writing. The agent shall have no duty to act and shall incur no liability to me or to my estate for failing to take any action under this power of attorney before receiving written notice from me requesting the agent to act or, alternatively, receiving written notice that, in the opinion of two licensed physicians, I am unable to act due to either physical or mental disability, in which case the agent shall immediately begin to act.

Reliance by third parties. Third parties may rely on the representations of the agent in all matters regarding powers granted to the agent. No person who acts in reliance on the representations of the agent or the authority granted under this power of attorney shall incur any liability to me or to my estate for permitting the agent to exercise any power before actual knowledge that the power of attorney has been revoked or terminated by operation of law or otherwise.

Indemnification of the agent. No agent named or substituted in this power shall incur any liability to me for acting or refraining from acting under this power, except for that agent's own misconduct or negligence.

Original counterparts. Photocopies of this signed power of attorney shall be treated as original counterparts.

Revocation. I revoke any previous power of attorney that I may have given to deal with my property and affairs as stated in this document.

Compensation. The agent shall be reimbursed for reasonable expenses incurred while acting as agent and may receive reasonable compensation for acting as agent.

Substitute agent. If MARY DOE is, at any time, unable or unwilling to act, I then appoint JACK DOE as my agent.

Dated: _____

    _____

    JOHN DOE
    123 Main St.
    Any City, Michigan

Signed in the presence of:

Witness 1

Dated: _____

    _____

    [Typed name]
    [Address and telephone]

Witness 2

Dated: _____

    _____

    [Typed name]
    [Address and telephone]

Subscribed and sworn to before me on

_____.

_____

Notary Public, _____ County

My commission expires _____.

FIGURE 3.4 Sample Durable Power of Attorney Effective on Disability

DURABLE POWER OF ATTORNEY EFFECTIVE ON DISABILITY

I, MARY DOE, a resident of Wayne County, Michigan, designate JOHN DOE as my attorney in fact (the agent) to act for me, if I should become disabled, on the following terms and conditions:

Authority to act. If I become disabled, the agent is authorized to act for me under this durable power of attorney until my death or recovery from the disability. I shall be considered to be disabled if a court determines that I am disabled or if two licensed physicians certify in writing that, in their opinion, I am unable to attend to financial matters due to either physical or mental disability. Recovery from disability shall be established in the same manner.

Powers of the agent. The agent, acting in my best interests and for my welfare, may perform any act and exercise any power with regard to my property and affairs during my disability that I could do personally, including exercising all of the specific powers set forth below:

Collect and manage. Collect, hold, maintain, improve, invest, lease, or otherwise manage any or all of my real or personal property or any interest in it.

Buy and sell. Purchase, sell, mortgage, grant options, or otherwise deal in any way with any real property, including real property described on the attached schedule; personal property, tangible or intangible; or any interest in it, on whatever terms the agent considers to be proper, including the power to buy U.S. Treasury bonds that may be redeemed at par; pay federal estate tax; and sell or transfer treasury securities.

Borrow. Borrow money, execute promissory notes, and secure any obligation by mortgage or pledge.

Business. Conduct and participate in any kind of lawful business of any kind, including the right to sign partnership agreements; continue, reorganize, merge, consolidate, recapitalize, close, liquidate, sell, or dissolve any business; and vote stock, including the exercise of any stock options and the carrying out of any buy-sell agreement.

Banking. Receive and endorse checks and other negotiable paper and deposit and withdraw funds (by check or withdrawal slip) that I now have on deposit or to which I may be entitled in the future, in or from any bank, savings and loan, or other institution.

Tax returns and reports. Prepare, sign, and file separate or joint income, gift, and other tax returns and other governmental reports and documents; consent to any gift; file any claim for a tax refund; and represent me in all matters before the Internal Revenue Service.

Safe-deposit boxes. Have access to and remove any property or papers from any safe-deposit box registered in my name alone or jointly with others.

Proxy rights. Act as my agent or proxy for any stocks, bonds, shares, or other investments, rights, or interests I may hold now or in the future.

Government benefits. Apply to any governmental agency for any benefit or government obligation to which I may be entitled.

Legal and administrative proceedings. Engage in any administrative or legal proceedings or lawsuits in connection with any matter under this power.

Life insurance. Exercise any incidents of ownership I may possess with respect to policies of insurance, except policies insuring the life of my agent.

Transfers in trust. Transfer any interest I may have in property, whether real or personal, tangible or intangible, to the trustee of any trust that I have created for my benefit.

Delegation of authority. Engage and dismiss agents, counsel, and employees, in connection with any matter, on whatever terms my agent determines.

Restrictions on the agent's powers. Regardless of the above statements, my agent (1) may not execute a Will, a codicil, or any Will substitute on my behalf; (2) may not change the beneficiary on any life insurance policy that I own; (3) may not make gifts on my behalf; and(4) may not exercise any powers that would cause assets of mine to be considered taxable to my agent or to my agent's estate for purposes of any income, estate, or inheritance tax.

Reliance by third parties. Third parties may rely on the representations of the agent in all matters regarding powers granted to the agent. No person who acts in reliance on the representations of the agent or the authority granted under this power of attorney shall incur any liability to me or to my estate for permitting the agent to exercise any power prior to actual knowledge that the power of attorney has been revoked or terminated by operation of law or otherwise.

Indemnification of the agent. No agent named or substituted in this power shall incur any liability to me for acting or refraining from acting under this power, except for that agent's own misconduct or negligence.

Original counterparts. Photocopies of this signed power of attorney shall be treated as original counterparts.

Revocation. I revoke any previous powers of attorney that I may have given to deal with my property and affairs as stated in this document.

Durability. This durable power of attorney shall not be affected by my disability. The agent shall be under no duty to act and shall incur no liability to me or to my estate for failing to take any action under this power of attorney before receiving written notice from two licensed physicians that, because of either physical or mental disability, I am unable to attend to financial matters, in which case it shall immediately begin to act for me.

Compensation. The agent shall be reimbursed for reasonable expenses incurred while acting as agent and may receive reasonable compensation for acting as agent.

Substitute agent. If JOHN DOE is, at any time, unable or unwilling to act, I then appoint JACK DOE as my agent.

Dated: _____

                                                                  _____
MARY DOE
123 Main St.
Any City, Michigan

Signed in the presence of:

Witness 1

Dated: _____

                                                                  _____
[Typed name]
[Address and telephone]

Witness 2

Dated: _____

                                                                  _____
[Typed name]
[Address and telephone]

Subscribed and sworn to before me on

_____ .

_____

Notary Public, _____ County

My commission expires _____ .

Exempted Powers

Some powers cannot be transferred to another person, including:

- The power to vote in a general election
- The power to execute a will
- The power to revoke a will
- The power to execute a living will (also known as right to die)

Major Drawbacks of Powers of Attorney

As good as durable power of attorney documents are, they do have some draw-backs. Banking and other financial institutions do not always accept them. Many banks and insurance companies want their own power of attorney forms used. This obviously can cause problems because you already may be disabled when these institutions request such forms. In this case, your family may need to hire an attorney to convince these companies to comply. Usually, the attorneys will prove successful. Many states are now forcing institutions to accept properly drafted durable power of attorney documents.

It is highly recommended that you not only have a durable power of attorney document, but that you consider a revocable living trust as well. A living trust operates as a legal entity that can hold real property assets such as real estate, investments, bank accounts, and business interests. You can appoint a successor trustee to serve for you in the event you are disabled. Your successor trustee or trustees can handle your affairs on your behalf with no court involvement. This is usually completed in private with no public records required. Consider also that a successor trustee can handle your affairs much easier for assets registered under your trust than by using a power of attorney document. Banks and other financial institutions are much more accepting of dealing with successor trustees. This is covered in much more detail in Chapter 5.

Note that even with a living trust, you still should have a durable power of attorney document because you cannot give all your financial powers to a trustee. For instance, it is impossible to give your successor trustee the power to cash Social Security checks due to the fact that this is not considered real property but a government benefit.

Disability Insurance

If you are still working, have you taken steps to insure your most valuable asset, yourself? While most other large assets such as a house, auto, or boat are insured, there are many cases where the largest asset, yourself, is underinsured. You and your ability to generate income are truly a valuable commodity. Insuring your future income is one of the smartest financial moves you can make.

Disability income policies are available that can provide two-thirds of your current income in the event of a disability. Good policies will provide ongoing income as long as you are disabled. A sound disability income policy would also provide for a partial disability if you are limited to part-time work. A good disability contract will make up the difference between what you usually make and what you are actually making because of a partial disability.

Look for an insurance company that offers the most liberal definition of what is a disability. Also, look for the longest benefit coverage period possible. If you have coverage available through work, make sure you check to see if your coverage is long-term disability coverage. Most employers only offer short-term accident and sickness policies, which usually provide only 26 weeks of coverage.

Don't depend on Uncle Sam either. Social Security benefits are provided only for the most severe disability situations. More than 70 percent of the claimants who make disability requests for Social Security benefits are denied. In fact, depending on your employer and the government for disability income is a recipe for disaster. You could easily expend what valuable energy and resources you have left trying to wrangle disability benefits from those two sources.

Usually, if you are successful in obtaining benefits from the federal government or state government agencies, you still lose. The amount of benefits they pay would keep you entrenched in poverty and cut short any long-term dreams you may have had. It is far better to take a small amount of time today to plan for a possible disability tomorrow, thereby ensuring the maintenance of your current lifestyle.

Plan for the Best, Prepare for the Worst

You will find insurance companies more than willing to insure you for a low premium, providing that you are relatively healthy, have a good occupation, and have good moral character. Make sure you select a financially strong company that will remain in business. There are countless variations in policy design so make sure that you obtain several quotes from different sources. Many companies will offer coverage that takes place when you are unable to perform the substantial duties of your own occupation. They pay policy benefits, usually for two years, and then only continue if you are unable to work in a occupation in which you have been trained or in which you have previous experience. Some companies will only offer five years of benefits while others readily cover you all the way to age 65.

Important Policy Benefits

Consider this, if you are in a professional career or high-skilled job, you should be able to find an insurance company that provides disability income benefits all the way to age 65 or longer based on you being unable to work in your specific occupation. Therefore, if you were a dentist and are now unable to use your hands because of a disability, you could receive up to two-thirds of your normal earned income for life.

If the policy states your occupation for life, then you would not have to worry about them asking you to deliver newspapers because that's how you paid your way through dental school. Always look for the term *your occupation* in a disability policy. A good insurance agent can shed much light on these definitions for you. If insurance agents know they are in a competitive situation for your business, they will usually attempt to obtain the best possible coverage for you, both definitionwise and pricewise.

One agent evaluating another agent's proposed coverage can also help educate you. Most people overlook the tremendous value of an insurance agent as a dependable source of information.

Not Having Good Long-Term Care Coverage

Most retirees work their entire lives to accumulate assets for retirement. They have no intention of using those assets for a nursing home stay! However, without proper planning retirees or those planning for retirement could find their valuable financial resources being used for their care or that of a loved one. Simple planning steps today could prove a godsend for your tomorrows. The previous chapter looked into who would take care of you if you were disabled. Now, the concern is not only who will provide care but how you will be able to afford this type of care.

The base problem lies in the belief that one way or another, long-term care coverage will be provided. Many people have never been involved in securing the services of a nursing home or assisted living facility and don't realize the tremendous costs involved. It simply takes a lot of time and resources to take care of anybody who requires constant medical supervision and attention. These resources that must be mustered are enormous and don't come cheaply.

A Case in Point: Without Resources

George was living alone after his wife, Martha, passed away. Slowly, he developed near-blindness from his diabetes and had extreme difficulty getting around. He would visit neighborhood restaurants to get his meals; however, with his vision failing, George didn't attempt to renew his driver's license. Soon George was only able to move around with the aid of an electric cart and had to have food delivered by local restaurants at an added expense.

His doctor considered amputation of his foot due to complications of his poor circulation. Luckily, he was able to postpone such surgery. Yet he remained home-bound and isolated. His family tried to help. His son would stop by periodically, but George could tell it was hard for his son to make the time, especially because his son was busy with his own children and the burden of a full-time business schedule.

George decided that he would be better off living at an assisted care facility, but was shocked to find out how expensive it was. Not only did it want a very large down payment, but the monthly fees were well above what he was collecting in Social Security benefits.

He checked with his local community center about senior services and discovered that he could receive free hot meals delivered to his home daily. This would help but George knew it wasn't the answer.

Who would take care of him when he could no longer take care of himself? Who would assist him in making it to the bathroom? Who would make sure that he received the proper amount of medicine, especially with his failing vision?

George discovered that he was alone in an unworkable situation with no one to turn to for full-time care. He knew that he should inquire about moving in with his son. Hopefully, his son and family would agree. George knew he had to ask but could never seem to get the courage up. Deep down, he was afraid of being told no. If his family couldn't help him, where could he turn?

If his son agreed to let him move in, would he be taken care of? Would he be treated right? George hated the feeling of helplessness. He grew depressed. The more depressed he became, the harder he was to be around. He checked into government programs and was dismayed to find no easy answers. It seemed that if he could get into a nursing home he would have to spend almost his entire savings and then go on government assistance.

What a lousy deal! He would have to sell off most of his assets, leaving virtually nothing, just to get into a nursing home facility. Once he went in, he felt there was no real way to get back out. What would he have to come home to? He simply couldn't afford the long-term care expenses as well as his normal home bills and expenses such as property taxes, utilities, and normal repair costs. He felt helpless.

He's Not Alone

Many conditions require the services of a long-term care facility: heart disease; diabetes; arthritis; accidents; weak bones caused by osteoporosis; mental conditions such as Alzheimer's disease, dementia, or other cognitive dysfunctions; multiple sclerosis; amyotrophic lateral sclerosis (ALS, better known as Lou Gehrig's disease); and strokes to name a few. In fact, stroke is considered the number one cause for disability in the United States today.

It is estimated that 60 percent of the U.S. population will require long-term medical treatment at some point in their lives. The actual statistics for seniors age 65 and older requiring long-term care in a long-term care facility are slightly lower at roughly 40 percent. That is, you have a 2 in 5 chance of needing long-term care. This is a real risk! This statistic is for each of us as an individual. If you are a married couple, your odds greatly increase because there are two of you!

The Fallacy of Medicare

Many seniors, like George, thought that government programs such as Medicare or private health insurance (also known as Medigap when used in conjunction with Medicare benefits) would take care of them if they had to go into a nursing home. They are dismayed to find Medicare only covers the first 20 days and, then, only partially covers the next 80 days. Here is how it works:

> You must have been in the hospital for at least three consecutive days and enter a skilled nursing center within 30 days of being discharged from the hospital. Medicare then will cover the first 20 days. After this time, Medicare covers expenses for the next 80 days, except for a daily deductible of $96 (Medicare part B or a Medigap policy may pay your deductible). Thereafter, you are on your own!

People assume Medicare or private hospital expense insurance coverage will provide ongoing coverage. This simply is not the case. According to various studies, Medicare pays for no more than 16 percent of all long-term care in the United States today!

If Medicare Doesn't Pay, Who Does?

Long-term care facilities are not cheap. You will need room and board, as well as constant medical assistance. Monthly costs easily exceed $3,000. If you cannot afford the coverage, there is Medicaid, a welfare program funded both by the federal government and state government. You qualify by being indigent, that is, without the necessary funds required to pay your own way.

Medicaid takes into account your sources of income and current assets. They then contribute the minimum amount required to pay for your nursing home stay. Therefore, they pay different amounts for different people, depending on each person's resources. How much you are allowed to keep in remaining assets varies from state to state.

People used to give their financial assets away just before applying for Medicaid. This strategy has become much more difficult since the Omnibus Budget Reconciliation Act of 1993 (OBRA '93). This act states that gifts of assets within three years (36 months) of your application for Medicaid could delay your eligibility for benefits. In other words, simply giving your financial assets to family members before applying for Medicaid and their claiming you are indigent will no longer be allowed.

Some folks would set up an irrevocable trust (sometimes referred to as a Medicaid trust), transfer their assets to this entity, and then claim they were without assets. This type of trust would hold your assets. The payment of income or principal for your benefit was optional at the discretion of the trustee. Upon your demise, the remaining balance of your trust is passed to the named beneficiaries, usually family members. The theory being that, because you no longer owned the assets, you should be eligible for government money. This actually worked for a great deal of people. So much in fact, that the government now states that if you transfer assets to such a trust you must wait 5 years (60 months) before being eligible to apply for Medicaid. Medicaid rules now assert that if trust assets can be used for your benefit, then those assets should be taken into account.

This change in the rules may delay your eligibility for Medicaid until those trust assets are spent down. Medicaid trusts may still work for some people. Make sure that you seek competent legal and financial advice before proceeding.

Should Your Goal Be to Impoverish Yourself and Your Spouse Just So You Can Qualify for Medicaid?

Many people are shocked when they see what they get from Medicaid facilities. Nursing homes are reimbursed only so much for Medicaid patients. While these homes claim you will be treated the same as other private pay patients, studies do not bear this out.

Their Goal, Your Goal

Some people feel that having Medicaid cover their long-term care needs will be sufficient. Don't fall into this trap. This type of attitude is one of the major problems facing retirees today. Do you really want to be on Medicaid stuck inside a Medicaid facility? What about your dignity? Why not have the best care money can buy? Stay at a facility where you are treated as a fully functioning human being. Stay at a facility where they want to make you better so that you may return to your old life. Plan, so that you have a life to return to.

How about Home Care?

Wouldn't it be nice to stay home and get better? Private insurance may provide for this but don't expect Medicaid to! Medicaid rules foster a negative environment for today's seniors. Be proactive and positive by checking into suitable coverage. Obtain proper insurance now to preserve your way of life for yourself or your loved one, such as your spouse or parent. Give serious consideration to a good long-term care insurance product that includes a home care rider. It usually costs more, but is worth it. Some home care riders will even pay family members to take care of you.

Long-Term Care Insurance

If the thought of losing your net worth due to a long-term care stay for yourself or spouse concerns you, consider purchasing a type of insurance known as long-term care coverage. Long-term care policies provide benefits when the insured is unable to care for himself and needs help with the activities of daily living, activities that we take for granted when we are healthy. These activities of daily life include bathing, dressing, transferring, toileting, continence, and eating. Severe cognitive impairment should also trigger policy benefits.

Insurance companies specializing in long-term care coverage will provide benefits based on which policy you purchase through them. Typically, you must be unable to perform two, sometimes three, of the activities of daily living in order for benefits to begin. The policy specifies which benefits will be payable, how much, and for what period. Most policies provide benefits for various levels of care such as the following:

- *Skilled care.* This is daily nursing care including rehabilitation under the supervision of licensed medical personnel such as registered nurses, physical therapists, and registered dieticians, providing that they are under a physician's orders.
- *Intermediate care (semi-skilled care).* This is the required care deemed necessary but with less intensity in regard to the daily care of a patient by a professional.
- *Custodial care.* This involves the assistance in helping you with your activities of daily living. People helping you with these functions need not be medically skilled but usually follow medical guidelines. This care is usually provided after a physician certifies that such care is required.

It is important to remember that the custodial care that most people in nursing homes require is not covered by Medicare or Medigap policies. The only nursing home care that Medicare covers is skilled nursing care or skilled rehabilitation care that is provided in a Medicare-certified skilled nursing facility. In addition, a physician must initially recommend such care. Long-term care coverage can help place your worried mind at peace by providing benefits at your time of need. As with all insurance policies, you must be knowledgeable in selecting the proper coverage with the right company.

Key Policy Features You Must Consider

When are benefits payable? When will you receive benefits under your policy? In other words, when will you be able to collect value from the insurance company for premiums paid? There are two main factors to consider: the elimination period and the insurance policy contract language used in detailing with when and how benefits are payable.

The Elimination Period

Depending on your insurance company, it is typical to see benefits payable after an elimination period of 30, 60, 90, or 180 days. The longer the elimination period, the lower your premium will be. Most common is a 90-day elimination period because Medicare usually will assist you during that time period. Having a 90-day elimination period also helps you avoid the expense of processing an insurance claim for short-term stays in a nursing home. Always get a quote for long-term care coverage that is based on your actual needs. If you have enough assets to support yourself for a while, you may wish to go with a 180-day elimination period (6 months). Your premiums could be 10 percent lower if you do.

When and How Will You Receive Benefits?

When and how will you actually receive benefits? Your policy will spell out in detail when and how you may collect benefits. At a minimum, a decent policy will provide benefits under either of the following conditions:

- You become disabled due to sickness, injury, or advanced age and are unable to perform two or more activities of daily living such as bathing, dressing, transferring, toileting, continence, or eating.
- A physician has certified that you are severely mentally impaired due to severe cognitive impairment or that you require constant supervision to protect you from hurting yourself or others.

If a policy fails to provide benefits under these minimum guidelines, do not even consider purchasing the policy. No other restrictions should be placed on your ability to receive benefits, such as language stating that you first must be in a hospital for a certain amount of days before being eligible for coverage. This language exists in some older long-term care contracts and should be totally avoided.

Always have another insurance agent or attorney review your policy. Make sure that you read and fully understand your policy. Insurance companies have their attorneys draft their policies so that the language favors them, not you, the consumer. The insurance company puts their obligations in writing and nothing else matters but that contract language. When it comes time to collect benefits, what you see is what you get.

Daily Benefits

Most policies are geared to pay a daily benefit. You select the daily amount you want to insure for. This is usually in $10 increments. A minimum of $100 per day is suggested in most areas of the country. This would provide an average of $3,000 per month for a total of $36,000 a year. Depending on your financial resources and the cost of nursing homes in your area, you may need to increase or decrease this daily benefit amount.

Benefit Period

Most insurance companies will issue policies for various time periods. It's common to see policies for three years, five years, or lifetime. While the average nursing home stay is less than three years, it would be very dangerous to rely on this average figure. If at all possible, insure for a lifetime of benefits. The premium will be higher for this valuable coverage, but well worth it. Why risk it? Insure for the possibility of needing a lifetime of care.

Indemnity Plans

Consumers may be wise to seek a type of plan called an *indemnity plan.* This type of policy is geared to pay you your policy benefits if you meet their definition of being eligible. Once you qualify, they send you the monthly benefit check.

Compare this to a *reimbursement plan,* which will only reimburse you for the actual charges incurred up to the benefit maximum stated in the policy. Imagine the aggravation of having to submit various claim forms for expenses. Worst of all, with a reimbursement plan you may be paying for a $40,000 a year policy and only collecting a portion of that in benefits! It simply is easier to do your planning with an indemnity plan of coverage.

Are Reimbursement Plans Bad?

Not at all, they're just harder to work with. Typically, a reimbursement plan requires you to submit claims and your coverage will only provide enough reimbursement to meet those claims up to your policy limits. Therefore, you may be paying for a daily nursing home benefit of $120 per day and only collecting a portion of that if your claims are less than that amount.

Insurance companies find this type of coverage to be less expensive to underwrite because they charge for the maximum benefit, yet pay out less in many claims. Many insurance companies take this into account and charge slightly less for their policies than an insurance policy that carries the indemnity language. Many advisors feel that reimbursement plans are more affordable for average consumers who are just trying to make sure that their long-term needs are covered.

If you are single and on a budget, you may want to look at reimbursement policies first. They may provide the coverage for actual expenses incurred and also get the insurance company more involved in the insured's medical situation. Simply put, because your policy is a reimbursement-only type of plan, your insurance company will be slightly more involved with the nursing home or your case worker regarding your ongoing plan of treatment or care due to the fact that they are checking invoices regarding your standard of care.

When purchasing reimbursement plans with benefit amounts of less than a lifetime, be sure to check on the language called *pooled funds*. This language can make a huge difference. For instance, a contract that has pooled funds language may provide reimbursement up to actual costs incurred. If all of your daily benefits are not used up, they add these funds back to a pooled account for use on future claims.

Don't Overinsure

Many people believe that they cannot afford long-term care coverage. With the quotes some of them receive from insurance agents, it is easy to see why they feel this way. Many agents load up a policy quote with all the bells and whistles they can think of. Sometimes this is well meaning and other times it may be done to get the premium higher for their own compensation purposes.

Many insurance agents will inform you of annual costs of nursing homes in your area. They will then quote you a rate based on those costs. If a nursing home costs an average of $36,000 per year in your area, then your agent might recommend $3,000 per month or more in benefits to cover this expense. While this indeed may cover your expenses, you and your agent should also take into account other sources of income.

For instance, let's take the case of Mary. Mary has Social Security benefits of over $500 per month and a monthly private pension of almost $700 per month. Combined, these two checks provide over $14,000 per year. Mary should take this income into account and calculate how much money would be required to provide annual long-term care expenses in her area and how much funds would be required to maintain her current home while she is away.

If nursing home care is running $36,000 per year in her area and she calculates that she needs roughly $5,000 to maintain her home annually while she is gone, we can see that her total combined annual cost would be around $41,000. She has over $14,000 a year coming in. It doesn't make sense to insure for a full $36,000 in long-term care benefits when all she needs is $27,000 in benefits to make up any potential shortfall.

She might be better off taking out a $30,000 indemnity, long-term care plan with an inflation rider, which should meet her needs just fine. This could save her a tidy sum in premiums from buying the more expensive policy of $36,000 or more in benefits. After all, while we do want to cover the need, we don't want to overinsure.

Indemnity policies are easier to work with because we know how much we will have coming in, in the event of disability. Reimbursement policies are harder to plan with. While you may have a $36,000 plan per year, your actual incurred expenses might be substantially lower. You, therefore, have overpaid.

Policy Exclusions

All policies include certain exclusions. Typical exclusions might include:

- Any loss that is intentionally self-inflicted or an attempted suicide
- A loss that was caused by the commission of a crime
- Losses caused by alcoholism or alcohol abuse
- Losses caused by a war or act of war, whether declared or undeclared
- Losses caused by certain classes of controlled substances
- Certain losses caused by several mental conditions including anxiety conditions, depression, personality disorders, and schizophrenia (policies usually cover conditions that are physical in nature such as Alzheimer's, brain injury, or Parkinson's)
- Losses when you are out of the country for more than 30 days

These exclusions will vary from company to company and must be considered. Many policies may initially look good until you read the small print. The fewer the exclusions, the better off you are. If a company has listed exclusions that you feel are unreasonable, look elsewhere!

FIGURE 4.1 Limitations of Deductibility for Long-Term Care Problems

Age (At End of Year)	2000 Limitation	2001 Limitation
40 or under	$ 220	$ 230
41-50	410	430
51-60	820	860
61-70	2,200	2,290
71 or over	2,750	2,860

Would You Like Your Policy Tax-Qualified or Nonqualified?

As if selecting policies were not hard enough, you now have to select what type of plan you wish to have. Under the Health Insurance Portability and Accountability Act of 1996, long-term care insurance plans that meet certain requirements may be eligible for favorable federal income tax treatment.

One major advantage with qualified programs is that your benefits may flow to you free of federal income tax. In other words, a portion of your benefits may not be taxable. Typically, up to $190 per day may qualify for such favorable tax treatment.

The second major benefit of a tax-qualified plan is the availability of a possible tax deduction for paid premiums. Certain amounts of premiums paid for long-term care policies can be added to other deductible medical expenses. To claim this actual deduction, all of your medical expenses just have to total more than 7.5 percent of your adjusted gross income.

The deductibility of premiums paid for a qualified long-term care contract is limited to a dollar amount that is based on the age of the covered individual at the end of the tax year. These amounts are adjusted for inflation. For your convenience, the table in Figure 4.1 shows the dollar limitation for 2000 and 2001.

A word of caution concerning tax-qualified plans. Due to the fact that they have favorable tax treatment afforded them, Congress insisted that certain language be inserted into such policies. This language affects the policy eligibility standards.

Basically the language states that you must be chronically ill as certified by a licensed health care professional and that you have a written plan of care drafted by medical staff. This chronically ill status must be recertified annually.

When Are You Considered Chronically Ill?

You can qualify for this status under the following two standards:

1. You are expected to be unable to perform all of the necessary activities of daily living (ADLs) without substantial help from another person for at least 90 days. If a person is unable to perform two or more of these ADLs, then they will be considered to be eligible for policy benefits. ADLs are bathing, dressing, toileting, transferring, eating, and continence. Each individual state may decide to allow insurance companies to choose which five ADLs to include or can require insurance companies to use all six.
2. You require substantial supervision to protect your health and safety because you have a cognitive impairment.

Generally, these new requirements apply to long-term care policies issued after January 1, 1997, in order to be considered tax-qualified. Policies issued before this date should automatically be considered tax-qualified. The purpose of such legislation was to provide uniformity for qualification and also to serve as an incentive for people to insure themselves. If more people would take out long-term care policies, both the federal government and state government could benefit by paying out far less in Medicaid benefits.

Nonqualified Policies

The following are the main issues surrounding nonqualified policies:

- Each company will define its nonqualified plan, if available.
- Generally, you are not assured the favorable tax treatment.
- Many nonqualified policies are easier from which to qualify for benefits.

A nonqualified policy may be easier to claim benefits under because the requirements may state that in order to receive benefits a physician, registered nurse, or licensed social worker acting under medical direction must certify that nursing care is necessary as part of a plan because

- your care is medically necessary,
- you cannot perform one or more ADLs without standby assistance, or
- you have a cognitive impairment that requires supervision or verbal cueing by another person to protect yourself or others.

As always, shop around for the policy that best meets your needs.

Who Should Consider Purchasing Long-Term Care Insurance or Home Care Coverage?

As an aging nation, we all should seriously consider the possible, if not probable, need for such coverage. The shifting demographics of our country show that our families are scattering to different living locations sometimes hundreds, if not thousands, of miles away.

Add to this the lack of family closeness and sense of responsibility that was more common in days gone by and you can see the importance of having solid long-term and home care coverage.

Those with the necessary resources will invariably receive better and more personal care than those without resources. Therefore, all of the following may want to consider coverage:

- Single women
- Single men
- Children, for a parent, to ensure that resources will be available to take care of that parent
- Children, for a parent, to ensure the protection of their inheritance
- People that have known medical conditions in their family such as strokes, osteoporosis, Alzheimer's, Parkinson's, etc.
- Married couples in order to provide care for their loved one and to help preserve their assets
- Friends or relatives who live together to ensure they can retain some of their dignity, freedom, mobility, and closeness
- Couples who wish to ensure that proper care and assistance will be there for themselves or a loved one when they are no longer capable of assisting each other
- Anyone wishing to stay home to receive care (consider a long-term care program with a meaningful home care rider)

Things to Look For in Your Contract

Guaranteed renewability. Make sure that the insurance carrier you select cannot cancel your coverage. Imagine paying for many years only to have your carrier drop you from its program at a point in time when you may no longer be healthy. This could prove disastrous to your financial well-being because you usually have to go through strict underwriting (a process where the insurance company evaluates you for approval in the programs) to be approved into another program.

Home health care. Imagine the flexibility of staying in your own home while health care providers come to you. This includes, among others, doctors, nurses, nurse's aids, trained attendees, dietitians, and rehabilitation professionals. This benefit usually has to be added as a rider on most policies. This rider could prove to be a godsend to you and possibly could preserve your dignity. Many married couples favor this type of coverage because they can still be together. Many times, people simply need professional assistance in dealing with the frailty of a loved one. Protect yourself by insisting that your policy covers home care as well as adult day care. Adult day care is a facility where you can drop off your loved one during the daytime while you attend to needed chores or for custodial relief.

Alzheimer's disease. Believe it or not, some policies try to exclude this condition from being covered primarily because the causes and accurate diagnosis of this dreaded disease are still uncertain. Avoid any and all policies that do not cover this condition.

Inflation protection. A policy that provides adequate protection today may be outdated five to ten years down the road. Medical expenses have been rising much quicker than other expenses. While this rider is not recommended for all cases, it's well worth considering. Obtain a premium quote with and without this rider. If it is affordable, go with this protection.

Lifetime benefits. Though a three-year policy is much less expensive than a five-year or a lifetime policy, the additional premium for a lifelong policy is usually worth it for your peace of mind. A good agent should be helpful is showing you how you can afford this coverage. If premium dollars are an issue, you may want to consider dropping other riders like inflation riders to make it possible to afford a lifetime benefit contract. Extending your elimination period to a longer time frame may also work.

No coordination with other coverage. Your policy should provide policy benefits regardless of any other health plans or government programs to which you may be entitled.

Spousal discount. Look for this discount if both you and your spouse are seeking coverage. The savings can be substantial! Remember that some companies offer a joint discount to persons living in the same home even if they are not married. This could prove advantageous to siblings living together or people who share resources.

Insurance company strength. At a minimum, you should insist that your insurance carrier is rated A or A+ by A.M. Best Rating Service. What good is a policy if the insurance company backing the policy goes bust?

No preexisting condition restrictions. Once you have been approved, the insurance company should not be able to assert that benefits are not payable to you for a condition that you had prior to obtaining coverage. It is also wise to disclose any medical conditions you have, or have had, when first obtaining coverage. Disclose everything; if you do not and the insurance company approves you, it can later allege that you committed fraud. Fraud is the misrepresentation of information or failure to disclose pertinent information to the insurance company. As long as you honestly disclose all pertinent information to an insurance company and it accepts you for coverage, then you should not have to worry about being cancelled or having your claim denied due to misrepresentation or fraud. Do not rely on the assurance of your insurance agent whether you should, or should not, disclose a prior medical condition. Disclose everything that is pertinent so that the insurance company cannot allege fraud later. An agent does not have the right to decide what is pertinent or not. Only the insurance company and its underwriters can make this decision.

Bed reservation clauses. Make sure your policy takes into account that if you are required to leave a nursing home for hospitalization, the insurance company will continue to pay the funds necessary to maintain the costs of your bed. Otherwise, you may lose your patient status in a facility and be forced to find another.

Rate guarantees. Very few companies will offer a policy premium rate guarantee. Usually the company will only guarantee that it won't single you out individually for a rate increase. They could, however, raise rates for certain classes or groups of policies, which may include your contract. A few companies will guarantee rates for a certain time period such as the first ten years. This type of rate guarantee is very rare but, if available, should be seriously considered.

In general, you are at the mercy of the insurance company and its officers with regard to rate increases. Choose reputable companies that have traditionally been good to their policyholders. Avoid companies that have a history of rate increases. The best way to find this out is by asking your agent or the company directly. Do some research. Avoid companies that are in the process of being merged into other financial companies. New owners of these companies may pass along rate increases to improve profit margins.

Ten pay programs. There are insurance companies that offer a *ten pay* solution. This allows you to make ten annual premium payments and have a paid-up policy. Always inquire if the company you are receiving a quote from offers this option. This rate will be higher, but well worth it in many cases. Imagine the peace of mind you would have in knowing that your policy will be paid up at the end of 10 years. This could save you a fortune in premium dollars.

Waiver of premium. This rider usually states that if you are collecting benefits under your policy, you will not have to make further premium payments. There are various forms of this rider. Check with the company you are considering because some will only cover long-term care facilities, while others will extend this benefit if you are receiving home care as well.

Third party notification. Wouldn't it be a shame to lose your coverage because you forgot to pay your premium? Third party notification helps prevent this because the insurance company will notify a named relative or friend in writing that your premium is due. People that are in the beginning stages of memory loss will also appreciate this safety feature. Also, this protection is a real benefit due to the common occurrence of misplaced or misdirected billing statements.

Restoration of benefits. This is a feature that restores your policy benefits to their original benefit amounts even if you have already used a portion of your policy's stated benefits. This type of rider or policy feature generally kicks in if you have been collecting benefits under your contract but have not yet exhausted your benefits. If you go for a certain length of time without collecting benefits, your coverage will revert back to its original stated amount.

This will prove a very valuable rider to those policyholders who cannot afford a lifetime benefit period. For example, consider a person with a five-year benefit amount that is in a nursing home for three years because of a hip fracture. Providing that she is properly discharged and does not collect any further benefits under the policy for one year, she may see coverage fully restored to a full five-year benefit program.

Nonforfeiture. Many long-term care policies offer a nonforfeiture option. This will vary from contract to contract, but usually states that you will be entitled to a full or partial refund of policy premiums paid in the event that you choose to terminate your coverage down the road. Typically, companies state that you must be with them 10 or 20 years before such benefits are payable.

Needless to say, these types of riders are probably the most expensive you could add to your policy. Certain companies offer a variation of this benefit by not refunding your money directly but instead giving you a paid-up policy for the premiums paid. Therefore, if you paid $30,000 over the years for your coverage, they may offer you a paid-up policy that can be used for future nursing home claims.

Death benefits (premium refund due to your demise). Some policies provide for a return of your premiums paid to your estate or named beneficiary if you die before receiving benefits. This rider varies so much from one insurance carrier to the next, it is hard to compare. Just make sure that you thoroughly understand when and how this rider might be payable before agreeing to it. Usually, this rider adds significantly to your premium and can make comparison shopping more difficult.

Substantial savings can be obtained by going with a longer waiting period such as 180 days or even 360 days.

Insurance companies consider the following factors when determining rates:

Type of coverage:

- Does it include long-term care?
- Does it include home care?
- Does it include other care such as adult day care or respite care?

Length of coverage:

- Typically, companies offer benefits for three years, five years, six years, or lifetime.
- What is the elimination period (when your benefits begin)? Substantial savings can be obtained.

Amount of benefits payable. Usually, most policyholders request a policy that will provide at least $100 per day in benefits. If after reviewing nursing home costs in your area, you determine that you require a $150 per day benefit, expect to pay more for coverage.

Riders that are added to your policy:

- Home care coverage riders will add substantially to your premiums but are usually well worth the added expense.
- Inflation riders will increase your policy benefits over time by increasing a set percentage each year to keep up with inflation. It is likely your benefits will rise by 4 to 5 percent each year or by actual inflation figures as given by government indexes such as the consumer price index.
- Other riders, which vary from company to company, may increase your premium such as refund options, paid-up policies, and waiver of premiums.

Tax-qualified or nonqualified policy. It pays to keep an open mind and look into both types of plans.

Your health:

- Many companies are seeking healthy applicants only. Rates can increase dramatically if you are being treated for certain medical conditions that could lead to the insurance company paying a claim.

- Your medical history, including your family's health history, can impact the rates that you may be charged.
- Physical characteristics such as weight can affect your rates.
- Your health habits, especially smoking and drinking, can impact your rates.
- Your bio-markers, which are indicators of your over all health, such as blood pressure, sugar levels, cholesterol levels, and dexterity may affect your rates.

Other factors such as current or prior occupation:

- Your moral character can affect your coverage.
- Your mental status may impact your rates.

Sample Rates

The sample rates shown in Figures 4.2 and 4.3 are quoted from the July 1999 issue of *Broker World* magazine, an insurance publication. Check with the actual companies for a full comparison. Actual rates could be different depending on riders and type of plan selected. A few companies offer rate guarantees for ten years, which may cause your premiums to be higher. These various companies are ranked by price only and not by policy features.

Obtaining Coverage

Many retirees wait too long to secure good long-term care policies. The time to apply for coverage is when you are healthy and able to obtain reasonable rates. The younger and healthier you are, the lower your premiums will be. Many retirees who receive quotes from insurance companies are often shocked by the amount of the premiums. Assuming you have done your comparison shopping, the reason that the rates seem so high is because you waited until you were older before seeking such coverage.

Look at these policies from the insurance company's standpoint. They may receive one annual premium payment from you and instantly be on the hook for a lifetime of benefits to be payable to you. They are in the business to make a profit. If they can't make a margin of profit from this type of business, they will first try to increase premiums. If this does not work, they may try to sell off that portion of their business to another insurance carrier. If this fails, they may be out of business. As always, you, the consumer, should make sure that your insurance company is financially strong. Try to obtain some rate guarantees or consider a policy that can be paid up in ten years.

FIGURE 4.2 Single Life Annual Premiums

AGE	Lincoln Benefit L-6301	CNA P1-N0100	GE Capital 7030	John Hancock LTC-96	Time Fortis 6063	Travelers H-LTC4J
60	$1,296	$1,972	$1,863	$1,720	$1,620	$1,872
Rank	1	6	5	3	2	4
65	$1,890	$2,725	$2,628	$2,190	$2,230	$2,547
Rank	1	6	5	2	3	4
70	$3,024	$3,999	$3,852	$3,190	$3,220	$3,771
Rank	1	6	5	2	3	4

How to Find Premium Dollars

The best reason to work with a good agent or financial advisor is that you can be clued into ways of finding premium dollars that you are currently overlooking.

For instance, an advisor may recommend transferring some funds from a low-paying bank account to a higher-yielding bond account or fixed annuity. Many of these accounts pay higher interest than bank accounts pay. That increase in interest may be all that is required to fund your coverage.

Today, more and more advisors are recommending tax-deferred annuities that are tied to the stock market. Generally, the principal is guaranteed, yet you are allowed to participate in the stock market gains. They typically tie your gains' increases to a well-known stock market index such as Standard & Poor's 500. Thus, they are commonly referred to as index annuities. An account such as this may serve you better as an inflation hedge, thereby, providing more dollars for long-term care premiums.

Popular among retirees are variable annuities. These are similar to mutual fund accounts. Some of the reasons for their popularity include:

- They usually guarantee your original investment as a death benefit, which could prove a blessing to your spouse.
- They allow you to defer paying taxes on your growth. You only pay taxes on the portion that you pull out. Therefore, you may save on federal income taxes, state income taxes, and even reduce the taxable portion of your Social Security benefits.
- You retain the right to annuitize. In other words, your principal is spread out over your life expectancy as monthly income. This can increase the amount of income you have to live on. At the same time, it may protect this pool of money from creditors.

FIGURE 4.3 Joint Life Annual Premiums

AGE	Lincoln Benefit L-6301	CNA P1-N0100	GE Capital 7030	John Hancock LTC-96	Time Fortis 6063	Travelers H-LTC4J
60	$1,944	$3,155	$2,981	$3,096	$2,754	$3,120
Rank	1	6	3	4	2	5
65	$2,835	$4,360	$4,205	$3,942	$3,791	$4,245
Rank	1	6	4	3	2	5
70	$4,536	$6,398	$6,163	$5,742	$5,474	$6,285
Rank	1	6	5	2	3	4

- You may be able to use a systematic withdrawal program with your equity variable annuity accounts and your equity mutual funds. See Chapter 1 for an example of a systematic withdrawal program.

Another Way to Reduce Premium Costs

If you flat out cannot afford a policy offering a lifetime of benefits, consider having a policy that offers three, four, or five years of benefits. This is suggested for several reasons. One reason is that the average nursing home stay is just under three years. Second, some coverage is definitely better than no coverage. Third, in order to qualify for Medicaid, you must have little in the way of financial assets.

Medicaid will not allow you to apply for benefits if you have just divested yourself of assets in order to qualify. It states that if you give assets away to family, friends, or others you must wait at least three years before applying for benefits. The wait may be even longer if you place your financial assets into a Medicaid Trust. Therefore, even a policy offering a three-year benefit may be useful in allowing you to reduce your financial assets in order to qualify for Medicaid.

You may end up giving your financial assets to your family, using your long-term care policy for the expense of a nursing home over the next three years in order to qualify for Medicaid just as your long-term care benefits diminish. Not bad planning if you don't mind being on Medicaid!

In summary, the ABCs of long-term care are:

- Always have a trusted, knowledgeable friend or advisor review the program you are considering before making your premium commitment.

- Be skeptical if a person only represents just one insurance carrier. This type of coverage is not a one-size-fits-all type of insurance.
- Certain companies that may be competitive for one age group may not be for another group.
- Don't delay—nothing worthwhile comes easily. Finding a good long-term care program that meets your needs will require time, energy, and effort on your part. Save yourself a lot of grief by consulting with a knowledgeable agent or financial advisor. A good advisor will have several quotes from various companies and will take the time to explain the differences between them.
- Expect to be educated. In fact, you should know the company and product you are purchasing well enough to explain it in complete detail to a friend or family member.
- Find a financial advisor that can show you a way to fund your long-term care program.

How to Check on the Financial Status of an Insurance Company

Always have the insurance company that you are considering provide you with independent reports on its financial status. There are certain rating companies that follow the insurance industry and report annually on its financial health. If an agent is reluctant to give you this information, you may take that as a possible warning sign.

Here's how to check on your own. Begin by contacting as least two of the rating services listed below:

- A.M. Best Company, 908-439-2200
- Duff & Phelps, 312-368-3198
- Moody's Investor Service, 800-811-6980
- Standard & Poor's, 212-208-1199
- Weiss Research, 800-289-9222

Most of the companies can be easily checked by calling A.M. Best Company and Standard & Poor's. See Chapter 8 for a brief overview of the ratings system. Only consider companies that are highly rated, A or A+, by A.M. Best Company. If not, they should at least have a favorable report from Weiss Research. For more information on interpretation of the ratings system, see Chapter 8.

5

Not Planning Properly for the Transfer of Your Estate

If you were to leave your home never to return or to be heard from again, what do you think would happen to your property, belongings, investments, and possessions? Think long and hard about this. Imagine that you are gone and unable to make your wishes known. This exercise requires that you write out a list of all that you own or control and then try to calculate what would happen to those possessions upon your demise.

Most people assume that their assets will flow to the proper people. However, reality shows that this will not necessarily transpire unless you have intelligently planned for it.

Put It in Writing

People assume that if they place their wishes in writing, those wishes will be carried out. Many retirees have made their wishes known and have even had their attorneys put their instructions to paper, thinking that their affairs were now in order. Little did they realize that after their demise, the written instructions might end up being totally useless. One reason for this is that so few people truly understand how property is transferred upon their demise. Furthermore, very few retirees and even financial professionals take into account the myriad tax consequences or legal aspects that are imposed upon an entire estate.

Loved Ones Can Be Left Out

Poor planning leads to poor results. Family members that were to receive a portion of your property may be left out.

A Case in Point: The Pitfalls of Joint Ownership

Suzie was very close to her father, Harold. She was there to take care of him after his wife, June, passed away. Apparently, June had taken care of their banking, investment planning, and bill paying. After she passed away, Harold had a hard time even remembering to pay the bills.

Suzie was a godsend because she stepped in and made sure that all of the bills were paid well ahead of time. Harold appreciated this because it gave him more time to indulge in card games with his friends down at the local VFW hall. It only seemed natural that Harold add Suzie's name to his checking and bank accounts. Harold liked what Suzie was doing for him yet he treated his other children equally. Just because Suzie lived the closest and was therefore able to assist him, Harold wasn't going to favor her at the expense of his other children. Shortly after his wife passed, Harold had a local attorney prepare his will to reflect this fact. He still wanted his estate to pass equally to all three of his children.

Harold suffered a massive stroke and died shortly after. His children were all shocked at his quick passing and went through the funeral proceedings in a sullen state of disbelief. Finally, as they got together to settle their father's estate, they were surprised to find out that because Suzie was joint owner of the bank accounts, she was entitled to the total proceeds of those accounts by virtue of being named joint owner with right of survivorship. Suzie's brother and sister each received a one-third share of their father's probate estate. However, they were not entitled to a penny of the jointly held assets that were passed on to Suzie.

Because Suzie's father had an estate that was under the federal estate size of $675,000, no federal estate tax return (Form 706) had to be filed. Therefore, Suzie's brother and sister were not even aware of how much Suzie actually received by virtue of being named joint owner on their father's accounts. Furthermore, Suzie was under no obligation to let them know. In fact, the amount that Suzie received was double the sum that the other children received. This was not Harold's intention. A brief overview of estate planning should prove helpful.

A Matter of Will

The majority of Americans believe that a will constitutes estate planning. Nothing could be further from the truth. What is a will? A will serves as your road map through probate. This written document will inform the probate court of your wishes via written instructions. Common instructions left in a will document include:

- Whom you want to serve as your personal representative. Your personal representative is the person or persons that will act on your behalf in carrying out your instructions and in representing your estate with regard to business and legal matters. The term personal representative is the name commonly used today because it is gender neutral. Many documents still refer to your personal representative as your executor (male) and executrix (female).
- How you would like your estate divided or whom you would like to receive your property.
- Whom you would want to serve as guardian and custodian of any minor children or dependents.

There are, of course, many other instructions you can leave in a will. A few more examples will give you some insight into how powerful this document can be. In a will you can

- name not only the primary beneficiaries, but also alternative beneficiaries in case your primary beneficiaries predecease you;
- name charities and organizations as the beneficiaries of your estate if you so desire;
- designate what assets should be used for payments of certain debts;
- notify the court whether or not you want your personal representative (executor) or successor personal representative to post bond;
- specify different custodians or guardians for each minor child if you desire different people for each;
- define how you want the issue of common disaster addressed;
- establish a definition and description within your will document of what length of time a spouse should survive you in order to inherit under your will;
- establish any gifts to minors to be made under the Uniform Transfer to Minors Act as well as who should be custodian of those accounts;
- establish testamentary trust provisions that could be used to establish a family trust for your family's well-being and protection;
- establish trusts for your children when they are minors and be sure to use the trust language that will ensure the most flexibility to the person managing those funds; and
- establish trusts through your will that would financially protect beneficiaries from themselves.

These are just a sampling of provisions that you may wish to think about inserting into your will document. This is why a knowledgeable estate planning attorney can prove so helpful.

The biggest misconception circulating today is that a written will is enough. A will has several limitations to it. Just because you state your desires in writing doesn't mean that the probate courts will agree. The biggest problem, in fact, can be that a will does go through probate. The process of probate opens up your set of instructions to interpretation by the court and all other interested parties.

Wills Are Not Private

Families often are disappointed to find that wills are open to public viewing by virtue of going through the probate process.

What Is Probate?

Probate is the process in which your will is admitted to the court. Once the court accepts that this is indeed your proper will, then the court will have your personal representative follow certain procedures.

Once these procedures are properly followed, the court may grant your personal representative the necessary papers to carry out your wishes. These papers are called *letters testamentary*. They allow your personal representative (also known in many states as executor) to transfer your property to the proper party.

Probate can be a very lengthy process due to the fact that it involves, among other duties, the following:

- *Collection of assets.* This task involves the collection and possible consolidation of the deceased's assets in order for them to be used for payment of taxes and bills as well as for the proper allocation to the intended heirs.
- *Accounting of inventory.* A complete listing of the deceased's assets and belongings will have to be made. This is crucial so that property is not overlooked and an accurate accounting can be made.
- *Payment of debts, expenses, and taxes.* The decedent may have medical bills, funeral expenses, credit card debt, business obligations, and taxes among other outstanding obligations. These issues must be addressed.
- *Determination of proper heirs.* Just because a deceased person has named certain heirs doesn't mean that the probate court will go along. A listing of relatives and heirs must be assembled before the court will sanction the instructions of the will. These relatives and heirs must be notified before final distributions can be made. This is known as *notice of probate*.

- *Acquisition of any necessary releases/disclosure of final accounting.* The representative of the estate needs to secure from heirs the necessary release forms and provide a proper accounting of the estate to both the heirs and the court.
- *Distribution of assets.* After all assets have been collected and debts, taxes, and other obligations paid, then distributions can be made to heirs. This part of the probate process can produce its own special problems, such as who should receive what particular assets.
- *Closure of the estate.* During the process of closing the estate, a final accounting is usually given when the estate's assets have been completely transferred to the proper parties. In addition, a final tax return is usually done.

As you can imagine, all of these duties and responsibilities can, and do, take time to complete. Most personal representatives spend numerous hours diligently trying to get through the process. Even when an attorney is hired, you will find them hard pressed to expedite the probate process as the probate process has a life of its own.

Hopefully, you will find an attorney to assist you who is competent and diligent in the matters of probate. Keep in mind that many attorneys are able to charge a percentage of the gross estate when handling a probate estate. This could mean that even if they only handle certain aspects of the probated situation, they could impose higher fees than you have estimated. The fees could run 5 percent or higher on large estates (estates valued at more than $675,000) and the percentage may be even greater on small estates. For instance, if an individual has an estate consisting of approximately $100,000 and the attorney charges $7,000 for directing that estate through probate, your estate has paid 7 percent in legal fees to settle that estate.

What If You Die without a Will?

Many people die without having a will document in place. Others have passed on without their heirs being able to locate their will document. In these cases, their estate will pass according to the laws of intestacy and by type and form of ownership.

Although the laws of intestacy share a common theme, they vary from state to state. That is because each individual state has adopted a certain distribution system concerning real property and those rules will come into play. This set of rules and body of laws are known as intestacy laws. People are considered to have died intestate when no legal will document can be found and there is either property to be distributed or claims to be filed on the deceased's behalf.

The laws of intestacy are in place to protect your heirs and to ensure that your estate falls into the right hands. In effect, if you die without a will, the state has written one for you. As nice as this sounds, you may not like what the state has come up with. Furthermore, it places your heirs at a disadvantage because someone must petition the court to represent your estate. Another major disadvantage occurs when you have minor children and have failed to name a guardian for them. Believe it or not, this is an issue for some retirees as well. It is becoming more common as grandparents are taking custody of their children's children due in part to the preponderance of broken families in today's world.

It is estimated that up to 75 percent of Americans die without leaving a proper will. This is indeed a shame when you consider how easy it is to obtain a proper will. Most individuals plan on getting around to the drafting of a will, but put it off for various reasons. A common comment often heard is "I will draft a will when I become severely ill and not before." They fail to realize that tomorrow comes very quickly and many times life catches us unprepared. People don't plan on becoming sick and when they do, they have a tendency to lose their energy. This makes it very difficult to do your estate planning. A few hours today could benefit your family tremendously tomorrow.

The laws of intestacy usually provide for your estate to be passed to immediate family first, followed by more distant relatives. Perhaps you wish to leave your estate to one particular family member and not another. If you die without having a proper will drafted, the state will pass on your property according to state guidelines. Therefore, your desire for one family member to receive more property than another family member could be out the window. Take decisive action now to ensure that the proper people receive your property. If you are married with children, the state usually insists that a third to half of your probate estate passes to your spouse. The laws of intestacy vary from state to state. Check to see how they are applied where you live. Better yet, have a will drafted.

State of Residence

Speaking of state laws, you may want to determine in which state you are considered to be a resident. This could have a tremendous impact on your probate estate. For instance, you may have real property in one or more states; therefore, your heirs may have to open up a probate estate in each state to settle your estate in order to pass your property to the appropriate parties. Additionally, the state in which you are considered a legal resident may impose additional state inheritance taxes or the equivalent. Worst of all, each state may want to exert authority over your probate estate. This could prove both costly and time consuming. Different states have different probate laws and intestate laws. Decide now which state you want to govern your will document. This can be accomplished by firmly establishing residency within that state and by having your will drafted in that state by a local attorney. However, if you are holding title to property in another state, be prepared by knowing that state's property laws and by seeking out competent legal advice to expedite the transfer of that property after you are gone.

The following questions will help you determine which state is your legal domicile:

- What state do you call home?
- In what state is your primary residence located?
- In what state are you registered to vote?
- What state issued your current driver's license?
- In what state do you file current state and federal income taxes?
- If still employed, what state do you work in?
- In what state do you hold your checking or savings accounts?

If the answer to all of the above is one state, then it's safe to say that you are a resident of that state. Contact a local attorney if you are unsure of your legal residence. This is an issue that must be addressed. It could very easily affect the legality of your will. Each state is different and thus you should have a new will drafted when establishing legal residency in a new state. When it comes to wills, one size does not fit all.

Will Substitutes

One of the most common ways to avoid probate is by holding real property with another person or persons as joint tenants with right of survivorship (JTWROS). In essence, when one person passes on, the property remains with the survivor(s). This is usually done without much fanfare. Most recipients receiving jointly owned property go about their business unconcerned with the hassle of opening a probate estate and all the procedures that go with the opening, administering, and closing of a probate situation.

The benefit of holding real property, such as real estate and investments, as joint tenants with right of survivorship is obvious—you have neither the aggravation of probate nor the delay of transferring title. It is also very quick to convey property and, in most cases, very private. In most situations, it is very hard to contest such a transfer of property as well. It's no wonder that so many laypeople use this method to convey property to loved ones.

As good as JTWROS may seem, there are some drawbacks. When you add someone to your account or property as a joint tenant, you have, in effect, made a gift. The new joint owner and you now both own the property. You cannot insist that the joint owner give back to you what you have given. He has as much right to the property or account as you do. You may not feel this way but, in the eyes of the law, you have made a completed gift. You have the legal right to make such a gift but no legal right to reverse such a gift. Only in extreme situations, where you can prove fraud or perhaps undue influence, could you have a legal case for reversing such a transaction. The following example illustrates this point exactly. Let's take a look at what happened to Anne and her daughter, Marcie.

A Case in Point: Anne and Her Completed Gift

Anne added her daughter, Marcie, to the property that she was living on by filing a new deed with the county. This deed reflected that Anne and Marcie now owned the home and the property it sat on as joint tenants with right of survivorship. Anne did this because she knew that she was getting up there in years and wanted to spare her daughter the agony of going through probate when she was gone.

Over the years, the home and property appreciated and Anne wanted to cash in on the recent price appreciation of the surrounding properties. Anne knew that she could take the proceeds from the sale of the home to buy a much nicer home in a warmer location and still have extra proceeds left over to supplement her retirement lifestyle. The real estate agent had set the closing date for the sale of the home and everything seemed to be going fine. That was until Anne asked her daughter to sign off on the deed.

Marcie explained to her mother that she didn't feel that her mother was making the right move. Marcie stated that because her mother had lived in that home for over 30 years, another 10 to 15 years wouldn't matter. In short, Marcie would not sign off. Marcie didn't want her mother moving away. Not only that, Marcie felt that Anne was acting impulsively. The end result was that Anne was now landlocked in her own home, all because she wanted to spare her daughter the aggravation of probate!

A Case in Point: Joan and Her Loss of Control

Anne's situation is not an isolated incident. Many children think that they know what is best for their parents. Even if your children will agree with your decisions, consider the case of Joan. Joan placed her only son, Glenn, on her vacation home deed to ensure that he and his family would inherit that property upon her passing. Glenn and his family were always there during the holidays with her and they had built up some great memories.

Imagine Joan's shock when she learned that Glenn's wife was filing for divorce. It seemed that Glenn's wife had taken a new position in the workplace and had met the true love of her life. Glenn's wife was proceeding full steam ahead with the divorce. In addition to wanting full custody of their children, Glenn's wife wanted the vacation property as well. Glenn and his mother talked to their attorney and were shocked to find out that Glenn's wife did indeed have a legal right to ask for that property. Joan could make a counteroffer in regard to Glenn's wife's request but, ultimately, it would be up to the judge who was deciding the divorce action and subsequent property settlement to make the final decision.

Loss of Some Tax Advantages

Most people have heard about the advantages of the step-up basis, but fail to inquire about how this affects their situation. Typically, when we pass on, we are allowed to pass certain assets on via a favorable step-up basis. This generally applies to real assets such as real estate and individual stocks that are not held inside of qualified plans. Qualified plans usually include such items as IRAs and profit sharing plans. The advantages can be tremendous.

Let's suppose that years ago you acquired 1,000 shares of IBM stock at $5 per share. Now, let's consider what would happen if at the time of your demise your IBM stock had grown in value to $150 per share. Your beneficiaries would receive the stock on the step-up basis, which means that they would owe no federal income tax on the sale of the stock as long as they sell it at $150 per share or lower. Essentially, the government states that they can treat the stock as if the beneficiaries bought it at that value on the date of your demise, which was in this case $150 per share. They would be free to redeem all of those shares tax-free if the stock stayed at $150 or under. This is much more advantageous to your beneficiaries than it was even to you.

While we are living, the government states that we have to pay taxes on the profit from the sale of a stock based on the difference between what we paid for it and the price that we sold it for. If, while living, you want to sell your IBM shares at $150 per share and you had originally purchased those shares for only $5 per share, you would have a $145 gain per share that would be taxable at your current federal capital gains tax bracket level.

Once you place another person on your account as joint tenants with right of survivorship, you have, in effect, given up the favorable step-up basis on the portion of the property that has been given. Therefore, in the case of a parent adding a child to a stock account, the child may receive the parent's portion on a favorable step-up basis, but will have to pay taxable gain on the portion given by virtue of the account being registered as JTWROS. Therefore, half of the account would be given the favorable step-up treatment and the other half would not.

The net result in this situation presents itself when the child sells the IBM stock. Half of the shares will have a cost basis for income tax purposes that stems from the date of the parent's demise, which in this case would be $150. The other half of the shares will be given the cost basis at time of original purchase, $5 per share. When the child sells the shares, half of those shares will have a huge gain because the child takes over the parent's cost basis on being added to the account as a joint tenant with right of survivorship. The remaining shares that passed upon death are always afforded the step-up basis assuming they were the right type of asset.

Typically Married Couples

Joint ownership appears to work better with married couples, but many couples don't take into account the possibility of both of them passing away at the same time as could occur in a common disaster such as a car accident or home fire. Even when one spouse survives, the surviving spouse often fails to do any further planning with the end result being a probated estate.

Alternatives to Joint Tenancy

The moral of these stories is to make you aware of what you are doing when placing people on as joint tenants on any accounts. There are other alternatives that allow you to remain in full control yet still allow you to avoid a probate situation. Consider some of the following strategies for avoiding probate while still maintaining control.

When dealing with checking and savings accounts, consider leaving the accounts in your name. By using the bank's own account forms, you can usually leave the accounts to your children or other intended heirs by use of something called the Totten Trust Provision. This is a form of joint bank account in which you name a co-owner or co-owners, who have no legal right while you are living, but who are entitled to receive such accounts after you have passed.

Consider using special language on securities accounts such as mutual funds and brokerage accounts. This is called a "transfer upon death" or "payable upon death" instruction. This language, which is not recognized in all states, will allow you to designate ahead of time whom you want to receive your account balances in the event of your passing. Check with your mutual fund company or brokerage firm to inquire if you are allowed to do this in your state.

With regard to certain retirement plans such as individual retirement accounts, profit sharing programs, pensions, and tax-sheltered annuity plans, keep in mind that you usually have the right to name a beneficiary to receive the proceeds from your account. Naming a person or persons as primary beneficiary of your plan will allow them in most cases to receive those proceeds without the grief of going through probate.

Special care must be taken if you are married. Certain states provide that your spouse must be named as primary beneficiary. You may need to obtain spousal consent before being allowed to alter your beneficiary. With married couples, federal law may also state that spouse approval is required before you are able to change the beneficiary of certain qualified plans. Check with your plan custodian or trustee to see if this is applicable.

Life insurance policies and nonqualified tax-deferred annuity policies have beneficiary designations. Naming a person or persons as direct beneficiary of such programs will allow you to pass those funds on without going through probate. People should very rarely name their estate as beneficiary as this would almost guarantee a probate situation every time.

With life insurance, it is wise to name a beneficiary other than your estate because these proceeds can make up the largest portion of your estate. These funds are usually payable immediately and can come in handy when settling an estate, especially when the other assets are less liquid.

Keep in mind that minors cannot hold title to real property by themselves. The main reason is that real property such as real estate or investment accounts may require that certain decisions are made that a minor would be incapable of making. Furthermore, those assets may require additional contributions of assets to maintain, manage, or improve that property.

A minor is simply not in the position to make such commitments or to vote on certain issues that may be required for those assets. Certain types of real property like real estate, autos, boats, land, and business interests may require the outside services of management companies, service personnel, contractors, and others to ensure their viability. Minors would be in no position to initiate those types of transactions due to the fact they are not legally able to enter into contracts. The age of majority for most young adults is between 18 and 21 years of age. Check with your state if you are unsure.

In most states, if a minor child has more than $2,500, then an adult must manage the child's assets. If there is no prearranged guardian, then the probate court will be involved in selecting an adult or professional company to act as guardian or custodian over those funds. Some states now permit a minor to hold up to $5,000 in assets before this requirement comes into play. This holds true for funds left by insurance policies, individual retirement accounts, group benefit programs, business interests, and outright inheritances as well as many other sources.

Gift to Minors

Most states have adopted the Uniform Transfers to Minors Act while a few states have adopted the Uniform Gifts to Minors Act. Both of these acts perform in the same fashion. That is, they allow an adult to leave various assets for a minor's benefit as long as there is an acting adult named under the registration of such assets. This adult, therefore, acts as a custodian for the minor's benefit.

Once the minor reaches a certain age, the minor is then entitled to those assets outright. Be careful when using these vehicles because the minor will usually have free access to those funds upon reaching the age of majority within that state. Certain states will allow you to extend that age by a small margin. Therefore, you may be able to extend the age at which the child has total access from age 18 to age 21 and even to age 25 in some states.

Most states will only allow a certain maximum dollar amount to be transferred this way such as $25,000 to $50,000. Some states will allow additional funds if they are being held for educational purposes. As with most estate planning issues, you should consult with a knowledgeable advisor in your state to check out complete details on what is available. Due to certain limitations regarding these accounts and because the minor will be able to access these funds at a relatively early age, the Uniform Transfers to Minors Act and the Uniform Gifts to Minors Act may not be sufficient. In many cases where substantial assets are involved or more flexibility is required, you would be better off having an actual trust drafted and established. This would allow you the advantage of appointing a longer succession of potential trustees, who would act in the same capacity as custodians. Consideration should also be given to prolonging the distribution period for the minor upon becoming a young adult. It takes a special type of young person to handle a substantial inheritance at such an early age.

Trusts are becoming increasingly popular as the vehicles of choice with regard to the transfer of property and avoidance of probate. The most popular type of trust that is used for this purpose is the revocable living trust (known in Latin as *inter vivos,* which simply means living). This type of document can be easily drafted due to the use of personal computers.

Using Living Trusts

A revocable living trust is a legal document that you have drafted while you are living. In essence, you create a legal container to hold title to your real property such as real estate and investments. The language of this document should allow your property to pass free from the probate process to whomever you designate as beneficiary.

The common advantages of having a revocable living trust include:

- Assets held within your trust will avoid probate.
- A trust is private and your financial affairs and financial situation can remain out of public records.
- Flexibility can be built into your trust to provide for family members and other beneficiaries. Unlike a probated estate where beneficiaries are to receive their inheritances outright upon obtaining legal age, a trust can stretch out the beneficiary's amount to be received over many years.

- Special provisions can be added to your trust that can provide for your beneficiaries based on their needs.
- Special provisions can be placed in the trust document allowing your successor trustee to handle the educational expenses and medical expenses of beneficiaries on an individual basis.
- Because the trust is considered a separate container for legal purposes, you can provide for a successor trustee to step in and manage your trusts assets in the advent of disability or diminished capacity.
- If married, special provisions can be placed into your trust document that can take advantage of the federal tax code and save your family large sums of money in estate taxes.
- A trust may retain the benefit of the step-up basis for tax purposes.

Careful Advice

Many retirees who approach their attorneys with questions concerning trusts are given unsuitable information. They are often told by attorneys, who have not really studied current trust strategies or who are not up to date on modern estate planning, that they don't need a revocable living trust.

Many of these attorneys simply are not up to speed on current trends impacting retirees. Quite often, these attorneys have never prepared a revocable living trust document and may feel intimidated by such a task. Other attorneys honestly feel that their clients don't need such a trust. Some common objections retirees may hear from their attorneys are:

- Your estate is too small to have a revocable living trust.
- A will document will be sufficient for your estate.
- Probate is not that expensive nor will it take very long.

Worst of all, in many cases an attorney who is unfamiliar with revocable living trusts will draft a trust for you within your will document. This type of trust is referred to as a testamentary trust. It is set up after your demise through the probate court.

Quite a few clients will leave their attorney's office with their estate documents in hand thinking that they have a revocable living trust and, therefore, will avoid probate. Imagine their surprise when they find out that even though they told their attorney that they wanted to avoid probate, the attorney drafted a document that guaranteed probate.

The practice of law is open to interpretation and every attorney has his or her own opinion. Expecting them all to agree on what is best for any given client is impossible. They are swayed by their upbringing, education, area of expertise, and other factors. An attorney who specializes in probate law may really believe that there is nothing wrong with having your estate go through probate. After all, the attorney may understand the probate system and feel you are best served by using such a system.

Make sure you visit an estate-planning attorney who is knowledgeable in the uses of trusts and other estate-planning strategies. It may cost a little bit more, but your heirs will be thankful that you did. The savings that you get from avoiding probate, just one useful strategy, could make all the difference in passing on as much of your wealth as possible.

The only advantage in having your real property transfer to your beneficiaries through probate via your will is when you want the supervision of the probate court, or if there are certain legal disputes that are of such a nature that you absolutely want them settled by the probate court to ensure that those disputes do not resurface later. Keep in mind, however, that a good estate attorney usually will include language within a revocable living trust that will allow the trustees to pass assets under the jurisdiction of the probate court if they deem it advisable. Therefore, a revocable living trust may still be the best choice.

Understanding the Jargon of Living Trusts

Like most areas of study, living trusts have their own language. At first, you may have a hard time connecting the jargon to its actual meaning. The most common terms used in a living trust include:

- *Grantor.* This term simply means the person who established the trust and provides the property to be placed into the trust.
- *Trustee.* This is the person or persons (can be a corporation as well) who has the task of handling the trust. Typically, the trustee will handle the day-to-day affairs involving the trust and be responsible for ensuring that the instructions given within the trust are carried out.
- *Beneficiary.* This is the person, persons, and/or entity that will benefit from the trust.

In many situations, the duties of the grantor, the trustee, and the beneficiary can and often are performed by the same person. When single persons (or married couples) establish a living trust, they are considered the grantor by virtue of having set up such an account and transferring assets to the trust. Because they usually are managing their own trust, they are considered the initial trustees. Also, because the trust is for their direct benefit while they are living, they are considered the primary beneficiary.

A few other terms that you will encounter:

- *Trustor.* This is the person or persons who initiates a trust and by transferring property into such trust causes the trust to be created. The trustor is also known as the grantor, donor, assignor, releaser, transferor, and settler.

- *Successor trustee.* This is the person, persons, or trust company that takes over the duties of trustee in the event of your complete disability or death. The language in the trust document will state when the successor trustee is to step in for this provision and what powers he or she have.

Only upon the grantor's disability or demise would other parties be involved. For instance, if a single person (grantor) had a living trust and she became disabled, most well-written documents would provide for a successor trustee to serve in her place. This successor trustee could make sure that the trust property or trust assets would be used for the benefit of the beneficiary (grantor also in this case).

If the grantor were to pass away, the successor trustee would follow the written trust instructions and pass the trust assets accordingly. Therefore, the successor trustee would pass the assets to the next beneficiary(ies) listed within the document. This can all be done without the court's intervention or supervision.

Typically, married couples will share a joint revocable living trust. Therefore, they both are usually considered the grantors. While living, they will typically both serve as cotrustees. Only upon the death or disability of one or both, will a successor trustee be necessary. While they both are living, they are usually the primary beneficiaries of their trust.

For Your Information

The enormous flexibility of a trust comes into play upon the demise of a spouse. Provisions can be inserted into the trust to provide investment management expertise into such trust documents to protect the surviving spouse from mismanagement of the trust assets. Provisions also can be made to protect the children born of either party, including from a prior marriage as the case may be.

Revocable living trusts can be tailored to fit your actual life situation. The trust typically starts with the declaration of trust, which is the formal, written expression of the grantor or trustor creating such trust. This body of written language will contain the names of the parties involved, the description of the property to be placed within the trust, and the actual terms of the trust.

You should always seek out the services of a specialist in regard to creating your own revocable living trust. They can be greatly beneficial when it comes to designing a document that meets your specific needs and desires. People that buy do-it-yourself kits think that they have all of their bases covered and will spend the rest of their lives with the smug conviction that they have taken care of their estate planning. Nothing could be further from the truth!

Many of the people who have a do-it-yourself plan have a haphazard collection of verbiage that boils down to an accident waiting to happen. There simply are too many details of law and specific situations that need to be properly addressed to ensure that your wishes are carried out effectively for a do-it-yourself trust to be a wise choice. The sad fact is these do-it-yourselfers will never know that their estate documents are flawed because they will be gone when the matter comes to light.

Pour Over Wills—A Necessity

Even if you have a revocable living trust drafted, your attorney will still draft a will document to go with it. This document is a special type of will called a *pour over will*. If you inadvertently miss registering any assets into your trust, a pour over will allows those assets to go through the probate system and be added to your trust at some future point in time. Because your revocable living trust has all of your written instructions, you need to have your will document direct any probate assets into the trust, so those instructions can be carried out.

A Few More Reasons

Many retirees feel that they have placed all of their real property such as real estate and investments into their trust and, therefore, no further action is needed. What these retirees fail to realize is that there may be property that will flow into their estate after they are gone, such as proceeds from a wrongful death lawsuit or a possible legal settlement from a medical malpractice lawsuit. The point being, we never know for sure what will flow into our probated estate. That is one of the reasons a pour over will is required.

If a person has to be given the authority to represent your estate to bring forth a legal action or to represent your estate in a legal action. A pour over will, similar to a regular will document, will appoint someone to handle these positions. That person will be known as your personal representative (executor). Will documents are also required to appoint a guardian or custodian for minor children.

About Living Trusts

Many people feel that they will lose control by having a revocable living trust. This simply is not the case in most situations. With most living trusts, you retain the right to change your mind at any time as well as to terminate the trust. That is why the trust is called *revocable*. You are also free to change the terms of your trust at any time.

The reason for this misconception is twofold. First, many people set up their trust so that it cannot be changed upon their death or disability. This is typically done in the cases where one of the parties involved in the creation of the trust has a family from a prior marriage. They may also have certain restrictions kick in upon their death and/or disability to protect the right to pass on certain property free of the federal estate tax.

Second, people see families on television shows such as *Dallas* struggling with the yoke of trusts established for them by their families or legal counsel. In fact, if you have a large amount of wealth, you may need to create certain trusts that are often irrevocable and may impose severe restrictions. This is done for tax reasons and for wealth protection. A revocable living trust is not that type of trust.

Larger Estates

You may need certain tax language placed into a revocable living trust to help save on federal estate taxes. Furthermore, you may require a special trust to hold your life insurance polices. If your estate is large or has the potential to increase dramatically, than you need to be aware of other issues as well.

A Brief History of Certain Tax Laws

There are various forms of taxation. Most people are familiar with federal and state income tax. They may, however, be totally unfamiliar with another tax which originated back in 1916. This tax is called the federal estate tax. This tax is imposed on the right to transfer property upon one's demise. The federal government also has a tax called the federal gift tax, which covers the giving of property while living. Either way, the government has rules governing the transfer of wealth in this country. The Tax Reform Act of 1976 combined both of these. These are the tax schedules people are referring to when they speak of the unified estate and gift tax.

Most people are stunned to find out that all the property they worked their life to accumulate will face the possibility of being taxed further when that wealth is transferred to family members or other heirs. Even if you have been paying current income taxes on this property, you must understand that the federal estate tax and federal gift tax are in addition to other taxes that the federal government and state and local governments may impose. The reason for the tax is based on a doctrine called Redistribution of Wealth.

Basically, this doctrine states that our government needs to take from the wealthy and redistribute this wealth to less fortunate people. Otherwise, the few multibillionaire families would control our country. The stranglehold that this would impose on the economy would be near impossible to break up. Look at our history and you will see points where many wealthy families were controlling the wealth of this country with near monopolies over most industries and services—the Rockefellers, Duponts, Morgans, etc. This federal estate tax and federal gift tax along with laws against monopolies proved very useful in breaking the grip that these wealthy families had over the U.S. population as a whole. The problem is not necessarily with the concept of estate and gift taxation, but with who must pay this tax. Originally, this tax was designed to tax the very wealthy. It is doubtful that past lawmakers intended this tax for middle-class families or for families that had small to midsize companies to pass on. The problem has been inflation. With inflation, you have estates growing much larger than any lawmaker could have anticipated. So, while this law was meant to tax the very wealthy, the net effect is that it has been taxing middle class and upper middle class families far too often. Especially hurt have been ranchers, farmers, and small business owners.

Estate Taxes

Many people have often heard of local businesses closing their doors due to tax liens. Perhaps it was a local establishment that got behind in its payroll taxes or behind in its state income tax collections. What many people fail to realize is how many small to midsize companies have to be shut down in order for the children of the deceased owner to pay the federal estate taxes on the value of the business that they just have inherited. There are not enough funds left over in many cases to allow these children to continue the business. The reason for this is the high amount of the federal estate tax imposed and how quickly it must be paid.

The Federal Estate Tax

Years ago, people would talk about the local rancher or farmer who had passed away. All the local people knew the rancher or farmer who had built up his estate from scratch and established a tract of land that had become prosperous by anyone's definition. The sad fact was that when the rancher or farmer passed away, his family would have to pay a tax on the value of his property. This tax was not only quite large in most cases, but had to be paid within nine months of the rancher's or farmer's passing. Talk about devastating a family.

In many cases, the widow would be forced to sell off precious land holdings and/or any material goods that were not absolutely necessary for the running of the business. This is how the expressions "They had to sell off the back forty" and "They had to sell the family farm" came into play.

Congressmen were being bombarded with these horror stories and took steps to ensure that at least the surviving spouse would be able to postpone these devastating taxes. Therefore, Congress decided that spouses should be allowed to pass an unlimited amount of property between themselves in order to not financially impoverish the surviving spouse. This is known as the unlimited marital deduction and was introduced in 1981 under the tax relief package known as the Economic Recovery Tax Act.

Therefore, be aware that the government imposes a tax on the right to transfer property in this country on its citizens. Even if U.S. citizens live outside of this country, our laws state that they still must pay these taxes. The tax rates were slightly different, depending on whether you were passing property on while you were living, which was called the federal gift tax, or passing property upon your demise, which was taxed under the federal estate tax rate. In order to simplify these two different tax schedules, Congress passed legislation in 1976 that combined the two taxes into one common schedule of taxes known as federal estate and gift taxes, as shown in Figure 5.1. Congress further allowed a credit amount that could be used for taxes due for amounts transferred while living or upon your demise. People were now free to apply any or all of this tax credit as they saw fit.

This tax credit is called the unified credit and can be used against the amount of property transferred, up to a certain allowable federal limit. To help mitigate the effects of inflation, this limit has been increasing gradually every few years. Many estate planners refer to this unified credit as the exemption equivalent. In other words, the government imposes a tax and you are able to apply the current tax credit available during the year of the gift or the year of death against the amount of property transferred. The amount one can leave at their demise or gift while living is $675,000 for tax year 2001. Under President Bush's tax plan enacted during 2001, the amount one can gift while living is capped at $1 million for tax year 2002 and beyond. The amount of property one can leave upon their demise, however, will start off at $1 million during year 2002, with further scheduled increases until the year 2009.

How Much Is a Tax Credit Worth?

A tax credit is a dollar-for-dollar credit against taxes due. For example, the government imposes a tax on the right of a parent to pass on property to her children. Let's assume that during tax year 1997, a parent leaves property valued at $1 million. During that year, the federal unified credit amount allowed to each individual was $192,800. That credit amount was enough to pay the tax on exactly $600,000 worth of property. Therefore, the parent passing $1 million to her children was able to pass on the first $600,000 free of tax. The difference, however, was taxed at quite a high amount.

The parent passing the assets needed to calculate what they would owe on the additional $400,000 of property, which doesn't have any tax credits to shelter it from taxes. The amount of tax owed would be around $153,000 with any further amounts transferred taxed at an effective rate of over 40 percent. Having said this, it is important that every U.S. citizen and U.S. resident understand that these taxes are due on

FIGURE 5.1

Federal Estate and Gift Tax Rates
(for tax year 2001 only)

If Taxable Estate:			Tentative Tax Is:	
Is Over	But Not Over	Tax	Plus %	Of Excess Over
$ 0	$ 10,000	$ 0	18%	$ 0
10,000	20,000	1,800	20	10,000
20,000	40,000	3,800	22	20,000
40,000	60,000	8,200	24	40,000
60,000	80,000	13,000	26	60,000
80,000	100,000	18,200	28	80,000
100,000	150,000	23,800	30	100,000
150,000	250,000	38,800	32	150,000
250,000	500,000	70,800	34	250,000
500,000	750,000	155,800	37	500,000
750,000	1,000,000	248,300	39	750,000
1,000,000	1,250,000	345,800	41	1,000,000
1,250,000	1,500,000	448,300	43	1,250,000
1,500,000	2,000,000	555,800	45	1,500,000
2,000,000	2,500,000	780,800	49	2,000,000
2,500,000	3,000,000	1,025,800	53	2,500,000
3,000,000	10,000,000	1,290,800	55	3,000,000
10,000,000	17,184,000	5,140,800	60	10,000,000
17,184,000	—	9,451,000	55	17,184,000

The Federal Gift Tax is intended to limit the amount that can be transferred to persons other than a spouse without incurring a tax. Gifts of up to $10,000 can be made during a year to an individual without incurring a tax. If the gift is made by a married couple from their jointly owned assets, it can be as much as $20,000 without being taxed. There is a lifetime gift tax exemption of $1,000,000 starting on January 1, 2002. Although the estate tax is being repealed, the gift tax will not be repealed. It will continue past 2009 at a tax rate equal to the highest income tax rate in effect for the year that the gift is made. Currently it appears that the tax rate will be 35 percent.

the transfer of property. The person who transfers the property needs to be aware that there are such taxes to be paid.

Speaking of gifting, the government allows you to gift only $10,000 per year to as many people as you wish without any taxes. This amount should increase with inflation. Any amount after that requires you to pay taxes. You are, of course, allowed to use some or all of your unified tax credit amount in order to reduce that tax.

FIGURE 5.2 Federal Estate Exclusion Amounts

Year	Exclusion Amount
2001	$ 675,000
2002	1,000,000
2003	1,000,000
2004	1,500,000
2005	1,500,000
2006	2,000,000
2007	2,500,000
2008	2,000,000
2009	3,500,000
2010	Repealed
2011	1,000,000

Figure 5.2 shows the amount that the current allowable Unified Credit Amount will shelter in the upcoming years. Rates are subject to change at any given time, depending on the mood of Congress.

Key Points to Remember about the Federal Estate Tax

- The federal estate tax is a tax on the right to transfer property.
- The tax is based on the fair market value of property.
- The tax must be paid before property is transferred to beneficiaries.
- The tax must be paid within nine months from the date of death.

You are allowed certain deductions against this tax such as:

- Debts
- Administration expenses associated with the estate
- Funeral expenses
- Casualty losses
- Charitable deductions
- Marital deductions

Keep in mind:

- Some states impose certain death taxes as well. Consult with your estate advisor.

- Everyone has the availability of the unified credit to shelter property to our heirs, but many of us fail to use it!

Imagine having a check in your pocket for $220,550 but you never cash it. That is what is happening all across the country because many retirees simply have not done the proper planning that is necessary to take advantage of the allowable tax credits.

Here is how it works. Everyone is allowed a one-time unified credit amount. We can use it now if we want to start a gifting program of over $10,000 per person or our estate can use it after we pass away. The only catch is that you have to have a taxable transaction to use it against. In other words, the government will only let you use that check against taxes that would be due if you die having property in your name.

A Case in Point: Harry and Sharon Make a Mistake

Harry and Sharon have been married for over 40 years. They have always owned everything as joint tenants with right of survivorship. In addition, Harry has named Sharon as primary beneficiary of his life insurance policy and his profit sharing plans. Harry has also named Sharon as the primary beneficiary of his will. In fact, his brother-in-law who is an attorney drafted a simple will. He joked to Harry that the will he drafted was called an "I Love You" will. He said that married couples typically have these types of wills, where one person leaves everything he has outright to his spouse.

Harry was glad that his brother-in-law was an attorney and had taken care of his estate planning for him and his wife. Harry knew that his brother-in-law was an attorney that specialized in corporate issues, however, his brother-in-law assured him that doing a will was a piece of cake. "No problem," he said.

Harry and Sharon were fortunate that their financial advisor routinely had an experienced estate-planning attorney review all clients' estate documents. This was done to ensure that as much property as possible would pass on to heirs in the event of a client's premature death. A major flaw was uncovered in Harry's planning.

Upon review of their documents, it was pointed out that if Harry passed away, his entire estate would pass to his wife, Sharon. You may be asking yourself, "What is wrong with that?"

In this case, Harry, in effect, had given his tax credit exemption amount away for free. Leaving everything outright to his wife would mean that the total estate would be in Sharon's name. In this case, assuming Sharon had passed away the same year, the following would have occurred:

- Harry died leaving his entire estate to Sharon.
- Harry's estate is valued at $675,000.

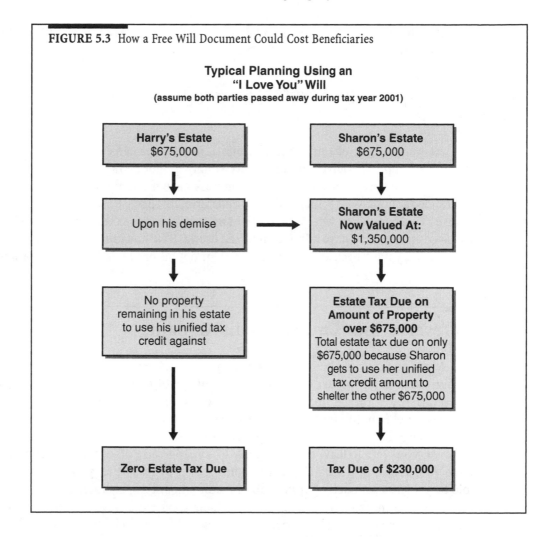

FIGURE 5.3 How a Free Will Document Could Cost Beneficiaries

**Typical Planning Using an
"I Love You" Will**
(assume both parties passed away during tax year 2001)

| Harry's Estate $675,000 | Sharon's Estate $675,000 |

| Upon his demise | → | Sharon's Estate Now Valued At: $1,350,000 |

| No property remaining in his estate to use his unified tax credit against | Estate Tax Due on Amount of Property over $675,000 — Total estate tax due on only $675,000 because Sharon gets to use her unified tax credit amount to shelter the other $675,000 |

| Zero Estate Tax Due | Tax Due of $230,000 |

- Because he left it outright to Sharon under the unlimited marital deduction, Sharon received the total amount free of any estate tax.
- Because nothing remained in Harry's estate, he did not get to use his credit of $220,550, which covers the taxes on real property such as investments and real estate of $675,000.
- Sharon passed away during the same year and Harry's funds transferred into her estate plus her own assets.

The example and the chart in Figure 5.3 illustrate how a free will document could cost your beneficiaries. In the case of Harry and Sharon's children, a sum of over $230,000 had to be paid. If Harry left his estate of $675,000 directly to his children or, better yet, had created a revocable living trust with an A-B provision (as discussed in the next section), he could have avoided the huge tax bill that his children were faced with.

Proper Planning Using a Revocable Living Trust with an A-B Provision

As the example of Harry and Sharon illustrates, one can easily lose the unified credit or exemption equivalent very easily simply by not taking into account how to preserve it. The problem started when Congress gave married couples the unlimited marital deduction. Most spouses simply transferred property to each other upon their demise. These transfers were now free of any federal estate taxes. Unfortunately, the deceased spouse may have left nothing in an estate. If he had left some property in his name, he may have been able to utilize some, if not his entire, unified credit amount.

How to Preserve Your Unified Credit Amount

Make sure that at the time of your demise, you leave enough of your property in your estate to allow your estate to take advantage of federal tax laws. If this property passes by contract, probate, or other means directly to your spouse, then the property would qualify for the unlimited marital deduction and would not be considered property left in your estate for purposes of using the unified credit amount. If, however, you were to leave your property to someone else other than your spouse or leave your estate in a special tax trust known as a bypass trust, you would then be able to preserve as much of your unified credit amount as possible.

Because most married couples want their spouses to have the full benefit of what they have worked so hard together to accumulate, they choose to use the bypass trust option. This trust can utilize the proper language, which states that your only wish is to include in your estate the amount that would qualify for the maximum unified credit amount that is applicable in the year of your demise. All excess value of your estate is passed on to your spouse's trust, which is known as a marital trust. The amount that is left in your estate in order to qualify for the unified tax credit amount is known interchangeably as the family trust or the bypass trust.

The Marital Trust is commonly referred to as an A trust, while the Bypass Trust is called the B trust. An easy way to remember the A-B trust concept is to keep in mind that the A trust typically passes to the surviving spouse, while the B trust belongs to the person who has passed away.

The property left in your estate or your bypass trust is ultimately for the benefit of your children or other nonspousal beneficiaries. This ensures that it doesn't pass to your spouse under the unlimited marital deduction. The trust, however, can utilize all of its income for the benefit of your spouse. The trustee, in fact, is allowed to utilize all the income and is allowed to access the principal in certain situations as well. In addition, a good bypass trust will state that the spouse is entitled to access the bypass trust for up to another 5 percent or $5,000, whichever is greater, for whatever reason she desires. This is known as the *frivolous withdrawal privilege* or *5/5 power.*

Also, a good bypass trust will have the language that states that the trustees are to exhaust the principal of the trust if need be for the health, education, maintenance, or support of the surviving spouse. Your surviving spouse, of course, does not have ultimate say of who is to receive the trust's final proceeds. The ultimate beneficiaries are usually your children. However, your spouse does obtain the full benefit of being able to live off of the trust. The spouse simply loses the ability to convert the trust into her personal account at her discretion. This may be of concern for smaller estates, but not to most midsize and large estates. After all, who wants to liquidate his or her assets and spend the entire principal all in one year? Living off your account and utilizing all the interest and perhaps a small amount of the principal will ensure that those funds are there to keep the surviving spouse company throughout the years.

How Harry and Sharon Could Have Saved on Their Federal Estate Tax Bill

Assuming Harry passed away first:

- Harry left his estate to their joint revocable living trust that included an A-B provision. Half of their trust funds are placed into Harry's B trust (known as a bypass trust, family trust, or credit shelter trust) up to $675,000.
- Sharon and her children are the cotrustees of the bypass trust. Sharon draws off all the income from this trust and also maintains the right to withdraw an additional 5 percent of the trust's assets per year for any reason. The trust's assets are to be used for the benefit of Sharon if she has health care expenses or any other urgent expenses deemed necessary to maintain her standard of living.
- The total amount of $675,000 held in this bypass trust could continue to grow through appreciation. This appreciation could pass to the children free of any estate taxes.
- Sharon maintains her own assets within her A trust (marital trust). If sharon passes away during the same year or shortly thereafter, her estate can pass on up to $675,000, free of federal estate taxes.
- Estate taxes due: $0.
- Result: Total estate savings to Harry and Sharon's family would be over $230,000.

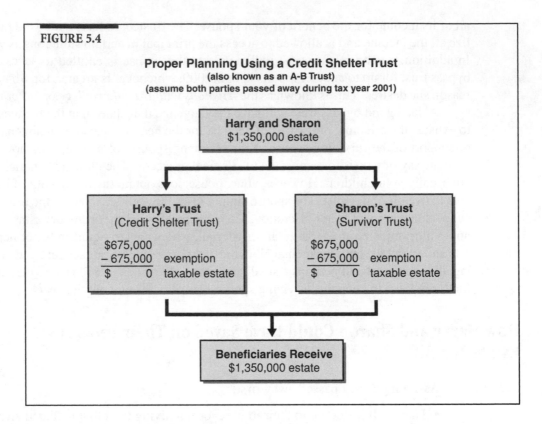

FIGURE 5.4

Proper Planning Using a Credit Shelter Trust
(also known as an A-B Trust)
(assume both parties passed away during tax year 2001)

Harry and Sharon
$1,350,000 estate

Harry's Trust
(Credit Shelter Trust)

$675,000
− 675,000   exemption
$ 0   taxable estate

Sharon's Trust
(Survivor Trust)

$675,000
− 675,000   exemption
$ 0   taxable estate

Beneficiaries Receive
$1,350,000 estate

This example, and the chart in Figure 5.4, illustrates what would occur if both Harry and Sharon were to retain property in their estates equal to their federal tax exemption amount. This could be accomplished by using individual trusts or a bypass trust (family trust).

Other Major Mistakes People Make

When working with the unlimited marital deduction, many couples are not aware of the small print contained within these various laws. For instance, a spouse who is not officially a citizen of the United States is treated differently than one that is a citizen. To prevent a noncitizen spouse from leaving our country with the married couple's assets, the unlimited marital deduction is simply not allowed to them. A quick example will help illustrate this point.

A Case in Point: A Foreign Spouse

Henry and his wife, Indira, have been living in the United States for over 40 years. Henry was born a U.S. citizen, but Indira, who Henry met at engineering school, chose to remain a citizen of Pakistan.

Upon Henry's death, any assets held in Henry's name couldn't legally be moved over to his wife, Indira, without federal estate taxes being considered and possibly due. Indira would most certainly find herself in the position of having to pay federal estate taxes before she could receive Henry's estate.

The Problem

The major reason that the U.S. government allows the unlimited marital deduction for its citizens is so that married couples can transfer property between each other without worrying about paying federal estate taxes on the first to die, as they had to do before 1981. That is when Congress introduced the unlimited marital deduction legislation under the Economic Recovery Tax Act. The government feels that there is a real chance that surviving spouses who are not U.S. citizens will simply choose to leave this country and return to their own. To make a long story short, our government could be out of their share of federal estate taxes that would be due upon the demise of surviving spouses.

Most experts feel the way around this rather large obstacle is to have the noncitizen spouse become a legal citizen of the United States, or have the spouse who is a citizen pass his property to a qualified domestic trust for the benefit of the noncitizen spouse. This language is easily inserted into most revocable living trusts. This should be done before the spouse who is a citizen passes away but may, in some circumstances, be done afterward as well.

U.S. citizens and residents may want to consider a gifting program to their noncitizen spouse. The federal government allows you to gift up to $100,000 a year to a noncitizen spouse without estate taxes being due. See a competent and knowledgeable estate-planning professional for more details.

Skipping Generations

If you intend to skip your children by passing assets to your grandchildren because you don't want your own children facing the prospect of paying federal estate taxes so soon, you need to be aware that the government is already ahead of you. Many people choose to bypass their children when passing on their estate because they know their own children are doing well. They don't wish to compound their children's estate problems by adding more property to their children's estate. Therefore, the parents decide to skip a generation by having their estate pass directly to their grandchildren.

The government will only allow a certain amount to be passed this way. Keep in mind that the government wants to tax larger estates and doesn't want you to extend for too long of a time the tax postponement of any federal estate taxes due. Passing property directly to your grandchildren or any other heirs two or more generations younger than yourself could dramatically delay the government's ability to further tax your estate.

The government has a tax called the Generation-Skipping Transfer Tax (GSTT). This tax is applied at the top level of the maximum unified gift and estate tax rate. Depending on the situation, this tax may be imposed—in addition to any estate taxes that may be due! This could eat up a large portion of any wealth being transferred. The government does allow an amount of $1,060,000 to be exempt from this tax. The GSTT exemption amount is subject to increases for inflation in 2002 and 2003, at which time it is scheduled to be the same amount as the estate tax exemption amount.

There are many in and outs to this tax and everybody should make sure that their estate plans address this issue. An estate's worth over extended periods seldom can be calculated with any degree of accuracy. So special attention should be given to avoid the GSTT through proper trust language and with frequent reviews of your assets and vehicles for transferring your family wealth.

Gifting Assets at the Wrong Time

If you have no real need for an asset you may be better off gifting this asset while you are living. This is especially important to consider if your estate is of such a size that federal estate taxes will be due upon your demise. Older people may gain more benefit by gifting an item while living and paying the estate and gift tax. This could be very beneficial because the tax could be paid now from their current estate. They could therefore reduce their total estate by both the gift they gave and the taxes that were due on that gift. The tax savings could be dramatic. If they waited to make the gift upon their demise, the federal estate tax may be due on the total amount transferred.

Another advantage of gifting while living is the person gifting can experience the pride and joy that comes from gifting! Assets that are most suitable for gifting are items such as cash or property that do not contain too much in the way of built-up capital gains. This is because the recipients receive your cost basis for tax purposes on a gift.

Property that holds mostly taxable gains may be best passed upon your demise because those receiving such property receive a step up in basis. They, in essence, receive a fresh start. No capital gains taxes would be due and the cost basis of the property reverts to the value on the date the person receives it.

Owning Life Insurance in Your Own Name

What seems very normal to people, in fact, can prove very damaging to your family's financial well-being. Many retirees have been told over and over again that their life insurance policies benefits will be paid out free from income tax. While it is true that generally life insurance death benefits are free from federal income tax, it is not true that the value of those proceeds will escape being included in the total of your estate if you have any incidence of ownership. An example will help illustrate.

Alex, who is a widower, holds an estate that is comprised of his home that is valued at $400,000 plus a substantial investment portfolio of $600,000. Assuming no debts, his taxable federal estate will be valued at $1,000,000. For the sake of this example, we will assume he passes away during the year 2001. The results are as follows:

- Total estate of $1,000,000
- Unified tax credit amount shelters property of $ 675,000
- His taxable estate would therefore be $325,000
- Taxes start at 38 percent on that $325,000 and go as high as 40 percent
- His estate will have to pay a federal estate tax of over $125,250

Now, let's assume that he is the owner of a $500,000 life insurance policy. Like many retirees, Alex assumed that the death benefits would flow directly to his named beneficiaries tax-free. He is partly correct in that the death benefits will be paid free of federal income tax, but he miscalculated greatly by not knowing that the government will take the total value of his insurance benefits and include them in his estate for federal estate purposes. He is expecting his heirs to receive his life insurance benefits of $500,000 to pay the federal estate taxes that he knows will be due of over $125,000. Alex is assuming that not only will his heirs have enough money to pay the federal estate tax, but they will have close to $370,000 additional dollars as well. Unfortunately, he is wrong.

Alex's revised federal estate tax situation is as follows:

- Home of $400,000
- Investments of $600,000
- Life insurance proceeds of $500,000
- Alex's total taxable estate equals $1,500,000

- Unified tax credit amount shelters property of $675,000
- His net taxable estate now totals $875,000
- Estate taxes due within nine months of his demise total over $335,250

His supposedly tax-free insurance benefits cost his estate over $210,000 in additional taxes. Put another way, Alex assumed his life insurance policy would pay his heirs $500,000. In reality, the heirs received just $290,000 simply because Alex was listed as the owner of the policy!

Avoiding Taxation on Life Insurance

Remember, in order to avoid estate taxes on your life insurance proceeds, you should make sure that the benefits are not included in your estate. The way to do this is to make sure that you are not the owner of the policy nor should you have any incidents of ownership in such policies. Having any rights or privileges in the policy, or access to life insurance cash values, reflects incidents of ownership.

In short, if you can effect any change of ownership of the policy or change the beneficiary, you are also assumed to have incidents of ownership. The Internal Revenue Service states that if you hold any incidents of ownership in any life insurance policies, coverage will be brought back into your gross estate to be taken into account for purposes of calculating the federal estate tax. Make sure that you review any and all life insurance policies including group term coverage. A simple change in ownership could save your estate enormous sums of money.

Using an Irrevocable Trust to Hold Your Life Insurance Policy

A vehicle called the irrevocable life insurance trust (ILIT) can be one of the best tools for removing life insurance proceeds from your estate. This works well when you create an irrevocable trust that holds your life insurance policy. The trust is also named as beneficiary. When you pass away, assuming that the trust has applied for your coverage or that the life insurance was transferred into the trust at least three years ago, the life insurance benefits will be excluded from your estate.

Any person who owns any substantial amounts of life insurance should look into the advisability of an ILIT for holding their life insurance policies. If you currently own any substantial polices, you should check with a knowledgeable estate advisor to determine your best course of action.

Advisors usually will suggest, at a minimum, to have an ILIT drafted and to transfer the ownership and beneficiary registration to that of your newly drafted ILIT document. Once the transfer is completed and you survive at least three years, those life insurance benefits will be excluded from your estate.

If you are in good health, they may suggest having your ILIT drafted first and having the trustee of your ILIT apply for another insurance policy that will replace your first policy. Once you are approved for the new coverage and that coverage is actually considered in force, then and only then, should the trustee cancel your previous life coverage. This strategy will allow the new coverage to be totally excluded from your estate without having to wait three years.

You can remove life insurance from your estate in other ways as well. Simply having someone else named as owner of your policy and making sure you retain no incidents of ownership can also remove the policy from your estate. The same three-year rule applies for current policies that are already in force.

You may be better off having the new owner or owners apply for a new policy. Once it is approved and issued, consider canceling your old policy. The value of this strategy is that you do not need to be concerned about the three-year rule.

Typically, people will effect transfer of ownership by placing the children as owners of the parent or parent's policy. The parents have to make sure that the children pay the premiums. If the parents were to make the premium payments, that would be considered incidents of ownership. Therefore, the policy would most likely be brought back into the parent's estate. Know and trust whomever you name as owner. Use a prudent and dependable person.

The main disadvantage of having children own your life insurance policies directly instead of an ILIT are as follows:

- Your children may fail to make premium payments thereby causing your policy to lapse.
- Your children may take advantage of any cash value within the policy, which in many programs could be substantial. If too much of the policy's cash assets are removed, your coverage could collapse.
- If your children are sued or go through a divorce action, these insurance asset values could be fair game.

However, there are a couple of advantages to having your children own your life insurance policies:

- You will not to have an ILIT drafted (a minor expense).
- Your children will have complete access to any policy cash value and could access those funds for your well-being if they felt so inclined.

Every family situation is different and professional advice should be sought before committing to either strategy. With most clients, it is more comfortable to go the ILIT route. As with most trust situations, you need to really focus on what you are trying to accomplish. Special care should always be given to whom you name as trustee. Always review your situation with an estate-planning professional. There are many ins and outs concerning these strategies that could trip up an unsuspecting retiree.

Other Irrevocable Trusts That Can Dramatically Reduce Taxes or Replace Wealth

There are various trusts that have the power of creating an estate, replacing an estate, and allowing an estate to escape taxes. There are many varied forms of these trusts.

Many times, retirees hold on to highly appreciated assets such as stocks or real estate. Typically, these assets have a low cost basis, meaning that the bulk of the asset would have taxable gains if sold. Adding to these retirees' dilemmas is the fact that, in most cases, these investment assets are not really diversified nor do they provide sufficient income.

Before Sale

- Retiree owns stocks or real estate worth $1,000,000.
- This asset is typically not diversified and produces very little income.
- If retiree sells assets, he or she will have large tax bill.
- Current asset will be included in the estate upon his or her demise.

Appreciated asset such as stocks
and real estate
$1,000,000
_____
$100,000 cost of asset

After Sale

- Retiree sells stocks or real estate for $1,000,000.
- Cost of asset is not taxable.
- Taxes due on growth are $180,000.
- Retiree only has $720,000 remaining to live on.
- Remaining asset will be included in the estate upon his or her demise.

Appreciated Asset (if sold)

Asset	$1,000,000
Cost Basis	−100,000
Taxable Gain	900,000
Tax	−180,000
Remaining Value	$ 720,000

While many of these retirees are wealthy on paper, they have very little in the way of income to live on. Many times, these same retirees' estates will face an estate tax because of the size of the assets that they leave behind. There is a solution.

Charitable Remainder Trusts

You may wish to consider using a charitable remainder annuity trust (CRAT). With this type of trust, you establish your trust and then transfer your appreciated property to that trust. Because the trust has been established with charitable intent, the trust can sell your appreciated property with no income tax due on your gains! Furthermore, the trust can pay you and your spouse or other named beneficiaries whom you've chosen an income for life or for a set period of years.

The trust could sell off your appreciated property free of income taxes and invest those proceeds into better income-producing investments. When the last of the income beneficiaries are gone, the remaining assets will pass to your favorite charity as designated.

A Partial Solution

Owner of $1,000,000 asset:

- Transfers asset to CRAT.
- Receives fixed percentage amount each year.
- Receives income tax deduction.
- Asset is not included in estate.

Charitable remainder annuity trust:

- Trustee sells asset with no taxable gains.
- Assets can be further diversified.
- Assets can be invested for income.
- Trustee can pay fixed income to trust beneficiaries.

Upon donor's or other named beneficiary's demise, trust passes to named charity.

Pros:

- Highly appreciated asset is removed from estate.
- Taxes are avoided on gains of property.
- Substantial tax deduction is received.
- Non–income-producing asset is converted to income-producing asset.
- Nondiversified asset becomes diversified.
- Charitable cause will be helped.

Cons:

- Heirs will lose out on inheritance.

If you give your appreciated asset to your charitable remainder annuity trust, your children or other heirs will be out of an inheritance. Therefore, you may wish to consider another type of irrevocable trust. If you create and fund a charitable remainder annuity trust while living, you are given a charitable income tax deduction. You can use the tax savings from these tax deductions or the income stream from your charitable remainder annuity trust to fund a wealth replacement trust.

A Full Solution

This scenario is the same as the partial solution except the donor or income beneficiary uses a portion of the annual income received from the charitable remainder annuity trust to fund insurance policy premiums within a wealth replacement trust. In many cases, the income tax deductions alone from establishing a charitable remainder annuity trust will be enough to fund such insurance.

Wealth replacement trust:

- Trust pays premiums on insurance held in irrevocable life insurance trust.
- $1,000,000 is available tax-free to heirs.

Charitable remainder annuity trust:

- Charitable remainder annuity trust diversified income streams to wealth replacement trust.
- Donor receives charitable write-offs.

Upon donor's or other named beneficiary's demise, trust passes to named charity.

Everybody wins (except Uncle Sam)!

A wealth replacement trust is nothing more than an irrevocable life insurance trust established for the benefit of your children. The wealth replacement trust is set up and purchases a life insurance policy on either yourself, your spouse, or both of you. Typically, insurance proceeds will be payable to the wealth replacement trust and then will flow to your heirs tax-free. Therefore, you still pass an equivalent amount of property to your heirs on a tax-favored basis!

An experienced estate-planning attorney can assist you greatly in this endeavor. Remember that you can be the trustee of your own charitable remainder annuity trust. Therefore, you still maintain financial control over the assets of the trust. Only upon your demise will the assets pass to the designated charity. You are allowed to change the charity while living if your trust document has been drafted properly.

Using the Wrong Beneficiary on Your IRA

Many retirees spend more time planning their grocery list or their next vacation than they do planning whom to name as beneficiary of their individual retirement account (IRA). IRAs represent a substantial amount of many retirees' investment assets. Therefore, any tax savings or asset-sparing strategies should be investigated.

Many retirees are told to name their living trusts as beneficiaries of their IRAs. Well-meaning attorneys want to make sure that the living trust is properly funded. This can be especially important when the owner of the IRA is on a second marriage and wants to ensure that the children from the prior marriage will receive the proper amount of the estate.

Trusts are often named as beneficiaries to ensure that enough property remains in the owner's estate to take advantage of the unified tax credit amount. Also, consider that many beneficiaries may be incapable of managing their own resources. Consequently, you may feel compelled to leave your retirement funds to a trust for their protection.

What most attorneys fail to inform their clients is that if an IRA is made payable to a trust, that distribution is immediately taxable to that individual's estate, either in the year of distribution or within five years. If that retiree were to pass away after reaching age 70½, the account may be taxable immediately by December 31 following the year of death. In order for a trust to receive an IRA and not be immediately taxable, certain guidelines have to be met, including:

- The trust beneficiaries are completely identifiable from the written trust document.
- The trustee must provide a list of all beneficiaries or an actual copy of the trust document to the IRA plan sponsor including any later changes that may be made to the trust document.
- The trust will have to become irrevocable upon the IRA owner's demise.
- The trust must be valid under state law upon being named as beneficiary or upon funding such trust.
- The beneficiaries are individuals (i.e., people instead of charities or organizations).

Many trusts do not meet these guidelines and thus will not work the way the client thinks it will when handling IRA distributions. Therefore, you may need to have your revocable living trust reexamined by an estate-planning attorney to make sure that it will comply. Your attorney will be able to draft a suitable document that will work. Have your attorney review your trust document to ensure that it will comply with the necessary language. This will allow your beneficiaries to postpone the immediate taxation of your IRA assets.

Many estate advisors recommend that clients name their spouse as the primary beneficiary with their appropriate trusts as the secondary beneficiary. That way, the surviving spouse retains the right to roll over the IRA into his or her own IRA to avoid current taxes on that distribution.

The main reason for naming the trust as secondary beneficiary is in case the IRA proceeds are required or desired to fund the deceased's unified tax credit amount. The surviving spouse, who is named as primary beneficiary, could decline the right to receive the IRA property. The property would then pass directly to the trust that is named as the secondary beneficiary. This is known as the power to disclaim. This method makes many couples feel more comfortable as the surviving spouse feels more in control of the final decision. This strategy should be discussed ahead of time as there are conditional time limits involved when disclaiming property.

Common Disasters and IRA Plans

If you were to pass away with your spouse in a common disaster such as an auto accident or home fire, do you know who would receive the proceeds of your pension, profit sharing plans, or IRAs? Most retirees think that their children would receive their account values but are not really sure. Take time to ensure that either your children are named as contingent beneficiaries of your retirement programs or that a qualified trust is. This can help you avoid passing money into your estate that will be immediately taxable. If children or a qualified trust are named, then distributions in many cases can be stretched out over the life of your children or the life expectancy of the oldest beneficiary named. The advantages could be tremendous due to the fact that the longer money can avoid taxes, the more it can grow.

Many retirees who hold their IRAs or rollover programs with a brokerage firm or mutual fund have no idea what would happen if they were to suffer a common disaster with their spouse. They assume that because they named their spouse as the primary beneficiary and their children or qualified trust as the secondary beneficiary, that in the event of their own and their spouse's passing, the funds would automatically pass to the secondary beneficiaries.

However, you must check to see what your IRA plan prototype or retirement plan summary actually states. For instance, many plans state that in the event of a common disaster, the account holder will have been deemed to have passed away first and therefore proceeds will be payable to the primary beneficiary, usually the spouse.

If the spouse has made no beneficiary arrangements, then the proceeds would be payable to the spouse's estate. Talk about undoing a lot of good planning work! This could also disinherit proper parties, including your children. These funds would also be subject to immediate taxation. The opportunity to fund a bypass trust in order to negate disastrous estate taxes may no longer be available.

Naming Children as Beneficiaries

Before age 70½. Generally, IRA balances must be distributed within five years of your demise, unless the IRA owner has designated a beneficiary. IRA balances must be distributed in full, on or before December 31 of the calendar year that contains the fifth anniversary date of the owner's demise. If an individual is designated as a beneficiary, they may take the account balance over their life expectancy. This is known as "stretching an IRA." To do this, they need to start the distribution before December 31 of the year that follows the owner's demise. If the designated beneficiary does not start these withdrawals by this deadline, then this valuable option is forfeited.

If more than one child, grandchild, or natural person is listed as beneficiary of an IRA, then the age of the oldest beneficiary is used when calculating the stretch out of an inherited IRA. Do not name your estate as beneficiary as this will negate the ability to stretch your IRA funds. Likewise, including a charity as one of your beneficiaries may also negate the ability to stretch your IRA. If naming individual children or grandchildren (or nieces, nephews, etc.) as beneficiaries, they may benefit by you establishing individual IRAs for each of them. This will give them the benefit of stretching an IRA over their own life expectancy as opposed to that of the oldest beneficiary. This may involve more work for the IRA holder but could turn a small, inherited IRA into a very large one for a younger beneficiary because the funds will grow tax-deferred over a longer time period. Recent IRA regulations changes may still allow each individual to stretch out an inherited IRA as long as the accounts are segregated by December 31 of the year following death. Segregation generally means having a deceased person's account held for the benefit of an individual.

Keep in mind that in order to stretch your IRA balance over the beneficiary's life expectancy, it is important to note that she will need to keep the account registered under the deceased person's name for her benefit! Inform your beneficiaries of this fact so they can make sure that the IRA plan custodian does not reregister the IRA into their name only. This would prevent your beneficiary from being able to stretch the IRA over her life expectancy.

The table in Figure 5.6 is used to calculate a beneficiary's required minimum distribution, or RMD. Simply divide the IRA account balance as of the preceding December 31 by the life expectancy factor associated with the beneficiary's age at the end of the distribution year. Each year thereafter you would reduce this amount of years by one for nonspouse beneficiaries. This is known as the nonrecalculation

FIGURE 5.6 Table V (Tres. Reg. § 1.72-9)

Age	Divisor	Age	Divisor	Age	Divisor
5	76.6	41	41.5	77	11.2
6	75.6	42	40.6	78	10.6
7	74.7	43	39.6	79	10.0
8	73.7	44	38.7	80	9.5
9	72.7	45	37.7	81	8.9
10	71.7	46	36.8	82	8.4
11	70.7	47	35.9	83	7.9
12	69.7	48	34.9	84	7.4
13	68.8	49	34.0	85	6.9
14	67.8	50	33.1	86	6.5
15	66.8	51	32.2	87	6.1
16	65.8	52	31.3	88	5.7
17	64.8	53	30.4	89	5.3
18	63.9	54	29.5	90	5.0
19	62.9	55	28.6	91	4.7
20	61.9	56	27.7	92	4.4
21	60.9	57	26.8	93	4.1
22	59.9	58	25.9	94	3.9
23	59.0	59	25.0	95	3.7
24	58.0	60	24.2	96	3.4
25	57.0	61	23.3	97	3.2
26	56.0	62	22.5	98	3.0
27	55.1	63	21.6	99	2.8
28	54.1	64	20.8	100	2.7
29	53.1	65	20.0	101	2.5
30	52.2	66	19.2	102	2.3
31	51.2	67	18.4	103	2.1
32	50.2	68	17.6	104	1.9
33	49.2	69	16.8	105	1.8
34	48.3	70	16.0	106	1.6
35	47.3	71	15.3	107	1.4
36	46.4	72	14.6	108	1.3
37	45.4	73	13.9	109	1.1
38	44.4	74	13.2	110	1.0
39	43.5	75	12.5		
40	42.5	76	11.9		

method. A spouse can use the actual figure stated each year for his age, which is known as the recalculating method. Of course, a spouse can wait to take distributions until the deceased account holder would have turned 70½ or simply roll over the account into his own name.

After age 70½. People don't realize that there are over two trillion dollars sitting in IRAs. The government estimates that over sixty billion dollars will be withdrawn during the next year. What would cause people to pull so much out of their IRAs? The answer is language in the tax code, which is referred to as *required minimum distributions*. These choices use to be extremely confusing and very complicated. In fact, up until the end of 2000, almost everybody was locked into whatever option they elected at age 70½. Now the rules are simpler to follow and, in most cases, more advantageous to IRA account holders.

Required Minimum Distributions

With IRAs, you, as the account owner, must make an election in the year that you turn age 70½. This election is in regard to how you wish to start drawing funds from your IRA, also known as your required minimum distribution amount. The government has let you defer these dollars and now it wants you to start pulling these funds out so it can start taxing those dollars. Generally, an account holder must take out a minimum amount each year based on the uniform table shown in Figure 5.7, or based on the person's and the spouse's actual joint age if more advantageous. The spouse method is more favorable if the spouse is at least ten years younger and the account holder wishes to reduce the IRA amount to be withdrawn each year. The IRS gives us a uniform table to calculate the required minimum distribution amount that must be taken each year.

Generally, children must take a required minimum distribution for the year of the decedent's death based upon the decedent's age in the year of death. Thereafter, the beneficiary will base their required distribution on their own actual age. That life expectancy will then be reduced by one in each subsequent year.

Spouses Are Special

When an IRA holder passes away, the spouse generally has the right to continue an IRA over her deceased spouse's life expectancy or to roll over the IRA proceeds into her own account. If a beneficiary spouse elects to roll over her spouse's IRA into her own account, then she is free to name new beneficiaries. This will give her maximum flexibility with which to plan her own finances. You can see why a consultation with a financial advisor would prove helpful in these matters. Most advisors have software that can show you the advantages of stretching out your IRA

FIGURE 5.7 Uniform Table

Age of Participant	Dist. Period	Age of Participant	Dist. Period
70	26.2	93	8.8
71	25.3	94	8.3
72	24.4	95	7.8
73	23.5	96	7.3
74	22.7	97	6.9
75	21.8	98	6.5
76	20.9	99	6.1
77	20.1	100	5.7
78	19.2	101	5.3
79	18.4	102	5.0
80	17.6	103	4.7
81	16.8	104	4.4
82	16.0	105	4.1
83	15.3	106	3.8
84	14.5	107	3.6
85	13.8	108	3.3
86	13.1	109	3.1
87	12.4	110	2.8
88	11.8	111	2.6
89	11.1	112	2.4
90	10.5	113	2.2
91	9.9	114	2.0
92	9.4	115 and older	1.8

assets over time. The power of compounding interest along with the favorable tax environment that an IRA offers can be tremendous. A financial advisor can also explain what your IRA plan document permits or doesn't permit.

A good advisor will point out that you can switch trustees of your IRA plans in most cases without switching investment managers. This is referred to as having a self-directed IRA. You select a good IRA trustee or custodian company that offers the IRA plan document that you wish to have and then transfer your current IRA holdings to that company. A trustee that uses a good plan document can give you the power of flexibility within your IRAs.

Seven Key Points to Keep in Mind

1. The rules for IRA beneficiaries are different depending on what age you are when you pass away. The main difference pertains to plans before age 70½ and after age 70½.
2. The rules are different depending on whom you name as beneficiary.
3. The rules are different depending on your relationship with whom you name as beneficiary.
4. The rules are different for spouses versus other beneficiaries.
5. This area of financial planning is very confusing even to those professionals who have being doing financial planning for years.
6. Make sure you consult your financial advisor or tax professional for proper guidance. He or she should be able to clearly show you your choices.
7. If your IRA funds are substantial, then it becomes imperative that you see the actual IRA plan document. Consideration should be given to having an estate-planning attorney review this document. Just because the IRS may allow certain options, doesn't mean that your current IRA plan document will. Also, do not hesitate to have an attorney review your beneficiary designation and choices in regard to your required minimum distributions options at age 70½.

6

Paying Too Much in Taxes

Many retirees are vaguely aware that they may be paying too much in taxes. Unfortunately, most of them don't do anything about it. They fail to realize the tremendous impact that taxes make throughout their lives, not to mention the significance that taxes will play in their financial affairs after their demise. Throughout history, people have had to deal with the burden of various tax systems. Regardless of what country you live in, historians will agree that taxes are the price we pay for a civilized society.

Most of us have no problem with the concept of a limited tax system. We know that our country requires such funds for the purpose of defense and to ensure that our country can maintain open trade patterns for the goods that we produce as well as for the goods that we import. What most retirees disdain is the thought of their tax dollars going toward unnecessary projects and expensive entitlement programs.

Face it, as long as this country has politicians and special interest groups that place their individual needs over the common good of this country as a whole, there will be wasteful spending. Wasteful spending along with escalating social programs can impose a heavy burden on the population as a whole via taxes.

Many individuals and government agencies now realize that individuals and private charities can do much more for the social good at a fraction of the price that bureaucracies charge for the equivalent services. As a result, private charities are encouraged in this country via social recognition and various tax deductions.

In fact, taking advantage of various charitable deductions can lower your tax bill, decrease the size of your taxable estate upon your demise, increase your spendable income, allow you better diversification, and give you a creditor-resistant income source.

Now once you accept the fact that taxes will be imposed, you can then logically create a financial strategy to ensure that you are paying only your fair share. No statues have ever been erected for those citizens who paid too much in taxes! When we compare the actions of two model citizens, both leaders in their communities, it never even crosses our minds to ask how much they pay in taxes.

There is simply nothing innately wrong with doing everything that you legally can to avoid paying too much in taxes. Dollars that you personally save that would have been lost in taxes could be used for the good of society in other ways. Extra funds that you have retained could be used in a myriad of ways: to improve your home, to make local purchases, and to support church and civic groups, just to name a few.

Tax Awareness

Many retirees have failed to pay attention to the various ways different investments are taxed. This lack of attention can be very damaging to your financial situation. The difference in how various investments are taxed can be the difference between being able to retire after years of hard work and sacrifice, and not being able to retire at all.

Lack of awareness of tax matters through ignorance or improper planning techniques is a major factor that determines the quality of your financial life during retirement. Later examples will illustrate dramatically the difference between knowing and implementing just one or two of the various tax reduction strategies.

Whoever said "Ignorance is bliss" was not referring to taxes! Take a few moments to become aware of how taxes are collected in this great country of ours. Realize that our tax system is not perfect and that some different investment strategies are afforded favorable tax treatments while others, including some of the most popular, are not. Ignorance may be bliss, but knowledge is power.

The Marginal Tax System

It is crucial that you understand the rules of the road. In this country, we have a progressive tax system known as the marginal tax system. The more you earn, the higher your tax rate.

Before you can calculate your marginal tax rate, you need to figure out what your total gross income will be for the year. From that figure, make sure that you subtract your personal and dependent exemption amounts and your standard deduction (or itemized deductions, if higher). You may also have other available adjustments to your gross income. This gives you your taxable income. You can use that number to find your marginal tax rate in the table in Figure 6.1.

Note: Claim yourself as well as other dependent exemption amounts.

FIGURE 6.1 Marginal Tax Table for Year 2000

Filing Status	If Your Taxable Income Is Between			Pay	And Then on Excess
Single Tax Payers	$ 0	–	$26,250	$ 0.00	15.0%
	26,250	–	63,550	3,937.50	28.0
	63,550	–	132,600	14,381.50	31.0
	132,600	–	288,350	35,787.00	36.0
	288,350	–	Up	91,857.00	39.6
Married Filing Jointly	0	–	43,850	0.00	15.0
	43,850	–	105,950	6,577.50	28.0
	105,950	–	161,450	23,965.50	31.0
	161,450	–	288,350	41,170.50	36.0
	288,350	–	Up	86,854.50	39.6
Married Filing Separately	0	–	21,925	0.00	15.0
	21,925	–	52,975	3,288.75	28.0
	52,975	–	80,725	11,982.75	31.0
	80,725	–	144,175	20,585.25	36.0
	144,175	–	Up	43,427.25	39.6
Head of Household	0	–	35,150	0.00	15.0
	35,150	–	90,800	5,272.50	28.0
	90,800	–	147,050	20,854.50	31.0
	147,050	–	288,350	38,292.00	36.0
	288,350	–	Up	89,160.00	39.6

The Economic Growth and Tax Relief Reconciliation Act of 2001 will affect most taxpayers. Probably the most beneficial change will be a gradual cut in income tax rates. A new 10 percent rate has been added and current rates will be lowered over time. Starting in 2006, the highest marginal income tax rate will be almost 5 percentage points lower.

The Act creates a new 10 percent income tax rate for a portion of taxable income that previously has been taxed at 15 percent. For tax years 2002–2007, a new 10 percent bracket will apply to the first $6,000 of taxable income for single individuals ($7,000 for 2008 and thereafter), $10,000 of taxable income for heads of households, and $12,000 for married couples filing joint returns ($14,000 for 2008 and thereafter).

Amount of Exemption for Year 2000:

- Taxpayer = $2,800   Personal Exemption Amount
- Spouse = $2,800   Exemption Amount
- Dependent Child = $2,800   Exemption Amount

FIGURE 6.2 Lower Tax Rates

Old Law	28.0%	31.0%	36.0%	39.6%
2001	27.5	30.5	35.5	39.1
2002–2003	27.0	30.0	35.0	38.6
2005–2005	26.0	29.0	34.0	37.6
2006 and after	25.0	28.0	33.0	35.0

For the year 2001 and beyond, these exemption amounts must be adjusted for inflation. If your adjusted gross income (AGI) is too high, then you will lose some or all of your personal exemption amount and dependent amount deductions.

The phase-out starts as follows:

- Single taxpayer, when AGI exceeds $128,950.
- Head of household taxpayer, when AGI exceeds $161,150.
- Married filing separate taxpayer, when AGI exceeds $96,700.
- Married filing jointly taxpayers, when AGI exceeds $193,400.

Standard deduction year 2000:

- Single taxpayer, $3,675
- Head of household taxpayer, $6,450
- Married couples filing jointly, $7,350

Factor in additional deductions if you are 65 or older:

- Single taxpayer, $1,100
- Married taxpayer (each), $850

If legally blind, you are allowed an additional deduction of:

- Single taxpayer, $1,100
- Married taxpayer (each if applicable), $850

Note: Claim the standard deduction if you are not itemizing your deductions.

Fully Taxed

Interestingly, some of the most popular accumulation vehicles in the country today are fully taxed. Bank accounts, including passbook savings accounts and certificates of deposit are fully taxable by both the state and federal governments. The interest that these vehicles pay is considered ordinary income.

As such, these accounts are taxed at your marginal tax bracket rate. They are even taken into account for the possible taxation of your Social Security benefits. One of the most popular accumulation vehicles that has attracted billions of dollars over the years, money market mutual funds, is also fully taxable at the ordinary tax level.

Why are some investment vehicles fully taxed while others are given more favorable tax treatment? The answer is threefold:

1. Government policies. A major reason for various tax treatments afforded different investment vehicles is that the government can direct dollars toward various segments of the economy where it feels the money will do the most good. Therefore, it passes various tax laws to favor, stimulate, and impact the sectors of the economy that it feels should be afforded such favorable tax treatment.

The government favors dollars that are being used for long-term investing versus short-term savings. Investment dollars that are used for the long-term good of our economy are afforded different tax treatment. These investments that are deemed favorable are usually given favorable capital gains treatment as well. Favorable capital gains status is great because you pay roughly half of what you would have paid on ordinary investment income at the top marginal tax bracket.

2. Politics. Politicians will enact legislation that favors different segments of the economy with various investment vehicles. Perhaps these vehicles will take the form of a federal tax subsidy or tax credit. In other cases, the government will allow favorable tax status to these investment vehicles or strategies. A few examples from years gone by include the energy credit, low-income housing tax credit, alternative fuel credit, and accelerated depreciation. This category also would include the many riders to legislation that Congress slips into various bills that permit favorable tax dodges to certain corporations.

3. Past laws and customs. With all the previous tax laws that have been passed, lawmakers may be hard-pressed to do away with the various laws that were legislated in previous years. People grow accustomed to prior laws and resist change. Therefore, lawmakers may be reluctant to change these laws. Tradition and custom are key factors that dictate the level of change in tax laws. We have a tradition in this country of rewarding the long-term investor versus the short-term saver. People investing in the long-term infrastructure of this country are, thus, rewarded.

Therefore, the government offers favorable capital gains treatment on many of these types of investments as well as allowing tax depreciation of other longer-term commitments. People would do well to remember how hard it originally was for the government to initiate federal taxes on our income. For many decades, the population at large simply would not accept the concept that our income should be taxable! In many other countries, taxes are raised in various manners such as value added taxes, instead of taxing personal income.

How to Obtain Favorable Tax Treatment

Probably the most favorable tax treatment afforded to investors is long-term capital gains. Congress changes this tax rate often, but usually it tends to be much more favorable than ordinary income tax rates. Typically, real property such as stocks and investment real estate are afforded this favorable tax treatment if such assets are held the required amount of time.

Capital gains investments are also given other favorable tax benefits such as tax deferral of the gains until sold and something called the step-up basis. This step-up basis comes into play upon your demise. Refer to Chapter 5 for more information on the step-up basis. This IRS code allows your heirs the right to receive such property free of any taxable gains. Your heirs will owe no federal income tax on the growth of such real property. The savings to your family could be substantial!

The Power of Deferring Capital Gains

Figure 6.3 illustrates the substantial tax savings you could realize if your investment was a capital asset.

Timing the Sale of Your Capital Assets Has Its Advantages

Note that when you own and control your capital assets such as stocks and real property, you can usually decide when to sell them. This puts you in control of when you wish to realize the capital gain or capital loss on such assets. You realize this gain or loss by actually selling the asset. The year of sale requires that you report that transaction on your income tax return. This advantage can give you great flexibility in planning you income taxes.

Keep in mind that capital assets held for less than one year will be taxed the same as wage, salary, and dividend income. Any short-term gain will be included on your return and taxed at the less favorable marginal federal income tax rates. This marginal rate could go as high as 39.6 percent if you are in the highest tax bracket.

Excess Capital Gains

Taxpayers are required to combine their realized capital gains and losses together at the end of each tax year. They are then required to report any excess gain or loss on their return. If you have excess capital gains, you are required to pay any taxes on a timely basis.

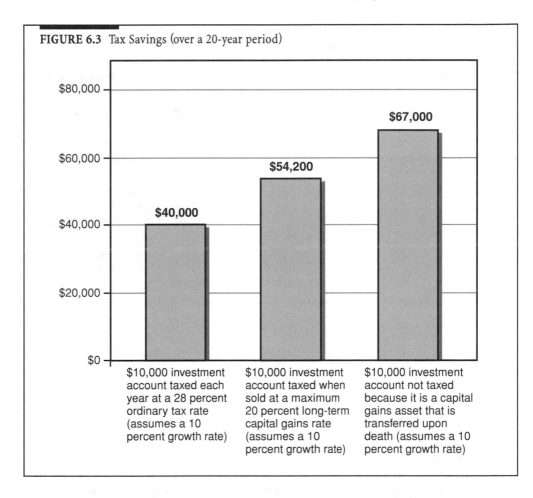

FIGURE 6.3 Tax Savings (over a 20-year period)

- $10,000 investment account taxed each year at a 28 percent ordinary tax rate (assumes a 10 percent growth rate): **$40,000**
- $10,000 investment account taxed when sold at a maximum 20 percent long-term capital gains rate (assumes a 10 percent growth rate): **$54,200**
- $10,000 investment account not taxed because it is a capital gains asset that is transferred upon death (assumes a 10 percent growth rate): **$67,000**

If you have an excess loss, you are only able to claim up to $1,500 of that loss if single or up to $3,000 of that loss if married. The government, however, does allow you to carry forward the losses to be used in future years. Be aware that a taxpayer who dies cannot carry forward any unused capital losses. These losses therefore become lost forever! Don't be afraid to sell capital assets that have gone down in value and appear to have little hope of making a comeback. One way to use these losses to your advantage is by selling them during a year that you have capital gains to offset. The table in Figure 6.4 details some types of capital gains and losses and related tax rates.

Primary Residence

Your personal residence is considered a capital asset. As such, you are offered the favorable capital gains rates on any increases of such property when sold. Unfor-

FIGURE 6.4 Capital Gains and Losses

Property Sold	Holding Period	Gain	Highest Tax Rate
Current sale of capital property	12 months or less	Short-term	Pay tax on gain at your marginal tax rate. Gain is considered ordinary income.
Sale of capital property after date of 12/31/1997	Longer than 12 months	Long-term	Maximum capital gains rate of 20%. If your marginal tax rate is 15%, then maximum capital gains rate of 10% applies.
Sale of certain collectibles	Longer than 12 months	Long-term	Generally a maximum capital gains rate of 28% applies.
Sale of capital property acquired after 12/31/2000	Longer than 5 years	Long-term	Maximum capital gains rate of 18% may apply.
Real estate where depreciation was taken	Longer than 12 months	Long-term	Maximum capital gains rates may be as high as 25% on portion of gain attributed to excess accelerated depreciation; otherwise, gains are usually taxed at a lower 20% rate.*

*See your tax advisor to determine your actual capital gains rates. These charts are general guidelines only and will not be accurate for all taxable transactions.

tunately, the government will not allow you to declare any capital losses on such property! This seems very unfair and there doesn't seem to be any legislation in the works to change this. This lack of ability to declare a capital loss on your personal residence takes away any tax incentive for people to settle in less than desirable neighborhoods. Perhaps Congress will wake up and realize that without such favorable tax treatment they may be impeding urban development.

Tax Break

The Taxpayer Relief Act of 1997 made some positive changes in how gains are treated on primary residences. A taxpayer may now exclude from their income up to $250,000 of gains received from the sale of a principal residence. You are required to have owned the property as your principal residence for at least two years out of the five-year period ending on the date of sale. You are allowed one such exclusion every two years.

Married couples that file a joint tax return may qualify for up to a $500,000 exclusion. It is always advisable to consult an accountant, CPA, or your tax advisor before selling any property to determine what the tax consequences will be. Find out before you sell, not afterwards!

The Word Is Not Out Yet

Many retirees are still living with the old real estate rules in their heads. They still believe that they only have a one-time exclusion from income of $125,000 and that they must be 55 years of age or older to use it. This simply is not true anymore.

Mutual Funds — The Hidden Tax

Mutual funds are the most popular investment vehicle in the country today. They have grown from a cottage industry in the early 1960s to become the dominant method for individual retirees to participate in the stock and bond markets. In most cases, they offer professional management and wide diversification. It's no wonder they have become the vehicle of choice for millions of Americans. While these mutual fund companies promote their investment track records, there is one disadvantage that they don't advertise very well. That disadvantage has to do with how mutual funds are taxed.

Mutual Fund Taxation

Mutual funds act as a tax funnel for their shareholders. Therefore, all dividends that an equity mutual fund earns will be reported to the government based on the shareholders' percentage of ownership of such shares. In short, if your mutual fund has stock dividends generated within your portfolio, expect a 1099 form for your taxable accounts. This dividend income is considered ordinary income for taxable accounts owned by individual retirees.

If you are investing in a high-yield bond fund, income fund, or government securities mutual fund, expect your taxable dividend interest to be taxable at ordinary income tax rates. There are exceptions for various municipal securities. The majority of these issues will not be taxed for federal income tax purposes.

What many retirees remain ignorant of is the fact that mutual funds can, and do, produce many short-term capital gains. These short-term gains are taxed as ordinary gains. In other words, if your mutual fund manager sells one of the fund's holdings without waiting the required 12-month period, then any gains will be taken as short-term gains. Your fund manager, of course, will first offset any short-term losses with those gains. But in a rising market, you may find yourself with unexpected short-term taxable gains. These gains will be taxed as ordinary income at your highest marginal tax bracket rate.

The Long Term

Most mutual fund brochures will espouse the wisdom of investing for the long term. However, the sad statistic is that the average equity fund turns over 70 percent of its portfolio each year. That certainly doesn't qualify as a long-term investment by the government's standards so the short-term sale is taxed as short-term capital gains.

Tax Time Bombs

What most mutual fund shareholders do not know is that you have no control over whether or not your fund manager sells a portfolio holding. The mutual fund may have purchased various stocks that have appreciated greatly in value over the years. If the manager happens to sell that stock while you are a shareholder of that fund, you could be faced with a rather large and nasty long-term capital gain.

For example, say you purchased a mutual fund and plan on holding on to it for the long term. You know that if your fund should increase in value over the years that you will pay tax on the gains when you sell your shares. What you didn't expect, however, was paying taxes on that fund's long-term gains that were accumulated long before you became a shareholder.

ABC Growth Fund Example

This fund has purchased the stock of XYZ Company. They paid $10 a share many years ago and have seen this stock increase to $150 per share. The managers of the ABC Growth Fund decide to sell shares to lock in their profits. They do this by selling their XYZ stock shares and realizing the gains. This means that they will have a long-term capital gain of $140 per share. That gain will be passed on to their shareholders in the year of sale!

Mutual Fund Tax Advice

Beware of the mutual funds that you are holding or are considering purchasing for your taxable accounts. There could be huge gains that the fund manager is sitting on. While the fund manager may claim to not plan on selling these stock positions, don't count on this. Many times fund managers are forced to sell certain stocks for liquidity purposes.

Sometimes, during times of market turmoil, fund managers have to redeem stocks to meet shareholders' redemption requests. Even if the market is doing fine, the fund managers may experience a shift in investments trends. This could cause different stocks in the market to be higher in demand. Your fund manager may have no choice but to sell off current holdings in order to acquire positions in other areas.

Most mutual funds are also registered as diversified mutual funds and by law are not allowed to hold more than 5 percent of the outstanding shares of any one individual company. Therefore, your fund manager may be forced to sell for this reason.

In addition, most mutual funds experience frequent changes in their investment managers. It is not uncommon to see a manager change an average of every five years. Unfortunately, for tax purposes, a new manager who takes the helm of a mutual fund usually makes substantial changes to the portfolio. A new manager will typically sell off certain stock positions to place his or her own management style on the fund. This could prove to be rather taxing.

Publications such as *Morningstar* allow you to access such information as the capital gains exposure that a fund may have built up within its shares. This service will also note the tax efficiency of any fund that you may be considering. It will give you details on the current manager or managers of funds including any recent management changes. Without this information, picking a fund is the equivalent of flying blind.

Tax-Free Investments

There are investments that pay out interest income that is free of federal income tax. These investments are known as municipal securities. They are usually issued as notes and bonds. They are deemed debt securities and are issued by municipalities, certain community projects, and states. They have one item in common—you loan these entities money. Therefore, you assume the position of being a debtor.

Think of a note or bond as an IOU that usually pays interest and that will give you a better understanding of what municipal securities are all about. Hopefully, you have selected a secured entity to which you will lend your money. Many retirees who are afraid of the stock market's gyrations will select highly rated municipal securities and sit back and collect their interest checks. Typically, these types of securities pay 25 percent less than comparable U.S. government securities that are offering the same maturities.

The reason that most municipal securities are federal income tax free is that the federal government doesn't directly tax a state's debt instruments and, likewise, the states generally do not tax the U.S. government's debt instruments. According to IRS code section 103, you can exclude all interest earned on obligations of a state, territory, municipality, or any political subdivision from gross income except in the case of arbitrage bonds issued after October 9, 1969.

There are exceptions to every rule and this one is no different. The federal government typically does not tax direct debt instruments offered by the state directly or certain local municipalities unless it considers a debt offering an arbitrage bond. The government will not allow you to exclude the interest earned from arbitrage bonds.

In the past, there were cases where municipalities would take advantage of their tax-favored status and issue low-yielding municipal securities while using the proceeds to purchase higher-yielding government securities. Clearly, the intent was to take advantage of current tax laws. These arbitrage bond offerings are rare now because most investors know better. Most bond offerings are accompanied with a legal opinion, which will give ample warning to perspective investors.

Selecting Tax-Free Issues

Tax-free municipal securities have their place in many retirees' portfolios. However, you must take care when selecting and constructing such a portfolio. If retirees have enough investment assets, they may wish to select individual municipal issues. The advantages would be that they know what they own and could therefore stagger the maturities of such a portfolio to meet their needs. A good broker could prove invaluable in this process. A broker could assist you in selecting individual municipal securities that were issued within your state. These securities could be free from both federal and state taxes! A broker also could point out what municipal issues would not be appropriate for your portfolio. If you cannot find a good bond broker, then you may wish to consider municipal mutual funds. Several well-known mutual fund companies including Kemper, Fidelity, and Franklin have numerous fund offerings. Figure 6.5 compares tax-free yields and their taxable equivalents.

Tax-Deferred Investments

Various investments offer the power of tax deferral, yet many retirees ignore such tax advantages in their pursuit for either investment returns or safety. Ironically, both are easily available on a tax-deferred basis. The conservative investor need look no further than one of the most popular tax-deferred investments available today, the U.S. government's EE savings bonds. While most retirees have learned to think of these types of bonds as being way too conservative, you may want to take a second look for the risk-adverse portion of your portfolio and for the cash portion of your investments.

FIGURE 6.5 Are Tax-Exempt Securities for You?

Comparison of tax-free yields and their taxable
equivalent based on 2000 tax rate tables.

If Your marginal tax rate is:	And your tax-exempt investment yields:					
	4%	5%	6%	6.5%	7%	7.5%
	It is the equivalent of a taxable investment yielding:					
15.0%	4.71%	5.88%	7.06%	7.65%	8.24%	8.82%
28.0	5.56	6.94	8.33	9.03	9.72	10.42
31.0	5.80	7.25	8.70	9.42	10.14	10.87
36.0	6.25	7.81	9.38	10.16	10.94	11.72
39.6	6.62	8.28	9.93	10.76	11.59	12.42

EE Savings Bonds Are Tax Favored in Two Major Ways

Interest earnings on EE savings bonds are exempt from state and local income taxes. They may, however, be subject to state and local estate, gift, and inheritance taxes.

You have the option of reporting your interest each year, which is called the annual reporting method, or deferring your interest growth until a later date, which is called the cash basis method. This later method is by far the most popular option. Be careful if you select the annual reporting method. If you do, you must use that method for all of your E and EE bonds.

If you decide to defer taxes on your EE savings bonds, you can only do so if your bond is currently earning interest. If your bond matures, you must then declare your interest growth at that time or exchange your EE bonds for Series HH bonds. Remember, after a EE savings bond matures it is no longer earning interest. This usually occurs in 30 years.

It is important to note that different series of savings bonds have different maturity dates. It is estimated that people are holding over $7 billion in savings bonds that are no longer earning interest. Check your bonds against the following maturity dates to make sure you are not one of these people:

- 40 years for Series E bonds issued before December 1965
- 30 years for Series E and EE bonds issued after November 1965
- 30 years for Series H bonds issued between 1959 and 1979
- 20 years for Series HH bonds issued since 1980
- 30 years for Series I bonds

Many retirees mistakenly assume that, because their bonds were purchased at half of their face value, the bond is only worth its face value upon maturity. However, most savings bonds are worth far more than their face amount upon maturity.

Because Series EE savings bonds can provide very valuable tax-deferral benefits, many workers use savings bonds as a cash accumulation tool and feel secure that they will be in a lower tax bracket during later years when they plan on making withdrawals.

If you are holding on to various E and EE bonds, you may want to obtain a booklet about savings bonds to help you calculate what your bonds are worth. The Department of Treasury has an excellent Web site at <www.savingsbonds.gov>, which includes a savings bond calculator and a downloadable program called The Savings Bond Wizard, which will allow you to calculate the current value of your bonds.

If you prefer to phone or write to the U.S. Treasury for information, here is the contact information:

U.S. Treasury
1500 Pennsylvania Avenue, NW
Washington, DC 20220
202-622-2000
Fax: 202-622-6415
<www.ustreas.gov>

In addition to EE savings bonds, the government is offering the newer Series I bond. These newer bonds offer a fixed rate of return and a variable semiannual inflation rate. The fixed rate will remain constant throughout the life of the I bond while the semiannual inflation rate that is paid will vary every six months. Therefore, if the economy experiences inflation your fixed rate will be augmented by an increasing variable rate. While I bonds have their advantages, there is one major disadvantage. They are not convertible to HH bonds. The major advantage of converting to HH bonds is that you can take tax-deferred bonds and convert them to bonds paying income without paying taxes on all of your accumulated gains at once. The conversion of E or EE bonds to HH bonds spares you the immediate taxation of previous gains until the HH bonds mature.

Many retirees like their savings bonds because they are safe and in most cases tax-deferred investments. If the tax-deferral option is selected on all of your savings bonds, then that income, while accumulating, is not taken into account for current federal income tax or taxation of your Social Security benefits. The major problem with this strategy is that savings bonds mature in 30 years and the government places restrictions on how much in savings bonds you may purchase in a given year.

The current limit is $15,000 issue price ($30,000 face amount) for EE bonds and $30,000 annual purchase limit for I bonds. You are allowed to purchase both types of savings bonds up to their allowable limit.

Now that you understand how easy it is to make your investments tax-deferred, you may want to consider tax-deferred annuities. These accounts are ideal for larger sums of money. Let's look at these popular tax-favored investments.

Tax-Deferred Annuities

There are investment vehicles offered by insurance companies that give an incredible advantage over traditional savings vehicles such as bank savings accounts and certificates of deposits. The life insurance companies in this country offer programs called fixed-rate, tax-deferred annuities.

They typically offer slightly higher rates than banks and, best of all, these annuity accounts accumulate interest on a tax-deferred basis. This means that your account earns interest without causing your marginal tax bracket to go up. Money that accumulates free of current income tax will grow much quicker than funds that are taxable each year. These accounts typically accumulate free of current state income tax as well. Many retirees have also figured out that while the interest in these accounts is in the accumulation phase, no 1099 statements are generated. Therefore, the interest from these accounts while accumulating is not taken into account for taxation of your Social Security benefits!

Fixed Annuities

This gives the fixed annuity distinct advantages over a regular taxable account. The only downside is that you will have to pay taxes later down the road. Taxes are due when you pull your interest out and, in most cases, upon your demise. If married, most insurance companies will allow the spouse to continue the annuity certificate without tax consequences if the surviving spouse is named as primary beneficiary.

Fixed annuities offer an excellent bond substitute. Purchasing individual bonds requires knowledge and effort. Investing in bond mutual funds can expose you to market volatility. These fixed annuities actually are a proxy for bonds, because an insurance company typically will have the majority of the funds backing your fixed annuity account invested in a portfolio of bonds. A competitive annuity company will offer high yields with security of principal. Many will offer guaranteed minimum interest rates while providing high current yields to the consumer. Look for a company that guarantees its rates for at least five years.

The only negative aspect associated with these types of accounts occurs if you purchase them through a weak insurance company or if you purchase an inferior type of certificate. The strength of the insurance company will protect your principal and interest. Select only top rated companies that are financially strong. Avoid policies that have long surrender penalties.

Any insurance agent who proposes that you lock up your funds for longer than seven years clearly has his or her own interest in mind, not yours. Most good annuity certificates will allow you to withdraw your interest each year if you so desire. Look at an insurance company's past track record to see what they have paid. Also look at their minimum guaranteed interest rate, which is required to be noted within the certificate.

Insurance companies operate under the legal reserve system. This is a method where the life insurance company must always maintain at least one hundred cents on the dollar plus 3 percent to 4 percent extra for any obligations that they may have outstanding. In other words, they must have enough assets to meet all their obligations plus some extra funds. Compare this to a bank where they typically have just a few pennies in reserve for each dollar of obligation. When banks were failing during the Great Depression, most insurance companies were not.

Their great track record has given many investors and policyholders great comfort over the years. Because life insurance companies are regulated by each of the individual states within the United States, it would be prudent to check your state's written regulations regarding its legal reserve requirements.

Typically, if an insurance company falls into a negative position where it may owe more than what it has in assets, the state insurance commissioner will step in to force the company to either liquidate or to go through a restructuring. In most cases, this is done so that policyholders will be made whole.

Various states offer additional protection through written agreements with other insurance carriers domiciled within their state that state they will provide additional funds as well. These programs are referred to as state guaranty funds. Insurance companies are not allowed to publicize such programs. Inquire from your insurance agent or company on specifics for your state. To add an extra margin of safety, always deal with an insurance company that is highly rated.

Index Annuities and Variable Annuities

Imagine being able to obtain stock market rates of return without worrying about current income taxes being created. All tax-deferred annuities offer the ability to defer the taxes on your account until some future point in time. While living, you usually control the timing of when you want to pay taxes. This can give you an extreme advantage over more traditional investments such as mutual funds.

Individual stocks operate much the same way in that your growth is tax-deferred until you sell the stock. The problem with individual stocks, however, is that it is much harder to obtain true diversification than with a variable annuity. Variable annuities typically offer very diversified subaccounts, which allow you to have adequate diversification. Also, variable annuities will allow you to switch from one type of subaccount to another without any current capital gains or income tax.

For example, if you have invested with a variable annuity and are currently invested in the overseas subaccount, you can transfer your investment dollars to its domestic stock account with no tax consequences. Try that with your regular mutual fund!

Index annuities are comparable to both the fixed annuity and the variable annuity. They are a relatively new type of product. They function much like a fixed annuity with minimum guarantees and like a variable annuity in the sense that you can participate in the stock market. Imagine participating in the growth of the stock market without risking your initial investment.

These types of annuities represent an interesting concept and should seriously be looked at by more conservative investors who want guarantees but also would like to participate in today's stock market returns.

Because so many insurance companies are rushing their products to the market, special care must be taken to evaluate any index annuity. These index annuities typically tie your account's performance to an index such as Standard & Poor's 500 Index. Make sure that your annuity certificate is credited the full amount of the index. Annuity certificates that credit your account via a method called monthly averaging generally end up paying you less than certificates that credit you with the annual performance of an index. More information on these types of annuities will be covered in the next chapter.

A Matter of Tax

The charts in Figures 6.6 and 6.7 detail the advantages a tax-deferred annuity can provide.

For the information in Figures 6.6 and 6.7 the following applies:

- Assumes 10 percent rate of return
- Combined 32 percent tax bracket (federal and state)
- Tax-deferred account will have taxes due upon withdrawal.
- Index annuities may average less or more than 10 percent per year depending on the structure of the account and the increase or decrease of the market index they are modeled after. Fixed annuity rates vary widely. Rates are not currently as high as 10 percent but could rise again if the economy were to experience more inflation.

For Figure 6.8, which shows the advantages of an annuity over a taxable account, the following facts apply:

- Earnings rates shown are expressed as annual effective yields.
- A portion of the value of the deferred annuity account may be subject to an IRS premature distribution penalty if withdrawn before age 59½.

FIGURE 6.6 The Value of Tax Deferment

End of Year	$10,000 at 10% Taxable Account	$10,000 at 10% Tax Deferred
5	$13,894	$ 16,105
10	19,306	25,937
15	26,826	41,772
20	37,275	67,275
25	51,974	108,347

A difference of over 100 percent in growth!

- A combined tax bracket rate of 32 percent is assumed (28 percent federal plus 4 percent state).

If You Are Younger

If you are younger, tax deferral could mean the difference between being able to retire and not being able to retire.

If You Are Retired

If you are retired, tax deferral could mean the difference between staying retired and having to seek out an additional income source.

How Tax-Deferred Accounts Can Save You from Having Your Social Security Benefits Taxed

Taxpayers must include in their gross income a set percentage of their Social Security benefits if their provisional income exceeds a certain amount. Obviously, you have to know what the government means by provisional income. This is defined as your adjusted gross income plus 50 to 85 percent of your Social Security benefits if, when taken into account, they exceed a certain threshold amount.

Up to half of your Social Security benefits can be deemed taxable if your provisional income exceeds the threshold amount of:

- $25,000 for a single person
- $32,000 for a married couple

Up to 85 percent of your Social Security benefits can be deemed taxable if your provisional income exceeds the threshold amount of:

FIGURE 6.7 The Value of Tax Deferment If Taking Income Each Year

	Taxable Account (at the end of year 25)	Tax-Deferred Account (at the end of year 25)
	$51,794	$108,347
Income if taken as a 10% systematic withdrawal	$5,180 per year	$10,835 per year

A difference of over 100 percent in income!

- $34,000 for a single person
- $44,000 for a married couple

If your provisional income exceeds the threshold amount for the 50 percent calculation, then the amount of Social Security benefits to be included in your taxable income would be the lesser of 50 percent of your Social Security benefits or 50 percent of the amount by which your provisional income exceeded the threshold.

If your provisional income exceeds the threshold amount for the 85 percent calculation, then you should add to your gross income up to 85 percent of your Social Security benefits or the sum of:

- The smaller of
  - the amount included under prior law (which is the amount that would have been taxed using the 50 percent formula); or
  - $4,500 (for single person) or $6,000 (for married couple who file a joint return); plus
- 85 percent of the excess of the taxpayer's provisional income over the threshold amount.

Taxation of Social Security Benefits

A portion of Social Security benefits may be subject to income taxation. The worksheet in Figure 6.9 will assist in determining that tax.

If you assume that Congress could simplify this formula, then you would be missing the point. Congress did not feel comfortable coming directly out and informing people that their Social Security benefits were now going to be taxable. So it started by announcing that a portion of your benefits could be taxable. Later it extended this tax to include even greater amounts of certain retirees' Social Security benefits. There are many that feel that sooner or later Congress will end up taxing all of our Social Security benefits.

FIGURE 6.8 The Annuity Advantage

$10,000 Invested at 10 Percent
(assumes a tax rate of 32 percent)

Yr.	Taxable Account Annual Earnings	Annual Income Tax	After Tax Balance	Deferred Annuity Annual Earnings	Account Balance Before Tax	After Tax	Annuity Advantage Before	After
1	$1,000	$ 320	$10,680	$1,000	$ 11,000	$10,680	$ 320	$ 0
2	1,068	341	11,406	1,100	12,100	11,428	693	21
3	1,140	365	12,181	1,210	13,310	12,250	1,128	68
4	1,218	389	13,010	1,331	14,641	13,155	1,630	145
5	1,301	416	13,894	1,464	16,105	14,151	2,210	256
6	1,389	444	14,839	1,610	17,715	15,246	2,875	406
7	1,483	474	15,848	1,771	19,487	16,451	3,638	602
8	1,584	507	16,926	1,948	21,435	17,776	4,509	849
9	1,692	541	18,077	2,143	23,579	19,234	5,501	1,156
10	1,807	578	19,306	2,357	25,937	20,837	6,630	1,530
11	1,930	617	20,619	2,593	28,531	22,601	7,911	1,981
12	2,061	659	22,021	2,853	31,384	24,541	9,362	2,519
13	2,202	704	23,519	3,138	34,522	26,675	11,003	3,156
14	2,351	752	25,118	3,452	37,974	29,022	12,856	3,904
15	2,511	803	26,826	3,797	41,772	31,605	14,945	4,778
16	2,682	858	28,651	4,177	45,949	34,445	17,298	5,794
17	2,865	916	30,599	4,594	50,544	37,570	19,945	6,971
18	3,059	979	32,680	5,054	55,599	41,007	22,919	8,327
19	3,268	1,045	34,902	5,559	61,159	44,788	26,256	9,885
20	3,490	1,116	37,275	6,115	67,275	48,947	29,999	11,671
21	3,727	1,192	39,810	6,727	74,002	53,521	34,192	13,711
22	3,981	1,273	42,517	7,400	81,402	58,553	38,885	16,036
23	4,251	1,360	45,408	8,140	89,543	64,089	44,134	18,680
24	4,540	1,453	48,496	8,954	98,497	70,178	50,000	21,681
25	4,849	1,551	51,794	9,849	108,347	76,876	56,552	25,081

What Is So Wrong with Congress Taxing Our Social Security benefits?

Plenty, when you consider that Social Security was a form of tax to begin with. Congress is in effect taxing a tax. Furthermore, it is taxing those retirees who were responsible enough to save for their retirements. Those that only have Social Security benefits to live on do not pay any taxes on their benefits. However, the retirees that saved hard, invested wisely, and acted frugally are being penalized.

FIGURE 6.9 Determining Income Tax on Social Security Benefits

1. Social Security benefits for the year _____
2. 50% of line 1 _____
3. Modified adjusted gross income:
   a. AGI less net Social Security benefits received _____
   b. Tax exempt interest and dividends received or accrued _____
   c. Line 3a plus line 3b _____
4. Provisional income (line 2 plus line 3c) _____
5. Applicable first-tier threshold (from table below) _____
6. Line 4 less line 5 (not less than zero) _____
7. 50% of line 6 _____
8. Amount of benefits subject to tax (smaller of line 2 or line 7) _____

If the provisional income (line 4 above) does not exceed the corresponding first-tier threshold, shown in the table below, no amount is taxable. However, if provisional income exceeds the corresponding threshold, continue with the worksheet below.

9. Applicable second-tier threshold (from table below) _____
10. Line 4 less line 9 (not less than zero) _____
11. 85% of line 10 _____
12. Amount taxable under first tier (from line 8) _____
13. Applicable dollar amount (from table below) _____
14. Smaller of line 12 or line 13 _____
15. Line 11 plus line 14 _____
16. 85% of line 1 _____
17. Amount of benefits subject to tax (smaller of line 15 or 16)

Filing Status	First-Tier Threshold (for line 5)	Second-Tier Threshold (for line 9)	Applicable Dollar Amount (for line 13)
Married Filing Jointly	$32,000	$44,000	$6,000
Married Filing Separately	0	0	0
All Others	25,000	34,000	4,500

Note: This is not an official IRS worksheet.

Caution: Any increase in income, such as from the sale of stock or a retirement plan distribution, may subject you to an unexpected tax on your Social Security benefits.

Many financial experts called the taxation of Social Security benefits a double tax because the government is taxing a benefit that originated from Social Security taxes in the first place. Actually, you could call this taxation of Social Security benefits a triple tax. The reason is that by taxing a portion of your Social Security benefits it is adding those dollars to your gross income, which raises your marginal tax bracket! An increase in your marginal tax bracket can kick up your taxation to a whole new level.

When retirees look into ways of avoiding the taxation of their Social Security benefits, they should consider any investments that have a tax-deferred nature. Investments like individual stocks and tax-deferred annuities can help reduce a retiree's investment income as long as the person lets these investments accumulate. Many retirees are disappointed to find out that the government takes into account any interest income that you make even if that income is from tax-free municipal securities! Talk with a good financial advisor, who should be able to demonstrate effective ways of possibly avoiding the taxation of your Social Security benefits.

Eight Major Tax Traps That You Should Be Aware Of

1. Mandatory Withholding for Qualified Plan Distributions

Upon retirement, many participants of qualified plans such as profit sharing plans or pension programs are offered a choice of several retirement options. Typically, they are offered a lump-sum payout, an annuity income payout, or the privilege to roll over their qualified funds to an individual retirement account.

If you choose the lump-sum payout or if you request that the funds be payable directly to you, then the government requires that the plan administrator withhold 20 percent of your distribution as income tax withholding. This withholding amount is to be sent directly to the government to go toward taxes that may be due from taking such distributions. The government was concerned about people taking taxable distributions and then failing to pay the proper amount of taxes due on such a transaction in a timely fashion. Many retirees were taking lump-sum payouts without considering the tax consequences. Typically, on retirement plan distributions you can expect to have the total amount of such distributions fully taxed.

Assume that you are requesting a distribution of $100,000 from your qualified plan. Because you requested the check be made payable to yourself, the administrator withholds the required 20 percent. You now only receive a check for $80,000. Assuming that you wanted to use income averaging, which is available for some retirees, this may not be a problem.

However, if you intended to initiate an IRA rollover you would have a major problem. Because of the mandatory 20 percent withholding you have only 80 percent of the funds left to complete the rollover. If you do not borrow the funds from another source you will only be rolling over 80 percent of your account while owing taxes on the 20 percent withheld! This was probably not your intent. In other words, because the government initiated mandatory withholding, you may be caught in the position of not being able to roll over all of your funds into an IRA because the government already received a 20 percent estimated tax payment from your proceeds!

In order to prevent this from happening, you must request that your plan administrator or trustee send you the proper paperwork in order to complete a direct rollover transaction. This is where you establish an IRA and have your plan proceeds directly sent to this account. Therefore, you must never have the funds made payable directly to you. This direct rollover transaction will occur between your plan administrator and your IRA trustee. With this method no 20 percent withholding is required. All of your funds will be available to work on your behalf.

2. Income in Respect to a Decedent

The combined tax whammy of having to pay both federal estate taxes and ordinary income taxes can quickly eat up an estate. The beneficiaries of such an estate may take what's left over, never knowing that they may be eligible to use a certain tax deduction against certain assets received as income in respect to a decedent (IRD) to recover some of those lost tax dollars. Worst of all, many accountants, brokers, and attorneys often overlook this valuable deduction as well.

Consider a person who dies during tax year 2001 when the unified tax credit amount is $675,000. Every dollar above this amount is taxed for federal estate tax purposes. Many of those assets may be taxed for federal income taxes as well. Imagine seeing a large estate exposed to a federal estate tax rate of up to 55 percent and an ordinary income tax rate of up to 39.6 percent. This would wipe out most of the funds to be passed on. This total tax, in theory, could exceed 94 percent of the estate. Because this could occur, the government allows a tax deduction for federal estate taxes paid against ordinary income taxes that are due from certain assets that must be either liquidated or claimed from the deceased.

However, when people inherit funds after someone's demise and after the deceased's final tax return has been filed, they may fail to claim a portion of those estate tax deductions against funds that they are currently receiving from the deceased's estate. Those deductions may be lost because the person inheriting IRD assets is usually not aware that such a deduction exists.

Internal Revenue Code Section 691(c) allows the recipient of IRD to claim a tax deduction for the estate taxes paid for the IRD portion that was included in the deceased's estate. This deduction for estate taxes paid can be used against current ordinary income taxes due on income that is being received as IRD. In other words, if a person's estate had estate taxes payable, is it fair that all those taxable assets should be fully taxed for ordinary income tax purposes? The government allows a deduction for income tax purposes for estate taxes that were paid already on such assets.

The most common sources of income in respect to a decedent are from the following:

- Interest on U.S. savings bonds
- Distributions from IRAs and qualified plans
- Subchapter S corporations
- Partnership interests
- Rental income
- Wages and other employee compensation
- Dividend income
- Growth on nonqualified tax-deferred annuities

3. Taking Withdrawals before Age 59½ and Paying a 10 Percent Penalty

This penalty can affect younger retirees that choose to leave the workforce before reaching normal retirement age. The problem occurs when people pull funds out of profit sharing plans, pensions, or other retirement plans such as IRAs and TSAs (403-B plans) before reaching at least age 59½. Not only do you pay ordinary income taxes on such distributions, you also pay a 10 percent penalty on those withdrawals.

Like most rules, this one offers some exceptions to the 10 percent penalty. The most common exception is for qualified plans such as profit sharing and pension plans. This exception also applies to most TSA (403-B) plans. If you are at least 55 years of age and are separating from service, you may be entitled to pull out funds without the 10 percent early withdrawal penalty.

The term *separation of service* usually refers to such events as retiring, being laid off, going on disability, quitting, or being fired. This exemption does not apply to other tax-deferred plans such as individual retirement accounts and nonqualified tax-deferred annuities. The intent of this exception is to allow people to retire early with employer sponsored programs that were designed to provide retirement income. Because you are simply opting for early retirement, the government doesn't want to penalize you.

One of the largest sources of retirement dollars is individual retirement accounts. The government does not allow you to make early withdrawals on these like they do on the qualified plans mentioned above. Note that the exceptions to the rules can prove complicated. Tax advice should be sought before proceeding with these exceptions.

The number one way to get around this early withdrawal penalty is to take the funds out according to IRS rules called the 72t Distribution Rules. One of the rules states that if you take the funds out as substantial equal payments, then you will be allowed to take that portion out with no excess 10 percent penalties.

There are three withdrawal methods that will qualify as substantial equal payments:

1. Life expectancy method
2. Amortization method
3. Annuity factor method

Any one of these methods can be used. I urge anyone who is considering such a move to investigate what the different options have to offer. If you require the maximum amount available without penalty, you may want to focus in on the amortization method or the annuity factor method. A knowledgeable advisor can illustrate what all three methods would produce.

Basically, the two factors considered for these calculations are your current age and an assumed interest rate factor. The older you are, the more you will be able to withdraw. The government allows you to assume a realistic interest rate factor, which can dramatically influence your penalty-free payout. In essence, your projected penalty-free withdrawal amount will be influenced by what interest rate assumption you use. A higher interest rate will allow more funds to be withdrawn.

Try to use a realistic assumption such as matching your rates to those of long-term government securities' yields or to current loan rates. While it may be tempting to use a much higher interest rate assumption, it could come back to haunt you if the IRS decides to challenge you later.

A good financial advisor will prove invaluable when it comes to calculating which method you should use and explaining all the details. Make sure that the advisor is using suitable tax planning software such as Brentmark's Pension Distribution Calculator. A word of caution is advised if you proceed with any of the withdrawal methods under 72t Distribution Rules. Once you start taking early distributions, you must continue for at least five years from the beginning date of your first distribution and/or until you reach age 59½, whichever comes later.

Other exclusions. Other general exemptions pertain to almost all plans. In order to qualify under these more general exclusions, distribution must be made because of your disability or your demise.

Individual retirement accounts are also allowed penalty-free withdrawals if the funds are used for certain medical expenses, certain educational expenses, or up to $10,000 for first-time homebuyers. Also, if you are involved in a divorce action, the rules allow you to make a distribution if it is so ordered under a qualified domestic relations order (QDRO).

4. Rolling Over Appreciated Employer Stock into an IRA without Careful Evaluation

Many retirees are sitting on various amounts of shares of highly appreciated stock that was issued by their employers. While many times these shares can be rolled over into an IRA, it may not be advantageous to do so. Favorable tax rules may apply to securities issued by the employee's company. When doing a lump-sum distribution, you are usually given the option to roll over all of the shares that you have acquired in connection with the various stock purchase programs that the employer may have offered.

If you roll over the shares into an individual retirement account, you will lose a very valuable tax benefit. Many soon-to-be-retired people will instruct their plan trustee to sell their shares so that they may direct cash assets into their IRAs. Their reasoning is based on the premise that their IRA plan will allow them many more investment options.

The only problem is that no one ever explained to them the tax doctrine known as net unrealized appreciation (NUA). NUA, as it is referred to, allows favorable tax treatment to the growth of stock purchased within various employer plans. If you choose to take these stocks outright, you will have to pay ordinary tax on the portion of stock that you purchased or that your employer purchased (known as the cost basis) but not on the gain of such shares. Those may be taxed at the more favorable capital gains rates when you decide to sell.

Therefore, if you retain highly appreciated shares of your employer's stock, you have some valuable advantages when they are taken as part of a lump-sum distribution, including:

- Any gains that may be realized upon the sale of such stock will usually be taxed at favorable long-term gains rates instead of as ordinary income.
- Your heirs will receive the favorable step-up basis on the appreciation of your shares upon your demise.
- Your shares will not be subject to the required mandatory distribution rules imposed on individual retirement accounts at age 70½.
- Withdrawals before age 59½ will only have a partial 10 percent penalty imposed. Cost basis is taken into account for the 10 percent penalty; the net unrealized appreciation is not.

The only negative is that in order to affect a rollout of employer stock you are required to report your cost basis as taxable income in the year of distribution. This usually is a small price to pay for all the noted advantages. This is why this course of action is usually recommended for shares of employer stock that have highly appreciated.

Check with your employer on the exact nature of any stocks you may be receiving as lump-sum distributions. Make a point of reviewing this transaction with your tax advisor and financial advisor before proceeding. Many times your advisors may suggest that you still roll over some of your stock shares into an IRA for diversification purposes.

5. Failure to Withdraw the Required Amount from Your IRA or Qualified Accounts

At age 70½, you must start taking funds from your qualified accounts, including your individual retirement accounts, no later than April 1 following the year that you turn age 70½.

There are a few exceptions to this rule that apply to a very small percentage of the population. Those exceptions are as follows:

- If you continue to work after reaching age 70½, you may delay your first required minimum distribution until April 1 following the year of retirement. This exception does not apply to those owning a business interest of more than 5 percent or for a regular IRA.
- Individuals who made a special election before 1984 to receive their distributions under the pre-1984 rules are not subject to the age 70½ required minimum distribution rules.
- Roth IRAs are not subject to the required minimum distribution rules of age 70½.

The penalty for not withdrawing the required minimum amount from your IRA or other tax-qualified accounts is a whopping 50 percent of the amount that should have been withdrawn. Many older retirees forget to withdraw the proper amount or are confused about how to calculate the proper amount to be distributed. There are, of course, many cases where retirees are simply given improper advice.

You can influence the amount you have to withdraw based on two main factors:

1. Whom you designate as beneficiary
2. What method you utilize for determining your life expectancy—the recalculation method or nonrecalculation method

These factors will determine the minimum amount that is required to be withdrawn. Of course, you can take more.

6. Failure to Use Your Unified Tax Credit Amount and GSTT Exemption

There is a tax on the right to transfer assets to your heirs after your demise. Most retirees will never have to pay this tax because they are currently given a unified tax credit amount that shelters property of $675,000 (amount for the years 2000 and 2001). This amount is usually enough to offset any potential estate taxes that would otherwise be due.

Generally, transfers and gifts to spouses while living or upon one's demise are exempt from these estate taxes (unless your spouse is a not a U.S. citizen). This simply defers the tax until the surviving spouse passes on. In essence, if you don't use your unified tax credit amount, you will lose it. While it may seem perfectly normal to leave your estate to your spouse outright, this strategy may cost your heirs plenty.

Simply having a fully funded trust in place that has language known as the credit shelter trust provision (also known as an A-B provision) can ensure that both you and your spouse each utilize your full current deduction. This credit shelter amount is slated to increase over the coming years.

Retirees who are aware of the federal estate tax will often take steps to avoid these taxes. Many of their children may already have large estates of their own. Rather than direct their funds toward these children and compound their children's own estate tax situations, they will bypass their children in favor of grandchildren.

While this is legal, the government considers this a skipped generation and has passed a Generation-Skipping Transfer Tax (GSTT). The government wants its portion of any estate taxes sooner rather than later. When you skip your own children in favor of grandchildren, you are usually postponing the time it will take for those assets to be taxed.

Each individual has a GSTT amount of $1,060,000. Both spouses of larger estates should utilize this exemption amount in order to preserve as much of their estate as possible for their heirs. Having the proper trust documents drafted and funded can do this.

Failure to shelter your GSTT exemption amount could mean a huge loss of unnecessary taxes to the government. As it is, any amount of transfer over and above your exemption amount can lead to a maximum estate and gift tax rate of 55 percent. This tax will be in addition to federal estate and gift taxes being imposed at the highest possible bracket amount of 55 percent! See Chapter 5 for more information on federal estate and gift taxes.

7. Losing Your Step-Up Basis

Most retirees are familiar with the advantages of a capital gain asset's growth being taxed at favorable long-term capital gains rates instead of ordinary income tax rates. What they may not know is that it is also quite easy to avoid any capital gains tax on the gain simply by passing the property upon your demise. Your heirs will receive the property on the step-up basis. This transfer of real property, often referred to as testamentary property, has the advantage of no current income taxes when passing the property at death. Note, while this method may drastically reduce federal capital gains tax it does not reduce any federal estate tax, if due.

The rules impacting various real property, such as real estate and securities, are known as cost-basis rules. Cost basis is the value of an asset at the time of purchase. Typically, when you sell an asset you must pay taxes on its appreciation. If you give away this asset as a gift while living, then the new owner assumes your original cost basis. There are definite advantages to holding on to property until you die. This will allow your heirs to escape paying capital gains taxes on the growth. Your heirs assume your basis for the property at the date of your demise. The government states that the basis will then be the market value of the property at the time of demise, not what you paid for the property!

You must consider what may be more advantageous to your heirs. Should you pass on property while living so that all future appreciation is transferred to the new owner or should you transfer such property at your demise in order to receive favorable stepped-up tax treatment? The risk associated with transferring property too late is that all that appreciation could cause a tremendous federal estate tax problem. All retirees should review their situations every few years in order to determine what may be best for them.

8. Doing a Roth IRA Conversion for the Wrong Reason

Many people are converting their individual retirement accounts to the newer Roth IRA. While in theory these newer Roth IRAs seem appealing, you should only do such a conversion after giving it careful consideration. The first question you must ask yourself is "Do you trust your government to never change the tax laws regarding the future taxability of the Roth IRA?" Congress gives and Congress takes away.

It is entirely possible that Congress could change the tax laws in the future and that these changes could directly or indirectly cause Roth IRAs to be partially or fully taxable. While the likelihood is very small for these Roth IRAs to be taxed in the next decade, the odds could increase if the government is running future budget deficits. This could occur as the baby boomer generation marches into its retirement years.

While total taxation of the Roth IRA is a small probability, the partial taxation of these accounts is not. Consider the history of tax laws. The federal income tax started off as a small tax not to exceed 3 percent. Social Security taxes started in 1937 with a maximum tax rate of 1 percent on taxable earnings of up to $3,000. Today, this tax rate is 7.65 percent on wage income of $76,200. This amount of tax does not include the portion that your employer must pay! Also consider when the government stated that Social Security benefits would be tax-free! We know that this is not the case for most retirees who are considered middle class or above.

Roth IRAs offer tax-free income if held for at least five years or until age 59½, whichever comes later. If your estate is getting to a point where federal estate taxes will be a problem, conversion to a Roth IRA is a good idea. Simply by paying the taxes on your IRA now, you could lower the size of your estate that will be exposed to the federal estate tax and achieve a tax-free return as well. Roth IRAs also are convenient assets to pass on to future heirs because they can pass free of federal income taxes.

Many retirees enjoy the fact that you do not need to take required minimum distributions from a Roth IRA at age 70½, unlike a regular IRA. The only major negative to a Roth IRA conversion is that when you transfer regular IRA funds to a Roth IRA you must pay the taxes in the year of the conversion. This could greatly diminish the amount of funds you have working on your behalf. You should only do a Roth IRA conversion after careful consideration of what taxes will have to be paid. Careful consideration must be given to your current marginal tax bracket as well as to your future tax bracket upon withdrawal.

Restrictions based on your adjusted gross income (AGI) have to be considered as well. If your AGI exceeds $100,000 (exclusive of the regular IRA amount being converted), you will not be able to transact a Roth conversion.

7

Using the Wrong Investment Strategies

Accumulation versus Investing

People act as individuals, yet collectively, share some common traits. This is especially noticeable with investors as a group. It is common for most people to follow certain steps and they typically do this in a logical sequence. The first step with investors is to accumulate money. This step is so crucial that without it most people will never have sufficient funds to invest. Like a baby that learns to crawl before it can walk, most people learn to accumulate money before they invest it. In the world of investing, you need funds in order to invest.

Average accumulators will do so by adding funds sporadically to their savings when they feel they have some additional funds. Good accumulators realize they need a consistent system in place to increase the likelihood of accumulating as much as possible. This typically takes the form of a steady savings program such as payroll deduction, monthly savings bond purchases, or other disciplined saving methods.

The more that you can follow a logical and systematic sequence of saving, the more you will accumulate. In other words, once you have set up your savings program so that it operates on automatic pilot, then you are well on your way. You are now moving from crawling to standing up. In order to start walking, however, you will need to learn the next step.

Taking the Next Step

While accumulation is necessary, you should not confuse accumulating funds with investing funds. A good accumulator can accomplish much by systematically setting aside funds in case of an emergency or in the event of an opportunity. Yet, this accumulation habit will not be enough to make a person wealthy or completely self-sufficient. That usually comes into play by taking your accumulated funds and investing them. This, for most people, is the next step.

An Investment Is

An investment, therefore, should be considered the intelligent use of resources to obtain the maximum results from your financial assets based on the amount of risk you are willing to accept. Seldom are people good at both accumulating and investing. It simply requires two separate sets of skills to perform either of these tasks well. Of course, your temperament, risk profile, experience, resources, and sophistication must be taken into account. That is why very few investments are suitable for everyone. Most investors start off by considering investments that are diversified and professionally managed. These investments are known as mutual funds.

Mutual Funds

Most investors discover mutual funds through stockbrokers, financial planners, or investment advisors. Many other investors are directed into mutual funds through articles that they have read in various financial publications. Others discover mutual funds through their work, where they are exposed to the various types of accumulation and investment programs that are available.

Mutual funds typically offer broad diversification with active management of the mutual fund's holdings by a set of portfolio managers. Obviously, this makes proceeding into the world of investing much easier than if you had to select your own basket of stocks or bonds. This ease of ownership has caused mutual funds to expand from a cottage industry in the late 1960s to one of the world's most popular methods of investing.

The most common type of mutual funds are called open-end investment companies. They continually offer new shares to the public via a document called a prospectus. These funds will allow you to redeem your shares on any business day, thereby providing ample marketability. Your percentage of ownership of the mutual fund is in direct relationship to the amount that you have invested in a particular fund. Therefore, if you were a shareholder who contributed a large investment that constituted 10 percent of the fund, you would own 10 percent of all of the holdings within the fund on a proportional basis. This would enable you to have good diversification among various financial assets. This is what has given mutual funds such a good reputation.

Diversified Funds versus Nondiversified Funds

Mutual funds are either considered diversified investment companies or nondiversified investment companies. Diversified investment companies have to follow certain guidelines. These diversified funds must have at least 75 percent of their assets invested as follows:

- No more than 5 percent of assets can be invested in the securities of any one company.
- The fund cannot purchase more than 10 percent of the voting stock of any one corporation.

This practice of diversification helps reduce risk by spreading the fund's assets over more stocks than a nondiversified fund would.

Therefore, a nondiversified fund would have a tendency to take on more financial and market risk. Performance could be magnified both in a negative or a positive manner. This will have a tendency to occur because the influence of a single stock could have much more impact on the portfolio. These nondiversified funds have their role in investment portfolios. They are most suitable for those investors who have clearly identified their investment objectives and have more financial experience.

Add to this that your mutual fund management group is typically compensated by a set percentage of the assets under management, and you will find that there is no shortage of fund managers offering their wares. You, as the consumer, are free to shop. Search for a fund management group with whom you feel comfortable and look for the specific funds that you feel meet and serve your financial objectives.

Liquidity versus Marketability

One aspect of investing should be pointed out. There is a big difference between accumulating money and investing money. While accumulating money, you typically have access to your funds with either low penalties or no penalties at all. This is referred to as having liquidity. This allows you to have access to your funds with the assurance that you will receive at least your principal at any given point.

With most financial investments, such as stock mutual funds and bond mutual funds, you are only guaranteed the ability to have your shares redeemed with the corresponding values sent to you. This process of redeeming your shares at the then current market price is known as marketability. This is not the same as true liquidity. With marketability, you will only receive back the value of your account on the date of sale. Because the stock and bond markets fluctuate, you could receive more or less than what you started with.

During turbulent times in the marketplace or during down times, you may receive quite a bit less than what you originally invested. Therefore, you should always be prepared for this lack of true liquidity and only allocate funds that you can afford to leave for the long term. Also, be prepared for the possibility of losing some or all of your funds. For these reasons, it is imperative that you do your homework before investing in any mutual funds. You should, of course, monitor not only the fund's progress but the world's changing economic environment as well, and then make adjustments as needed.

The reason for the popularity of mutual funds is that they have an outstanding track record of safety. This does not mean that your shares are guaranteed by anybody but that a transfer agent who receives investment instructions from your fund management group typically handles your shares. Therefore, this system helps to ensure that your fund manager, no matter how honest he or she may or may not be, cannot run off with all of the investment funds. This came about under various regulations passed by Congress and the Securities and Exchange Commission (SEC), and has worked out very nicely for all concerned.

Various types of mutual funds are offered. In fact, there are more mutual fund offerings than there are individual stocks listed on the New York Stock Exchange. These mutual funds fall into various categories.

Money Market Mutual Funds

Typically, these are the mutual funds that investors place their money into when they are not sure in which area of the economy they wish to invest. Also, these funds serve as an excellent holding tank for your cash position and are perfect for funds you wish to have in case of an emergency or upcoming purchasing needs. These funds have an excellent track record with their shares staying at one dollar per share while paying very competitive interest. Typically, they are competitive with most certificates of deposits and are much more competitive than simple passbook accounts.

Many consumers think that money market mutual funds are guaranteed and are surprised to find out that they are not. If you were to select the wrong money market mutual fund, you could get back less than what you had originally deposited. This has only happened in a few cases, and in these cases the investors received very close to what they should have received in actual share value. The moral of the story is to understand that as nice and competitive as money market mutual funds are, they are not backed by the Federal Deposit Insurance Corporation (FDIC) like bank accounts.

The mutual fund industry has done a wonderful job of establishing a formidable track record of safety with these investments. To add a margin of safety, one would be wise to find out what the money market mutual fund you are considering actually invests in. Typically, these funds will purchase corporate debt notes, certificates of deposit, government obligations, and other commercial paper instruments. You should not necessarily be looking for the highest yielding money market fund, because the fund may have taken on more risk in order to achieve this rate of return.

Many funds will lower their management fees on money market mutual funds to attract new investors. This is an acceptable business practice. Because they have lowered their management fees, the money market fund's yield will go up by that same amount. These funds are under no obligation to keep their fees low and typically will raise them as time goes by.

Another way to add a margin of safety is to purchase only money market mutual funds that invest in U.S. government obligations. These obligations are either direct or indirect obligations of the government. As such, the likelihood of any default risk is greatly reduced.

Most money market mutual funds offer check-writing services as well as debit cards. These make them excellent vehicles for overall money management services. Typically, most brokerage companies make these accounts available for any funds you have sitting with them that are not directly invested in the stock or bond market. Therefore, you are earning interest on your money while you are deciding what you wish to do.

Common Stock Funds

These accounts have become extremely popular since the stock market started its great ascent back in 1982. When interest rates started to drop after hitting their high point during 1981, investors quickly figured out that lower interest rates would be good for the economy.

There are several methods for categorizing these types of funds. These methods are typically as follows:

- By size
- By category
- By style of investing
- By charges involved

By size. In the world of stock investing, it is common to place an individual stock into a particular category depending on the company's size. The size of a company is usually determined by taking into account all of its outstanding shares and then multiplying that number by its current market price. This typically gives you an accurate picture of its market capitalization. Mutual funds may state via their prospectus or through reports to shareholders what areas of market capitalization they favor.

Many funds will limit their investments to only large companies. A significant and positive appeal of larger companies is their ability to raise money from investors via secondary stock offerings and bond issues. Larger companies' stocks also tend to have more shares that are freely traded in the marketplace. This provides more liquidity to mutual funds and larger investors. This is very important in the event that the investors need to reduce their stock positions without causing any downturn in the stock. Therefore, these types of investors prefer such companies. Larger companies often continue to grow by acquiring smaller companies whose prospects look promising. This ability to buy the competition is considered a good benefit to owning stock in large companies. Another important point to consider is how hard it would be to compete with a large company like McDonald's. New companies probably could not raise the necessary capital to compete with them head to head. Most investors would be too impatient to fund the venture due to the tremendous expense in resources and time that would be required to make the venture profitable.

These larger companies typically have more exposure to international markets because many of them have expanded overseas. This could be positive or negative depending on your world view. A company having exposure overseas could have more volatility attached to its shares, because currencies tend to fluctuate up and down and international economies may be weaker at times. Of course, the opposite may be true. International markets may offer the most growth potential in years to come. An investor should always be aware of the markets in which the companies are actually participating.

Other stock mutual funds may prefer midsize capitalized or small companies. These companies typically have less international exposure and may have more room to grow. Midsize companies tend to have more experienced management teams in place than smaller companies would, especially a start-up company. Investors have a tendency to favor midcap stocks over small companies because they tend to hold up in value and don't carry as much risk as a small company carries. Smaller companies may not be able to secure adequate financing or compete with larger companies especially over the long term. Midsize companies are large enough to secure adequate financing in most cases, while having a greater ability to exploit certain niches.

Other fund managers may prefer smaller capitalized companies because of their growth potential. Who wouldn't like to own the next Microsoft? Many funds will not limit themselves to any one category but will look for suitable selections from companies of all sizes.

The stock market seems to have been favoring larger capitalized companies over the last decade. However, long-term smaller companies have given higher returns.

Therefore, one may wish to have a mixture of such funds or find a fund manager who is flexible enough and nimble enough to venture into any of these areas depending on changing market conditions.

Keep in mind that a mutual fund that has grown very large due to its past success may find it harder to take advantage of smaller-capitalized companies. Even if the fund is successful in finding suitable small companies, their effect on the overall portfolio may be mitigated by the sheer size of their other holdings. The simple fact is that even if your fund manager has successfully invested in a rising small company, the value of that growth may be diluted from the performance of their other holdings. Therefore, you may wish to select a smaller mutual fund or allocate some of your funds strictly to a small-cap or midsize fund category to ensure that you are obtaining ample exposure to this area of investing.

The definitions of the three market capitalization groups are as follows:

- *Small cap.* Companies with market capitalization of $1.5 billion or less
- *Midcap.* Companies with market capitalization between $1.5 billion and $10 billion
- *Large cap.* Companies with market capitalization of $10 billion or greater

Please note that some funds may have different definitions as to what they consider a small-cap company, a midcap company, and a large-cap company. Read the prospectus that they offer for clarification.

By category. Common stock funds are further categorized by either their general area of interest or their stated investment objective. Therefore, you have funds that are considered aggressive growth, regular growth, moderate growth, growth and income, income, balanced funds, blue chip funds, utility funds, and international funds among others. Investors are advised to pay attention to the nature of their fund and to read the prospectus of their actual fund to ensure that the fund is investing the way the client wants. Many fund companies will drift from their intended goals for myriad reasons. For example, sometimes the fund manager may be chasing higher returns or perhaps is becoming more protective. While these traits are not necessarily bad, they may interfere with the investment plans that you have laid out.

In summary, you may have allocated funds according to your investment and personality profile. You may not want a fund manager moving into a different investment allocation without your full knowledge. Because fund managers are free to do this without contacting their shareholders, you need to stay abreast of these factors. The tendency of fund managers to change their portfolio allocation or mixture dramatically in a manner that is different from its initial objective is known as style drift.

Many mutual fund groups are offering various funds, with a concentration in one or several particular areas. These are known as sector funds or specialized funds. A fund that only invests in telecommunication companies or computer stocks would fall into this category. While these may offer the growth potential that you may be seeking, they are generally considered to be more aggressive in nature. The performance may be there if you pick the correct sector of the market, but losses can be intensified if you are incorrect.

By style of investing. Most mutual funds have their own distinct style of investing. This management style is usually fairly consistent, for better or worse. Because your fund's management style can dramatically impact your mutual fund's performance in a given year, be fully aware of the management style that your fund is following. Some common management styles are:

- *Growth.* This type of fund looks for stocks of companies that have higher than average earnings over the last few years and look like they will continue to do so for the near future. Growth stocks typically pay little, if any, dividends.
- *Value.* This type of fund typically looks for stocks that may be trading at a discount from their real value. This is usually based on the company's earnings or its book value.
- *Blended.* This type of fund will invest in both growth and value stocks. It will also invest in companies that are not labeled as either growth or value. These could be companies that are considered middle of the road.

By charges involved. Mutual funds typically are distributed directly by the mutual fund or through a network of registered representatives known as brokers or financial advisors. Depending on the distributor of the funds, a fund may fall into one of these categories:

- *No load.* Funds that are distributed directly to the public typically add no sales charges (which are referred to as the load) up front. A true no-load fund will not impose any charges up front, during the period when you own the fund, or when you leave the fund. The only charges you should incur are the management fees and the operating fees of the fund due to recordkeeping and portfolio trading costs. If a fund charges fees known as 12b-1 distribution fees, then that fund is not a true no-load mutual fund.
- *Load.* Funds that are typically sold through brokers or financial advisors have some form of sales charges priced in them. These charges may be up front, levied while you are holding the funds, or imposed upon the mutual fund shareholder if the shares are redeemed before a set period of years, which is detailed within the fund's prospectus. Adding to this confusion is the common practice of mutual funds using a combination of these charges.

More on No-Load Funds versus Load Funds

All things being equal, you want the no-load funds because they are typically less expensive to own. However, you must dig deeper to find the real charges in most funds. You should also consider the performance track record of the fund, as well as your own personal needs.

Much energy has been spent analyzing the pros and cons of no-load funds versus load funds. Countless articles have been written on this topic and people will have no shortage of opinions as they do their research. Primarily as a result of these types of articles being published, the distribution system for mutual funds is changing. The line between these two types of funds is becoming increasingly more blurred.

Load mutual funds were taking many critical reviews from various financial publications for the high charges that consumers were incurring for their financial products. Many load mutual funds in the past would charge up to 9 percent in up-front sales charges!

What most financial publications failed to mention was that those same funds would give a greatly reduced sales charge to those shareholders who invested higher amounts of money in their funds. The majority of load funds would start dropping their sales charges as soon as an investor placed over $10,000 in their funds. The discounts would start to increase substantially when deposits reached $50,000.

Load funds were compensating their representatives with a higher percent in sales commission for smaller accounts. Their reasoning was that a smaller client could take up as much time as a larger client and, therefore, the financial representative needed to be compensated. In addition, many clients with smaller investments also needed to be educated about mutual funds before they would invest.

12b-1 Fees

Starting about ten years ago, many mutual funds began using a little known provision called 12b-1 distribution and service fees. Many load funds added these charges to their funds so they could reduce their up-front sales charges without dramatically reducing what they paid out to their financial representatives that brought in new business.

These charges are very easy to add to a group of mutual funds. Typically, the fund's management group states in a letter to current shareholders that these 12b-1 fees would be beneficial for the funds involved. The group generally states that the value of such a fee will allow it to reduce up-front sales charges and, thereby, add more shareholders. These additional shareholders, in theory, should allow the fund to increase its investment asset base, which, in turn, should allow the fund to lower annual management fees. Therefore, most current shareholders approve such 12b-1 distribution plans.

Many no-load funds saw the financial success that these load funds were having by adding these 12b-1 fees to their accounts, and they soon joined in with their own 12b-1 fees. In fairness to the no-load funds, their 12b-1 fees were typically less than half of what many load funds were assessing. The average range for 12b-1 fees is just under ½ of 1 percent to as high as 1 percent. Therefore, regardless of whether or not a fund states that it is load or no-load, check to see what its 12b-1 fee is. A higher 12b-1 fee may cause a drag on investment returns.

In addition to 12b-1 fees, many load funds may impose additional sales charges. The most common structure of load funds is as follows:

- Up-front sales charges ranging from 2 percent to 5 percent. Expect to see a small 12b-1 charge of just under ½ of 1 percent.
- No charges up front, but a deferred sales charge if you remove all of your funds within a set time period. Typically, this time frame is four to six years long. Your sales charge will start off at one amount and reduce over the surrender period. Expect to pay a 12b-1 fee of at least 1 percent per year. This fee should fall after your surrender period is over with.
- No charges up front. No charges upon withdrawal. Expect to pay a 12b-1 fee of at least 1 percent each year.

Managed Accounts

Recent developments have added further confusion to the issue of no-load funds versus load funds. Many load funds are available with no sales charges when they are used in managed money accounts. Financial advisors set up these accounts for clients on a fee managed basis. The financial advisor charges a yearly management fee for allocating the clients' financial resources among various investment asset classes. Because these types of accounts have become very popular in gathering billions of dollars in investor's assets, the mutual funds involved will in many cases make their funds load exempt.

When clients have a managed money account, they can have access to load funds and no-load funds all for one low fee. These are sometimes referred to as wrap accounts or by a proprietary name when used by regional and national broker-dealers. Registered investment advisors and registered representatives offer these accounts.

Most of these accounts will impose a set amount of fees based on the size of your account. Consumers should be wary of any accounts charging more than 1½ percent per year based on their account value. Larger accounts of over $1 million will typically pay less than 1 percent per year in fees. Research any money managers you are considering to see if there are any 12b-1 fees being deducted as well.

Most of these managed money accounts are set up after the client fills out a questionnaire. This allows the financial consultant to select an appropriate portfolio blend that will match the client's investment profile and time frame. Your advisor should prepare an investment policy statement detailing:

- What your investment objectives are
- What expected time horizon should be used for your investments
- What assets classes are to be used
- What your expected rate of return is for various asset classes
- How you will be kept informed of your portfolio's progress and how often your portfolio will be reviewed

Many managed accounts will use institutional fund managers. These managers typically invest for the longer term and are not as swayed by popular trends or investment fads. They are used to dealing with more sophisticated institutional clients. These clients prefer a stable investment style because they usually have selected this institutional manager to handle a set portion of their portfolio based on the investment style established by the institutional manager through the years. The added benefits of institutional managers are typically lower fund expenses and lower turnover of the underlying portfolio. These advantages may add 1 to 2 percent to your performance during the year. These savings may be enough to offset any fees you are paying to your advisor.

Unit Investment Trusts

Many years ago, closed-end mutual funds dominated the landscape. Especially popular in England, these investment vehicles were considered the preferred way to invest. Over the years, however, people found that these closed-end funds were not convenient to own. Unlike an open-end mutual fund that could be redeemed by contacting your mutual fund group, a closed-end fund had to be redeemed by selling your shares on a stock exchange.

These closed-end mutual funds are also known as unit investment trusts. In addition to the above disadvantage, these types of investments fell out of favor for two more reasons. First, in order to purchase more shares, you had to find available shares in the marketplace. Open-end mutual funds, on the other hand, continually offer new shares that make them ideal for an investor investing a sum of money each month. Second, these funds would be offered at one point in time with no termination date given for the liquidation of the portfolio. This caused many closed-end funds to trade at a discounted share price compared to their real portfolio value.

Recently, several marketing firms, such as Nuveen Investments and First Trust Investments sponsored by Nike Securities LP, have addressed these concerns. These firms began to package individual securities in unit investment trusts, which were slated to terminate at the end of 13 months, 18 months, or 5 years. This solved the problem of these shares trading at a discount. This also ensured that any capital gains from those shares appreciating in value would be taxed at the favorable long-term capital gains rates. These same marketing firms also made sure that they priced the units at an initially low price, usually $10 per share, and that they would consistently offer new unit investment trusts with similar investment objectives.

These newer unit investment trusts are becoming increasingly more popular and investors are gravitating toward them. The reasons for this are fivefold:

1. These unit investment trusts are tax efficient.
2. Professional portfolio selection is typically used to select the initial hold- ings within a unit investment trust.
3. Investors will have an identifiable portfolio that they know will remain con- sistent.
4. Investors can focus on certain sectors of the market without being overly diversified
5. Investors will own a bucket of securities without being diluted with high amounts of money market instruments that many open-end mutual funds are holding within their portfolios in order to meet redemptions by share- holders.

In addition to these reasons, unit investment trusts typically have much lower management fees, if any, assessed each year, unlike open-end mutual funds. Unit investment trusts typically have an up-front sales charge that will equate to a cost of roughly 1 percent per year for ownership of such shares. The purchaser of these shares also does not have to worry about additional portfolio trading costs, which is a great unknown with most actively managed mutual funds.

This ability to focus on various segments of the economy and to employ various investment strategies will make these types of investments extremely popular in years to come. The ability to focus on various sectors of the economy, such as municipal securities, brought these types of funds back in popularity. Marketing firms quickly found out that there was a market for investments that allowed an individual investor to invest in various sectors of the economy.

As a result, these companies are offering portfolios consisting of securities such as telecommunications stocks, pharmaceutical stocks, and Internet stocks, among others. Therefore, investors can purchase unit investment trusts and receive relative diversification within a particular industry. Typically, these portfolios would hold 20 to 30 stocks. Investors can now focus on the sectors of the economy that they feel will perform the best, instead of relying on a fund management group that may have its own agenda.

Typical Example of a Unit Investment Trust Investing in One Area of the Economy

The telecommunications sector. This sector fund focuses on a diversified basket of stocks in the communications service area as well as data networking/communications equipment companies and wireless companies.

The following portfolios shown are for illustration purposes only. No recommendation is being made or given.

Telecommunication Companies

- ALLTEL Corporation
- AT&T Corp.
- Bell Atlantic Corporation
- BellSouth Corporation
- Cable & Wireless Plc.
- Deutsche Telekom AG
- MCI WorldCom, Inc.
- Qwest Communications International Inc.
- SBC Communications, Inc.
- Telefonica S.A.
- ADC Telecommunications, Inc.
- Applied Micro Circuits Corporation
- Broadcom Corporation (Class A)
- Cisco Systems, Inc.
- Comverse Technologies, Inc.
- ECI Telecom Limited
- Lucent Technologies, Inc.
- Nortel Networks Corporation
- PMC-Sierra, Inc.
- Tellabs, Inc.
- Vitesse Semiconductor Corporation
- Motorola, Inc.
- Nokia Oy (ADR)
- QUALCOMM Incorporated
- Vodafone AirTouch Plc.

The pharmaceutical sector. This sector fund focuses on a diversified basket of both traditional drug stocks and some biotech drug companies.

Pharmaceutical Companies

- Abbott Laboratories
- American Home Products
- Amgen Inc.
- Biogen, Inc.
- Bristol-Myers Squibb Co.
- Elan Corporation Plc.
- Genzyme Corporation
- Glaxo Wellcome Plc.
- Johnson & Johnson
- Jones Pharma, Inc.
- Eli Lilly and Company
- Merck & Company
- Mylan Laboratories, Inc.
- Novartis AG
- Pfizer Inc.
- Roche Holdings AG
- Schering-Plough Corporation
- SmithKline Beecham Plc.
- Warner-Lambert Company
- Watson Pharmaceuticals, Inc.

Examples of Various Trading Strategies for Unit Investment Trusts

These marketing firms that were responsible for bringing out unit investment trusts followed various investment strategies. Many of these investment strategies would be very difficult for a regular open-end mutual fund to employ. These strategies are many and are based on past historical information.

These strategies have not been actually used by any specific management group for the length of time illustrated. Many of these strategies could have the potential to outperform the markets if followed. Of course, no guarantee is ever made for future performance of any investment. Investors seeking out these strategies would do well to look at offerings from such firms as First Trust Investments sponsored by Nike Securities.

The S&P Target 10 strategy. The S&P Target 10 strategy seeks to outperform the S&P 500 Index through the following process:

- Only the largest half of the S&P 500 stocks is taken in account. This is done by ranking the stocks by market capitalization.
- These stocks are then screened for value by selecting the half of the stocks with the lowest price-to-sales ratios.

FIGURE 7.1 The Target 10 Strategy versus the S&P 500

	S&P Total Returns	
Year	500 Index	Target 10 Strategy
1980	32.11%	51.31%
1981	-4.92	-15.39
1982	21.14	35.49
1983	22.28	17.95
1984	6.22	13.79
1985	31.77	44.32
1986	18.31	19.22
1987	5.33	6.68
1988	16.64	17.77
1989	31.35	36.88
1990	-3.30	-7.98
1991	30.40	22.03
1992	7.62	20.69
1993	9.95	39.40
1994	1.34	5.70
1995	37.22	22.64
1996	22.82	23.98
1997	33.21	59.74
1998	28.57	47.20
1999	20.94	1.06
2000	-9.08	-11.24

Average Annual Total Return:

	16.31%	19.76%

- These stocks are then screened for growth by identifying the companies with the greatest one-year price appreciation. The top ten stocks are then selected for inclusion within the portfolio.
- This process is repeated annually.

Figures 7.1 and 7.2 illustrate the returns and growth of the S&P Target 10 strategy compared to that of the S&P 500 Index.

The results of Figures 7.1 and 7.2 are based on this hypothetical strategy. This information is based on historical data had this strategy been followed. No particular fund has actually been set up and in existence for the time frame illustrated. The S&P Target 10 strategy is not associated in any way with Standard & Poor's company.

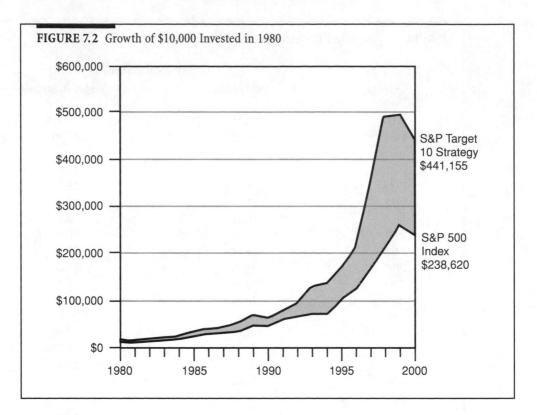

FIGURE 7.2 Growth of $10,000 Invested in 1980

The Nasdaq Target 15 strategy. This strategy begins with the Nasdaq 100 Index. It consists of the 15 stocks with the best overall ranking based on the following criteria:

- 12-month price appreciation
- 6-month price appreciation
- Return on assets
- Price to cash flow
- Repeat this process annually

Figures 7.3 and 7.4 illustrate the returns and growth of the Nasdaq Target 15 strategy compared to that of the Nasdaq 100 Index.

The results shown in Figures 7.3 and 7.4 are based on this hypothetical strategy. This information is based on historical data had this strategy been followed. No particular fund has actually been set up and in existence for this time frame illustrated. The Nasdaq Target 15 strategy is in no way connected with the Nasdaq Exchange.

The Value Line Target strategy. The Value Line Target strategy begins with the 100 stocks that Value Line currently gives a number one ranking for timeliness.

FIGURE 7.3   The Target 15 Strategy versus the Nasdaq 100

Year	Nasdaq Total Returns 100 Index	Target 15 Strategy
1986	6.89%	19.22%
1987	10.49	11.65
1988	13.54	-2.91
1989	26.17	34.70
1990	-10.41	-7.67
1991	64.99	106.13
1992	8.86	-2.47
1993	11.67	25.98
1994	1.74	8.08
1995	43.01	51.04
1996	42.74	57.22
1997	20.76	32.53
1998	85.43	119.86
1999	102.08	97.46
2000	-36.82	-16.90
Average Annual Total Return:	21.27%	29.79%

The 25 stocks with the best overall ranking based on the following criteria will be included:

- 12-month price appreciation
- 6-month price appreciation
- Return on assets
- Price to cash flow
- Repeat this process annually

Figures 7.5 and 7.6 illustrate the returns and growth of the Value Line Target strategy compared to that of the S&P 500 Index.

The results shown in Figures 7.5 and 7.6 are based on this hypothetical strategy. This information is based on historical data had this strategy been followed. No particular fund has actually been set up and in existence for this time frame illustrated. The Value Line Target strategy is in no way connected with Value Line.

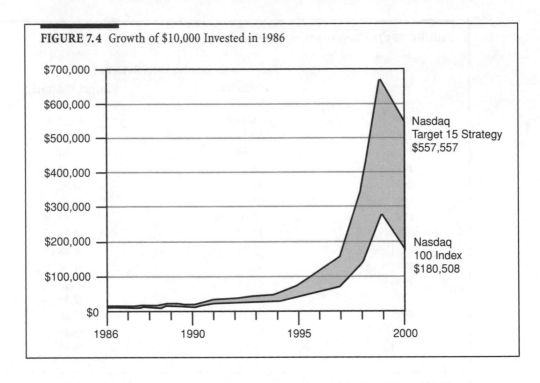

FIGURE 7.4 Growth of $10,000 Invested in 1986

Individual Stocks

Many retirees currently hold some individual stocks. Perhaps they received them from their employer's stock plan while they were working. Other retirees will purchase individual stocks based on news stories, local companies being talked up within their communities, or hot tips that they've received from friends and relatives. Many retirees are anxious to purchase individual stocks after they have invested with mutual funds for several years. They feel that it is time to step up and participate more directly in their investments. They realize that individual stocks can magnify your portfolio returns if you select the right stocks.

The fact of the matter is that owning individual stocks can be more exciting. You call the shots by selecting just those areas of the economy that you wish to participate in. You do not have to be diversified as most mutual funds must be. This concentration of financial resources in just a few individual stocks can make it easier to keep track of your portfolio. Share prices of larger stocks are reported in the newspapers daily. Many retirees also like the pride that comes from owning good performing stocks. Positive performance gives you some good topics of conversation among friends.

FIGURE 7.5 The Value Line Target Strategy versus the S&P 500

| | Value Line Total Returns | |
Year	S&P 500 Index	Value Line Target Strategy
1985	31.77%	31.99%
1986	18.31	20.00
1987	5.33	16.77
1988	16.64	-9.35
1989	31.35	46.29
1990	-3.30	3.12
1991	30.40	83.73
1992	7.62	-2.49
1993	9.95	25.26
1994	1.34	13.40
1995	37.22	52.64
1996	22.82	54.86
1997	33.21	34.45
1998	28.57	91.50
1999	20.94	112.45
2000	-9.08	-10.83
Average Annual Total Return:	16.85%	30.89%

The tax effects of owning individual stocks are much more advantageous than owning mutual funds. With mutual funds, you may be faced with a tax bill even if you did not sell any of your mutual fund shares. This is due to the nature of how mutual funds have been established and how they report various transactions. A mutual fund acts as a pass-through vehicle for taxable transactions that take place within its portfolio. If a mutual fund sells stocks or bonds, it must report any net gains to the shareholders via a 1099 report. Therefore, you may end up with a taxable event at the end of the year even though you never sold a share! Even worse, you have no control over this process.

The fund manager must report any net gains to the individual shareholders but not any excess losses. Therefore, you can really get hurt from a mutual fund that has huge trading gains on its portfolio but not receive the value of all the losses. Any net excess losses will be carried forward within the fund to offset future gains. This causes many individual retiree investors to favor individual stocks and bonds for the taxable portion of their portfolios. They, of course, may continue to use mutual funds for their tax-favored accounts such as individual retirement accounts and profit sharing plans.

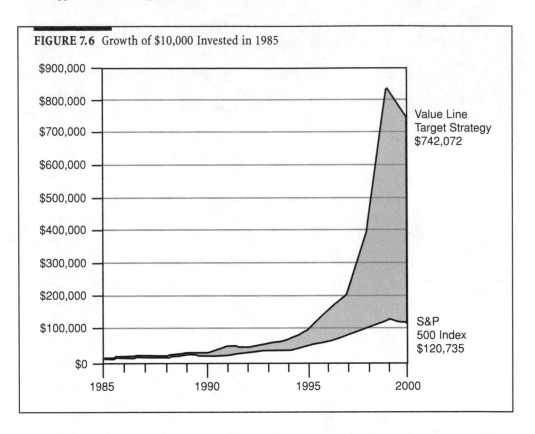

FIGURE 7.6 Growth of $10,000 Invested in 1985

Individual stocks also receive another very favorable tax treatment. They receive a step-up basis upon your demise if you hold them outside of a tax-favored plan such as an individual retirement account, tax-sheltered annuity, or profit sharing plan. This tax treatment is covered in detail in Chapter 6.

The same investment strategies discussed previously for mutual funds are applicable for individual stocks. You may decide to invest for growth or perhaps income. You may decide that you are a value investor or perhaps a growth investor. You may choose to invest in larger company stock shares or perhaps you favor small to midsize companies. The bottom line is that you should determine which area of the economy you wish to participate in.

In addition, with individual stocks, you may want to further analyze your stocks. There are two main methods for making a stock selection or for evaluating whether you should hold a certain stock position. Those two approaches are called *fundamental analysis* and *technical analysis*. There are many books available covering each of these methods in detail.

A fundamental approach involves thoroughly examining a company. This would include looking at:

- The company's operating efficiency and financial performance

- The company's product line or services it provides
- The management of the company

Some of the tools used by a fundamental analysis approach include:

- The company's annual report, balance sheets, and income statements
- Value Line and Standard & Poor's report services
- Earnings per share (EPS) ratios, which represent the company's net income after taxes divided by the average number of common shares outstanding. Look typically for a company that has a steady and increasing EPS ratio. This may be a sign of consistent growth.
- Price-earnings ratio (PE), which is calculated by taking the company's current stock price and dividing it by the earnings per share. This ratio proves helpful when you compare it to a company's past PE history. You may wish to compare one company's PE with other similar companies' figures.

Other ratios are available such as dividend yield, debt ratio, current ratio, and many others from services such as Value Line and Standard & Poor's. Many local libraries have information from such services available. Stock brokerage firms typically can supply you with such reports as well. They usually do this free for their customers.

The other major method of analysis for individual stocks is called the technical approach. This is when you believe that individual stocks and the market in general move in certain trends over periods of time. Past and current price movements are used to try and forecast where stock shares might go. Some of the tool's used by technicians are graphs and charts such as:

- Bar charts that show the price movement of a stock over time
- Moving averages, which is a chart illustrating a stock's daily closing price or an index closing price over a set period such as 30 days, 60 days, etc.

One of your best sources of information on this topic is *Investor's Business Daily,* which may prove helpful in bringing you up to speed on this particular approach. There are also numerous software programs that can illustrate how to track market trends and market movements.

Securities Registered in Street Name

Common dilemmas facing retirees owning individual stock certificates is whether to take actual delivery of their shares or leave them registered in street name with a broker-dealer. When you purchase an individual stock, you usually have the right to take delivery of the actual stock certificate. When you want to sell that stock, you must deliver your outstanding certificate or make arrangements with the transfer agent in the event of losing your stock certificates. This process can add to the hassle factor of owning individual securities.

Many retirees are looking to make their lives easier, not more complicated, so they opt to have their stock brokerage firm hold onto the stock certificates. The stock brokerage firm keeps the stock certificates at their offices or another proper facility for safekeeping. This makes it much easier for a retiree to sell their shares at a future date. This is known as keeping your shares registered in street name. The shares are held in the broker-dealer's name for your benefit, thereby facilitating any transactions with those shares.

Broker-dealers are the firms that take sell and buy orders from the public to help complete such securities transactions. They are insured for a set amount against losses resulting from the failure of a broker-dealer firm. This coverage is mandated under the Securities Investor Protection Act passed by Congress in 1970.

This law created the Securities Investor Protection Corporation (SIPC). This coverage provided by SIPC member firms is a maximum of $500,000 per customer. This amount of full coverage pertains to securities held within your account, not the cash balance. The cash portion of your account is insured for only $100,000. Generally, most broker-dealers purchase additional coverage from private insurance firms.

It's important to note that this is protection from the broker-dealer firm failing, not from market losses of your individual securities. Keep in mind that broker-dealers do fail. Make sure any broker-dealer firm you are dealing with has adequate coverage over and above the SIPC limits. Consider using more than one broker-dealer firm if your accounts are significant in size. When you exceed SIPC limits of protection, your excess claims are placed in the same category with other general creditors.

Most investors are not aware of how SIPC coverage works. For instance, SIPC coverage with a broker-dealer firm is based per customer and not per account. Therefore, if you are holding a regular brokerage account and a margin account, you will find that your SIPC coverage is still limited in total to $500,000. In order to increase your SIPC coverage, you would have to have different registrations on your accounts. An example of this would be to have one account listed under your name alone and another account listed under your spouse's name. You could also have a separate account registered jointly between you and your spouse. This will allow you to easily expand your SIPC coverage.

Should the SIPC member fail, trustees are sent in to facilitate the liquidation of the brokerage firm in a proper manner. Security values are determined on the day the trustees arrive on the scene. For example, if a client is holding 100 shares of XYZ stock, which closed at 50 that day, then that would be the value used for purposes of SIPC coverage. When the client is sent the distribution, the security might be trading at a lower or higher price, but the same value of 50 would be used. This could hurt you in a rapidly rising market. Consider this information when you are evaluating a broker-dealer to handle your securities.

Taking Delivery of Your Securities

Many retirees prefer to take actual delivery of their shares. They have these shares sent to their home, if possible. Some corporations are no longer issuing actual certificates, but are holding such shares in book form. This is a method where you are noted as owner of a certain amount of shares via paperwork that is sent to your address of record, but you never actually take delivery of any certificates.

These methods may be preferred if you plan on holding onto such corporate shares for the long-term. You avoid the possibility of any failures of any broker-dealer firms and the subsequent problems that may accompany such matters. A second great advantage of holding your shares is that you always have ownership evidence of your stock position.

Typically, when a broker-dealer firm holds your shares and it loses contact with you for a period of years, there is a chance that your shares could pass to the state. This is true of mutual funds as well. This occurs when the fund companies or broker-dealers lose touch with your current address. Various states insist that those funds revert to the state after a number of years. The presumption is that the account holder has passed away and the state wants the money to pass to the proper state department so any beneficiaries will have an easier time finding the funds. The risk of this is small, yet this does occur while the account holders are still alive and well.

Individual Bonds

Many retirees require the steady income that can only be secured by investing in fixed investments such as money market funds, fixed-rate annuities, and bonds. The advantage of bonds is that they typically pay the highest investment yield to the investor. They usually pay this bond interest semiannually.

There is certainly no shortage of bonds for the individual investor. Corporations, municipalities, individual states, the federal government, and many of its agencies are offering various bond instruments. They all share one common characteristic—they are considered debt instruments.

Remember, bonds all have one thing in common, they are sophisticated versions of an IOU. When purchasing a bond, you are making a loan of your investment dollars to the entity issuing the bond. In return for the use of your money, it will pay you interest. Bonds pay interest because your money is tied up. This is the way they compensate you for the use of your funds. Just like you would do with a friend, make sure that the issuing entity can pay you back your money. This payback of your investment is known as returning your principal.

Therefore, it is crucial that you deal only with high-quality corporations, municipalities, etc. If you are unfamiliar with how to evaluate a bond issuer, do yourself a favor and just stick to U.S. government issues. They may pay a little bit less in bond interest, but you won't be as worried about their financial condition.

Because bonds are considered debt instruments, you need to find out how long the bond will last. This is known as the maturity date. A bond maturing in 30 years will be riskier then a bond maturing in 10 years. The longer time increases risk because events could change more in a longer span of time than in a shorter time frame. Interest rates are very difficult to predict over the long term. This risk is known as the interest rate risk factor and can impact you in two major ways.

The first way this risk factor impacts you is if newer bonds start coming to market with higher yields than what you are currently receiving. You will find yourself locked in the lower-yielding bonds. This may not seem like a problem if newer bonds start yielding a half of a percentage point more in interest yield, but could prove a severe problem if rates go up by two or three percentage points or more in yield. The main reason interest rates go up is because inflation ignites and the cost of goods goes up. Unless your income goes up with inflation, you could be faced with having to make cuts in your standard of living.

The second major way interest rate risk can impact you is when you want to sell your current bonds. When interest rates go up, you will find that you will not be able to sell your current bonds for as much. The reason is quite simple. Who is going to want to buy your bond yielding 7 percent that matures in 20 years when they can buy a new bond yielding 9 percent that matures in 20 years? If they purchase the newer bonds they will obtain 2 percent more in interest each year for the next 20 years. The only way you will find a buyer for your bond is if you sell at a discount. This is the major reason why many investors lose principal with bonds.

To protect yourself, you should be in a position to hold your bonds for the long term until they mature. Of course, if you really believe that interest rates are going higher and will stay up, you may choose to take some initial losses so that you realign your portfolio to take advantage of higher bond interest rates. This, however, can prove a dangerous game. A better method is to stagger your bond maturities.

A Bond Investor's Best Defense

Sophisticated bond investors figured out a long time ago that it is hard to calculate which way interest rates will move. Their best defense was to employ a strategy that would not fully expose them to interest rate risk, yet, at the same time, take advantage of a changing interest rate environment. This method ensured that they did not commit all of their bond positions to one set maturity.

These investors would purchase bonds with varying maturity dates. This method is referred to as *laddering* your maturities. They might stagger the bonds with maturity dates of 5, 10, 15, and 20 years. This way, they would have funds coming due every five years. They would then deploy those funds in current bond yields that were available at that time. If rates were increasing, they would be able to take advantage of the higher rates without sacrificing current principal.

When interest rates begin to go down, bond investors discover some exciting news. This good news is that their current bonds are going up in value. The reason for this is that bonds react to interest rates. When current interest rates on newer bonds are lower than the bonds in your portfolio, you will find that you can sell your bonds for a higher price. Would you rather own a new bond yielding 6 percent or an existing bond that is still yielding 8 percent?

The problem with selling your bonds at a profit if you are an income investor is that you have just given yourself a pay cut. The reason being is that the proceeds from selling your old bonds will purchase similar bonds but at a lower yield. In this case, you may be better off to just sit on the bonds in your portfolio and hold them to maturity as planned.

Bond Speculators

Many bond investors cannot resist the temptation to trade out of their current bond positions at a profit. They should know that they are placing themselves in the position of being a speculator. While this feeling of taking a profit feels good at the time, remember that you are giving up the value of the higher-yielding bond and the impact it could have on your standard of living in future years. Many retirees realize that they cannot resist the temptation and, therefore, purposely keep their bond maturities short. Purchasing bonds with low maturities will allow you to be relatively free to sell out at any given point in time. Many financial advisors will keep their income clients invested in debt instruments that mature in less than five years for this reason.

The worst offenders of frequent bond selling are not individual investors but bond fund managers. These bond managers are constantly fighting for a better track record. A bond fund, which can advertise that it is yielding higher income yields then the competition, will attract a lot more investors. While this may be good for the fund manager and the fund group, it is not necessarily in your best interest. Therefore, many retirees might well be served to avoid bond funds with debt instruments maturing later then five years in their portfolio all together. Failure to do so may result in normal market fluctuation turning in actual loss of money. This is often referred to as market risk turning into financial risk.

While bond mutual funds do a great job of advertising their current interest rate yield, they do a poor job of educating retirees of the risk factors involved. Many income investors start off with bond mutual funds and enjoy the monthly income. However, years later when these same investors go to cash out of their funds, they are often dismayed to find out that they are receiving less in principal than the original investment. A good securities firm or qualified financial advisor can go a long way in assisting you in constructing a suitable bond portfolio.

Most Investors Should Avoid GNMAs

There is one type of bond fund that is very difficult to win with. Known as the GNMA (Government National Mortgage Association) fund, this type of debt instrument typically pays higher interest than the more traditional government securities. These funds purchase certificates of mortgage debt from the government. This debt represents a pool of existing outstanding mortgage loans.

In theory, these investments sound good. In practice, however, they can prove a disaster to the unsophisticated investor. Typically, when interest rates go up, debt instruments go down in value. This is because newer investors will purchase current securities that are yielding more interest. This is a risk that all bond buyers assume.

The primary problem with GNMA certificates occurs when interest rates go down. Usually, bonds go up in value when interest rates go down because your bond, which is yielding more, is more valuable in the marketplace than a newer bond being issued at a lower rate. The catch with GNMA funds is that they represent mortgages and homeowners have a tendency to refinance their mortgages to obtain a lower rate.

Therefore, you receive all the risks of owning a bond, but none of the rewards. Not too good of a deal! You should only consider venturing in GNMA certificates when interest rates are trading in a steady and narrow pattern and the consensus is that they will remain in that range. But there are better options.

In summary, before looking at individual bonds for building an income portfolio, you should educate yourself. Your best source for an education on corporate bonds and municipal bonds is a reputable securities firm or financial advisor. Each can inform you of the different bonds that are available and the various risk factors. You should always insist on having a diversified portfolio of high-quality bonds. If using corporate or municipal bonds, you should make sure they have the financial strength backing them in order for them to make good on paying you back your funds at the time of maturity.

Many corporate and municipal bonds include a call provision. This allows the issuer to call in the bond before it matures. Bond issuers will place this provision on many bond issues to ensure that they have the flexibility to refinance the debt issue if interest rates should fall. They would then call in the bonds as they issue newer bonds at a lower rate. These call provisions very seldom favor the investor. You may receive a premium from the bond being called in, but then you are faced with trying to find another bond at an equivalent rate during a time of lower interest rates. Rarely, do government issues have these call provisions.

Obtaining a diversified portfolio of quality corporate bonds can prove difficult for the smaller investor. Therefore, government debt obligations would make more sense. You can purchase these directly through the government. Write to them for more information:

U.S. Treasury   202-622-2000
1500 Pennsylvania Avenue, NW   Fax: 202-622-6415
Washington, DC 20220   <www.ustreas.gov>

Other government debt is best purchased through a reputable securities firm. These issues typically include U.S. government agency securities.

Tax-free municipal securities are available and can be a nice match for many retirees' portfolios. These typically offer more safety then corporate bonds and they usually have a tax-favored status in regard to their income. Chapter 6 details more information on these types of debt securities.

Variable Annuities

Billions of dollars are flowing in investment vehicles called tax-deferred variable annuities. There are several features that draw investors. The most noticeable is the tax-deferral aspect of these investments. Funds that are left alone, free from annual taxation by the federal and state governments, have a tendency to grow much more quickly. The higher your marginal tax bracket rate, the more beneficial these accounts are to you.

Basically, your growth is tax deferred until withdrawn. This places account holders in charge of their tax situation. Investors also like the fact that they can move from one account to another within these annuities without income tax ramifications. Retirees like these accounts because not only is the tax deferred on their growth but the tax-deferred growth is not used in calculating taxation of their Social Security benefits if left on deposit. Chances are if you talk to several different investment advisors, you will receive conflicting viewpoints on these investments. To understand this, we will discuss what a variable annuity is and the pros and cons about it.

Tax-deferred variable annuities are only offered through insurance companies. The reason for this is that the variable annuity is both an insurance product and an investment product. Because of its insurance benefits, this product can only legally be offered through an insurance carrier.

The insurance benefits vary from one insurance company to another. Typically, the insurance company will allow you to place your funds with their company and, in return, you are given the guaranteed future right to annuitize your funds with that insurance company. Annuitization is when you assign funds to an insurance company with the assurance given by the company that it will give you a series of income payments for a guaranteed amount or for a guaranteed time period. Therefore, many policyholders of annuities will select these vehicles in case they need a secure source of income in their future.

You are under no obligation to annuitize your annuity with an insurance company. This is one of the biggest misconceptions circulating today. Many investors only half read their annuity policies or, worse, they listen to others who are confusing a tax-deferred annuity with another annuity product called an immediate annuity.

A tax-deferred annuity gives you the option to annuitize, not the obligation. Most tax-deferred annuities will never be annuitized. Typically, an insurance company states that if you still have your funds with the company at age 90 and up, it will want you to annuitize. If you let the insurance company know in writing that you don't want to, it will usually give you another five years to make a decision. If an insurance company puts pressure on you to annuitize, you always have the option of cashing in your account or moving your annuity account to another insurance company.

An immediate annuity is typically purchased for qualified retirement accounts or for legal settlements. It is very different from a tax-deferred annuity. An immediate annuity is purchased with the annuity payment starting right away. Pension plans will typically purchase these for funding employee obligations such as paying workers' monthly retirement benefits. Retired workers are probably better off having their retirement income flow to them via an insurance company rather than counting on their former employer to make good on its promises. What happens if the employer were to sell out to another company or, worse yet, disappear?

Legal settlements typically use immediate annuities to ensure that claimants have a secure source of income for an agreed upon time period. This is usually done instead of giving a claimant a lump sum of money, which could be spent well ahead of future expenses yet to be incurred. In short, it is done for the claimant's protection.

Variable Annuity Death Benefits

Other insurance benefits offered by various variable annuity companies today are death benefits. These typically come in play if the account owner or annuitant passes away before a certain age. In these cases, the insurance company will usually pay out the account holder's original deposit amount or current account value, whichever is greater. Keep in mind that mutual funds and variable annuity subaccounts typically are not protected against normal market volatility while the account holder is living. Therefore, a client can feel more secure investing in a variable annuity knowing that perhaps the spouse or family would be taken care of in the event the market value of the annuity was down drastically at the time of his or her demise.

Critics of variable annuities state that these types of death benefit guarantees are nothing more than expensive gimmicks. In other words, these critics are not against the insurance benefits, they are just against the insurance company charging too much for them. Typically, insurance companies charge between 1 and 1½ per-

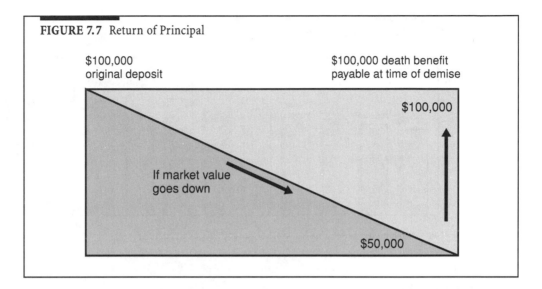

FIGURE 7.7 Return of Principal

$100,000
original deposit

$100,000 death benefit
payable at time of demise

$100,000

If market value
goes down

$50,000

cent per year of assets on deposit for various death benefits and for other policy guarantees that involve annuitization features. While it's easy for critics to comment on these insurance charges during a bull market, they may feel differently if the stock market experiences a long protracted bear market.

Common Death Benefit Available on Most Variable Annuities

Figure 7.7 illustrates that the full death benefit is payable upon your demise despite the actual value of your accumulation. The account will pay the higher of your actual accumulation value or guaranteed death benefit, whichever is greater. Any withdrawals already taken will be subtracted.

An enhanced death benefit states that your beneficiaries will receive back the amount you have invested plus a 5 percent increase each year, as illustrated in Figure 7.8. Therefore, you have a rising death benefit. Withdrawals already taken are deducted from this death benefit. Of course, if your actual account value is greater, then your beneficiaries receive that amount. This death benefit may prove helpful to couples that want to participate in the stock market but are concerned about leaving their loved ones impoverished. Larger insurance companies such as Pacific Life, Hartford, American Skandia, Anchor National, and Jackson National offer these types of death benefit options. Recently even more innovative death benefits are being made available at low costs. One such rider will pay out a percentage of the growth on your account up to 40 to 50 percent as a death benefit. Therefore, if you experience good growth on your accounts, these enhanced death benefits could be enough to cover any taxes due! Each company has its own riders and limitations so be sure to shop around.

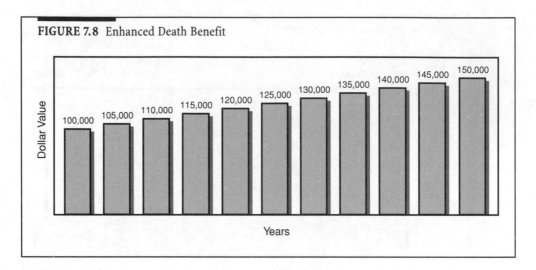

FIGURE 7.8 Enhanced Death Benefit

Living Benefits

Several annuity companies offer living benefits as well as death benefits. These are offered in two ways. The first living benefit offered is based on your initial deposit plus a set interest rate factor that is tracked over the life of the annuity. If you choose to annuitize your policy with the insurance company, it guarantees to use whichever is greater between your actual accumulated contract value or the living benefit account value.

Therefore, even if your account value should plummet because of poor investment choices on your part or a declining market, you can be assured of receiving a guaranteed annuity payout based on the higher amount offered by the living benefit rider. The only problem with these riders is that they tend to add slightly to your annual expenses and the interest rate assumption used at annuitization may be too low for most retirees' benefit.

The second living benefit being offered may prove to be more valuable. This rider states that the insurance company will guarantee the return of your original deposit in a certain time period regardless of your annuity's account performance. This benefit could provide some security for an equity portfolio against a protected bear market. You do not need to annuitize to take advantage of this benefit.

The fee for this is usually very small. Insurance companies typically charge ¼ to ½ of 1 percent for this protection. The upside is that you are assured of receiving your original funds back regardless of your account's performance. This could prove crucial if the stock and bond markets move against investors.

Aetna Life Insurance Co. currently offers a five-year guaranteed return of principal if you use their Aetna Total Return Fund subaccount. The New York Life and the ING Insurance companies offer a ten-year guaranteed return of principal regardless of what investment subaccount you use.

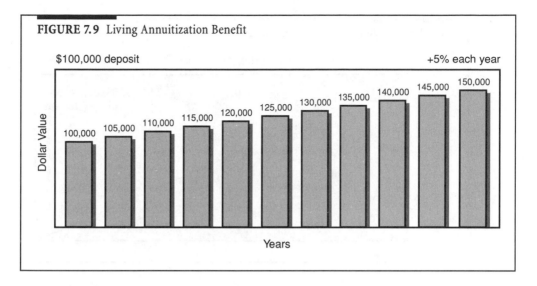

FIGURE 7.9 Living Annuitization Benefit

$100,000 deposit   +5% each year

In order to take advantage of these guarantee features, you must make your intentions known beforehand. The companies will have you sign the proper forms to ensure this protection is provided.

Annuitization Values

$100,000 annuitization value grows at 5 percent per year regardless of market performance, as shown in Figure 7.9. This is the minimum account value that the insurance company will use to calculate your annuity income value. The guaranteed annuitization rates are typically very low. If your actual contract value is greater, then you will get the benefit of using the higher account value.

With the return of principal guarantee, the account will pay out the return of your original deposit at the end of ten years regardless of market performance, as shown in Figure 7.10. If your account value is greater, you would receive that amount. Any withdrawals already taken will be subtracted from this guarantee.

Variable Annuity Performance

Variable annuities have subaccounts that are very similar to mutual fund accounts. They both are usually actively managed accounts that offer diversification. Critics point out that variable annuities are more expensive to own because in addition to normal management fees imposed by the fund manager of the subaccount, you have the added insurance expenses. They point out that mutual funds don't have these added expenses and, therefore, are a better choice.

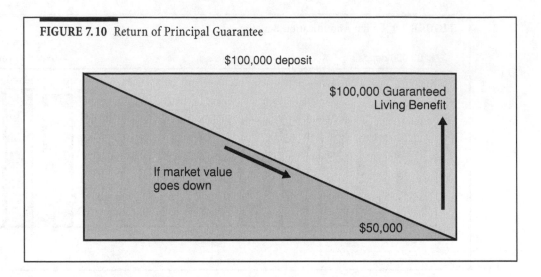

FIGURE 7.10 Return of Principal Guarantee

$100,000 deposit

$100,000 Guaranteed Living Benefit

If market value goes down

$50,000

What most critics fail to take in account is that the actual performance of variable annuities and mutual funds are, in fact, different. Mutual fund managers typically carry a higher cash balance within their portfolios due to frequent redemptions. How the portfolios are usually allocated creates a difference in the performance numbers.

The average returns on variable annuity subaccounts in the categories of growth, growth and income, and international funds are equivalent, if not greater, than the average mutual fund's performance, even after insurance expenses. Figure 7.11 illustrates this fact.

Therefore, the annuity is actually a better choice. Mutual funds were the clear winner in the categories of balanced funds and money market funds. This is because balanced funds and money markets typically earn less in returns than stock funds. Therefore, a higher expense rate would be noticed more.

Taxes Matter

A second point of contention between variable annuities and mutual funds is how they are taxed. Critics point out that variable annuity gains are taxed as ordinary income when withdrawn. Mutual funds may be afforded the more favorable long-term capital gains treatment and, therefore, are a much better deal for the consumer. What these critics fail to mention is that all gains on a mutual fund are not taxed at the more favorable long-term gains rate. In fact, much of a mutual fund's gain could be taxed as short-term capital gains and the taxes due could be the same as your ordinary marginal tax rate. This could occur because the average stock mutual fund has an annual turnover within its portfolio of over 70 percent.

FIGURE 7.11

	Average Growth Rate between Mutual Funds and Variable Annuity Subaccounts in Ten Years			
	Mutual Funds	Number of Funds	Variable Annuities	Number of Subaccounts
Aggressive Growth	16.17%	176	16.37%	1,082
Growth	16.12	2,138	17.10	3,362
Growth and Income	13.79	860	14.03	1,656
International	9.09	1,579	9.73	1,665
Balanced	11.35	444	11.24	1,181
Bond	6.66	4,052	7.35	1,980

Data taken from Morningstar, Inc., database as of 6/30/00.

In addition, you have very little control over when these taxable gains are generated. A mutual fund is required to pass on its net gains from sales each year or face paying taxes at the corporate level. If a fund manager decides to sell off a stock within the fund's portfolio that has had much appreciation, you could be looking at a large unexpected capital gain.

A Comparison of a Tax-Efficient Mutual Fund and a Tax-Deferred Variable Annuity Account

Assuming you could find a tax-efficient mutual fund that could manage to obtain the most favorable long-term capital gains rate available of 18 percent (which became available starting December 31, 2000, for capital gains assets purchased from that date and beyond and held five years), the tax-deferred variable annuity could still be the better investment after taxes! The following illustrations in Figures 7.12 and 7.13 assumes the same rate of return for each account.

Remember, when it comes to your wealth, use common sense and do the math! A 28 percent marginal tax rate was used for illustration purposes only. Your own individual tax rate should be taken into account. Be certain to include state taxes, if applicable.

In Addition

Critics fail to point out the changing nature of capital gains rates. Favorable capital gains rates might be available today while the government is experiencing

FIGURE 7.12 Investing in Taxable Mutual Funds

Investor 1 places $50,000 in taxable mutual funds.
Invests assertively for a 12 percent return. Assumes 18 percent capital gains rate paid per year.

Year   5 — $ 81,599
Year 10 — $133,168
Year 15 — $217,327
Year 20 — $354,673
Year 25 — $578,820

Taking income after year 25:
Before tax = $69,458
After tax = $56,955

If taken as a lump sum:
Before tax = $578,820
After tax = $578,820 (taxes have been paid each year)

favorable annual budget surpluses, but those rates could change for the worse in future years if we experience budget shortages or changes in tax laws.

The problem with variable annuities is that they are not given the favorable step-up tax basis afforded real property, such as real estate or individual stocks. This favorable step-up basis allows the growth from real property to pass without current capital gains tax being owed upon your demise.

Of course, if any federal estate taxes were due, they would have to be paid. Mutual funds are afforded the favorable step-up basis as well, but keep in mind that the account holder has typically been paying taxes each year on taxable gains. Also, any investment being held by an IRA or qualified plan does not qualify for the stepped-up tax treatment, but is taxed as ordinary income.

A variable annuity's growth will be taxable upon your demise unless your spouse continues the program on a tax-deferred basis. This option is usually available with most annuity companies. Therefore, your heirs, who are usually your children, will end up paying income taxes on your annuity gains. Typically, they will have to pay taxes on these accounts in the year of the annuitant's demise or within five years. They will, of course, be disappointed that they will have to pay taxes at the ordinary income tax rates. They should keep in mind, though, the peace, security, and tax benefits that the accounts offered their parents through their retirement years. If estate taxes are involved, then your children could benefit from an income tax deduction, which is available on the portion of an annuity's gains that were

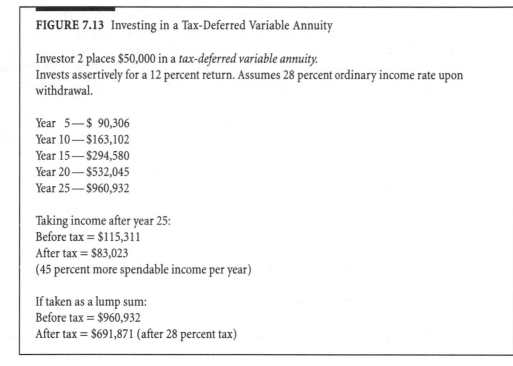

FIGURE 7.13 Investing in a Tax-Deferred Variable Annuity

Investor 2 places $50,000 in a *tax-deferred variable annuity.*
Invests assertively for a 12 percent return. Assumes 28 percent ordinary income rate upon withdrawal.

Year 5 — $ 90,306
Year 10 — $163,102
Year 15 — $294,580
Year 20 — $532,045
Year 25 — $960,932

Taking income after year 25:
Before tax = $115,311
After tax = $83,023
(45 percent more spendable income per year)

If taken as a lump sum:
Before tax = $960,932
After tax = $691,871 (after 28 percent tax)

included in calculating any federal estate taxes. This is known as income in respect to a decedent and is often overlooked as a tax deduction.

Many retirees are using variable annuities in conjunction with single premium variable life (SPVL) policies. These types of policies are very similar to tax-deferred annuities in allowing tax deferral and movement of the investments within these accounts without tax ramifications. Their annual expense fees are generally higher because they offer life insurance benefits over and above the amount of dollars you have invested. Retirees can use this strategy by directing 70 percent of their funds in variable annuities and 30 percent in SPVL policies. The additional life insurance benefits provided by SPVLs, which are free of federal income taxes, will usually be sufficient to make up for any income taxes due on the annuity certificates. Therefore, your children could end up receiving your total investment account balance without worrying about any tax losses. This method is known as the blended method of tax deferral. Additional information on SPVLs is discussed in the next chapter.

Fixed and variable annuities are meant to be retirement vehicles. As such, any withdrawals made before age 59½ will not only be taxable as ordinary income in the year of withdrawal, but will incur a 10 percent early withdrawal penalty as well. There are several exclusions for this penalty that are almost identical to the 10 percent penalty exclusion for IRAs covered in Chapter 6.

Because variable annuities are often used as long-term investment vehicles or as tax shelters, they tend to have long surrender charges. Typically, these charges will last for six to seven years. While these accounts often allow you to remove up to 10 percent per year in income without any charges, you might be better served by looking at the newer variable annuity certificates that are available with no surrender charges. With these, if you are not happy with their performance, you are free to exchange your certificate for another company's annuities.

Exercise caution when making these types of exchanges to prevent taxable gains from being due. For IRAs, you should do a qualified direct transfer. For regular accounts, use proper forms for a 1035 Exchange. These forms are made available from the variable annuity company that you transfer to.

Rules for Being a Successful Investor

Define Your Investment Objective

This sounds so simple, yet most retirees have not clearly articulated their real investment objective. Are they seeking growth from investment assets or income?

The successful investors know exactly what their investment goals are. They can write out these goals on the back of a napkin. They are that sure of their goals. Typically, they can explain them to a complete stranger in less than two minutes. Think of the most successful investors you know. You will find individuals who have focused on what they want to accomplish.

Let's take the case of the real estate developer who knows his investment objective. He may be seeking parcels of land at an attractive price that could be rezoned and sold for a much higher price. Perhaps he selected raw land and made added improvements such as water lines and sewage facilities. These improvements usually increase the underlying value of the land dramatically. In another case, a developer took inexpensive land and built homes on this property. She made a dramatic profit from the land value increasing in addition to a fair sum from the new house construction.

Many value-oriented stock investors know what they are seeking. Perhaps, they will look for company shares that are trading at a deep discount to their potential value. These investors put the adage of buy low and sell high to work for themselves. Simply by keeping an open mind and an open eye on the marketplace, they can find countless stock opportunities in the course of each month.

In each of these cases, these investors have decided on an investment strategy and then put it to work. These investors have focused on a set strategy for investing.

They have their investment objectives and are working toward making their goals reality.

Whatever your method of investing, it helps to clarify your goals. Set out what you want to accomplish on paper and decide how you wish to measure your progress. This simple exercise is what sets the successful investment experts apart from the multitude of amateurs. This simple routine of establishing your objectives and keeping track of your progress is what separates the wealthy retiree from the average retiree. You must first know what you are trying to accomplish so you may profit from the lessons that are to be learned in the pursuit of your endeavors.

Not only will knowing your objectives increase your knowledge in specific areas, but you will become much more immune to the negative thought processes that abound in the world today. Many people start off on the right track only to become easily persuaded to abandon their plans due to self-doubt. These precursors to self-doubt can originate from many different sources.

The most common are:

- *The news media.* Most news sources are just reporting news events. The shows and publications that report on actual financial topics are forced to report on such topics each and every month. They inadvertently make financial topics confusing by writing about them from too many viewpoints, with every writer's opinion coming across as some sort of fact. Remember, these media sources have to publish often. They may research a story for only a few days before they go to print or to film. This knowledge alone should make you cautious.
- *Other investors.* If all your friends are investing in auto companies or computer companies, chances are you will consider that avenue of investment as well. Likewise, if most of your fellow retirees are investing in government bonds, you will possibly be looking at this type of investment. Another example is when homebuyers purchase their homes with a 30-year mortgage because that is what the majority of people are doing. Most of these homebuyers ignore the shorter 15-year note and do not even know that there are 20-year mortgages as well. People of all ages seem to act in a manner that is typical for their times. Some of this is the result of traditions, customs, and current trends that people assume are the right and only way to proceed.

Typically, when the majority of Americans are investing in the stock market, the group talk is that the market is a safe place to keep your investments. The group thinking is that there is safety in numbers. A saying that has been said many times, bears repeating: "Just because everybody is doing it, doesn't make it right."

This lesson was driven home during the 1980s when investors who were used to having high certificate of deposit returns kept trying to squeeze every last dime from their accounts. They were doing this at a time when the stock market was just starting to take off. These bank investors missed out on one of the longest stock market rallies ever. Most of these investors took over ten years to finally start entering in the stock market. With stock market performances at an all-time high with risk increasing yearly, these investors were just starting to invest in the stock market. Ironically, they were doing this at a time when real rates of return being offered by certificates of deposit were at a very favorable rate of return compared to inflation. And these accounts are guaranteed, whereas stocks are not.

With regard to determining your true investment objectives you will need to ask yourself some real life questions:

- What are you really trying to accomplish?
- Will your current program keep up with inflation?
- Are you trying to build funds for your heirs or do you just need to be concerned about yourself or perhaps a spouse?
- Do you have adequate life, health, disability, and long-term care insurance programs in place including adequate sources or resources for making those premium payments?
- What risk factors are you taking on?
- Will your current investment program allow you to achieve your goals?
- What time constraints are you under?
- What are all of the ramifications of your program as they relate to various tax laws in this country?

After taking all of these questions into consideration, you may come to the conclusion that perhaps you are not only investing for income, but maybe you need to emphasize growth as well. Only when you evaluate your objectives will you start to realize how complicated real investing can become. A good relationship with a quality Certified Financial Planner (CFP) could assist you greatly with these and many other questions that will confront you. Best of all, a CFP could bring to your attention many questions that you have not even thought of asking.

Determine Your Time Horizon

Serious investors know their true time line. Many of today's investors get involved in investments that they are not prepared to hold on to for the long haul. As such, they will be tempted to sell those investments, either when they rise rapidly in price or when they drop in price.

Had those investors really known their true time horizon, they would have been more inclined to hold to their original strategies. Knowing your time horizon will allow you to articulate what strategy you should be pursuing. In doing this, you will also develop the ability to stick with your financial program for the long-term. This will more than likely give you the real results you are seeking.

Knowing your true time line will require that you evaluate what you are trying to accomplish both in the short term and the long term. A prime example would be someone in their mid-50s saving for retirement at age 65 and assuming that their goal is roughly a ten-year goal. Upon further reflection, they may realize that their true goal is to save for retirement at age 65 and to ensure that they can stay retired. They might also realize that they need to keep up with the rising costs of inflation. Considering that an average person in his mid-50s is expected to live for another 30 years, he may now realize his goal is quite a longer term.

Be careful when evaluating your goals and selecting your real time horizon. The influence it will have on your portfolio composition can be dramatic. Short-term investors are known to favor low volatility over higher returns. Therefore, a short-term investor would have a much higher tendency to go with bonds or money market instruments instead of equities.

Quantify Your Risk Level

Some retirees will put their money in various investments that are fraught with risk. Had these retirees been fully informed of these risks, they most certainly would not have gone forward. The main problem is that the majority of retirees are not aware of all the various risks involved with most investment programs.

Add to this the fact that most retirees have never completed a risk profile questionnaire. This type of fact finder will help you to determine how much risk you are willing to tolerate in order to achieve certain results. The more accurate you are in determining your true risk profile, the better investor you will be. Many times, these questionnaires will tell you or your financial advisor if you have the ability to hold on to your portfolio during tough times. This could also serve as a wake-up call to tone down your current portfolio before market volatility shakes you up so much that you end up selling in a down market. This phenomenon of panic selling has the ability of turning normal market fluctuation (volatility) into financial risk (the loss of principal).

Quantify Your Knowledge Level

Many people feel that they have to know everything about every investment. This, of course, is simply impossible. You would be well served to limit your circle of expertise to areas that you feel comfortable and knowledgeable navigating. Investing in the unfamiliar is a common mistake that investors make. You increase the likelihood of losses when you invest in the areas about which you lack good and reliable information.

Investment advisors report on how common it is to see people investing in areas in that they lack knowledge. Physicians will insist on investing in software start-up ventures which they know next to nothing about while ignoring the very drug companies of which they have detailed knowledge. Likewise, computer programmers will often ignore investing in strong, proven computer software provider companies in favor of some new start-up biotech firm that they read about in a popular science magazine.

Perhaps this is simply the story of the grass always looking greener on the other side. You would do well to remember the answer a young student gave to his teacher when asked to think of a reply to the question "Why does the grass always look greener on the other side of the fence?" The young student replied, "Actually, the grass is always greener where it gets watered!" From the mouths of babes can come true pearls of wisdom. Make sure you take time to research opportunities within your field of experience. Chances are that many great investment opportunities are waiting right there. Research the investments you are familiar with and find out as much as possible before you invest, not afterward. Make sure you water your own grass!

Many successful investors stick to one or two types of investments. Perhaps they switch back and forth between Treasury bills and Treasury bonds depending on the outlook of interest rates. They are often able to generate returns in the double digits with little room for financial loss. These investors believe in keeping it simple.

Other investors will focus on just one family of mutual funds, moving from one type of fund to another within the family of funds. Many times, they are able to increase their overall return by several additional percentage points each year. Compare this to the investor who simply stays with the same fund, year in and year out.

Still other investors have found success simply by watching their employer's stock within their profit sharing plan. When they see their company's stock reaching a new high for no apparent reason, they sell in this market rally. Once the stock drops in price, they move back in at the low price after evaluating that the company is financially strong and on the right track. This strategy of buying one or more company stocks during that stock's high point and selling during the low point is known as the rolling stock strategy. It is also known as "buy what you understand." Through the informal network of coworkers and your own knowledge, you may be more tuned in to the future and prospects of your company than many stock analysts.

Know What You Own

Knowledge is power—if it is knowledge worth knowing and properly used. Knowing what you own is one of your best defenses to avoiding mistakes. This assumes you have evaluated what you own beforehand and made the tactical decision to proceed with your purchase based on your knowledge level and research. You should weigh the many pros and cons of making such a commitment to any investment before investing.

Many retirees confuse gambling with investing. They will take a position in a company's stock based on what they hear and not on what they know. Perhaps a favorable news story motivated them. This is very common and is nothing short of gambling. This still can produce favorable results, if the stock market continues to increase at a torrid pace and if somebody is willing to pay a higher price for your investment than what you paid for it. There are a lot of *ifs,* however.

True investors know why they should buy a certain investment. They know if a company is being properly managed as well as other important aspects of a company's business. Typically, they know who the company's largest customers are, as well as who the company's competitors are. They will have a firm grasp on the company's marketing and business plan. In addition, they will be firmly familiar with the company's financials. They will have evaluated the company's debt level, profit margins, cash flow, and any pending actions against the company. They will know what a reasonable price might be for that company's stock and when it may be overvalued.

Know Why You Own It

Purchasing stock in a company or buying in a particular mutual fund should only be done when you have answered the question, "Why do you want to own these shares?"

A prudent investor will know what an investment is capable of and, in general terms, what this investment will achieve in the near future and, more importantly, in the long term. Will your investment provide a steady stream of dividend income or a steady stream of profits to be retained by the company for future growth? Is this company or fund situated to take advantage of our changing economy or to profit from the current improvements in technology that are being seen daily?

As a current example, many retirees have purchased stocks in companies that specialize in real estate investments. They are typically given a very high cash dividend of over 8 percent plus the prospects of capital appreciation. These stocks typically do very well during times of moderate to high inflation. These investors know why they have purchased these stocks. They are able to garner current income to live on as well as having an excellent inflation hedge against future price increases from the ravages of inflation.

Other investors will purchase fixed annuities instead of bank certificates of deposit because they are targeting a different agenda. They want security of principal along with higher interest rates. Because they know that fixed annuities are also tax deferred until funds are withdrawn, they know that their money will grow much more quickly in most cases. Therefore, they know why they are buying these types of investments and the benefits that they are reaping.

Many of today's investors are jumping on the current trend of owning high-tech stocks or mutual funds that invest in these companies. Prudent investors will stop to analyze how they can take advantage of the technology boom in a safer and more reasonable manner. They may see that the safe money is to be made by owning the companies that supply the many start-up companies. They may decide that communication companies are a better choice because all of these new companies will need phone lines, fax lines, Internet lines, and other related equipment. Furthermore, they may see that communication companies will further benefit from the increased usage of this type of equipment.

As a business and, consequently, as an investor, it may be more prudent to focus on high-tech supply companies instead of high-tech companies. Take the case of Internet companies. Their goods have to be delivered. Often this favors companies such as United Parcel Service and Airborne Express instead of the actual Internet companies. The competition is simply too fierce among most Internet retailers. A compelling example: during the California Gold Rush, it was the stores and equipment suppliers that became rich, not the miners.

Know How Your Investment Performs under Various Market Conditions

Most investors proceed along with their portfolio without the benefit of knowing how those investments have performed during similar markets. Crucial to your financial health is a firm understanding of how various investments perform in relationship to our economy. For instance, higher interest rates may negatively impact the current value of bonds. The longer you have until the bonds mature, the greater the impact. Likewise, higher interest rates and increasing inflation rates can impact stocks. Ironically, stocks are an excellent long-term inflation hedge, yet short term, they often move downward based on reports of stronger inflation.

The Spill Out Effect

When interest rates move too high because of inflation concerns and the stock market reacts badly to the news, investors should be aware of the spill out effect. This effect comes into play when certificates of deposit and ten-year corporate bonds are paying high yields relative to inflation.

An example of an attractive rate for a consumer is a current rate of 8 to 9 percent guaranteed for five to ten years when inflation is running at a 3 percent rate. The real rate of return in this example would be 5 to 6 percent. Investors may start moving their funds out of the stock market to lock in safer rates of return. This could pose a problem for you if you need to liquidate some or all of your stock holdings because fewer buyers could mean lower market prices for your securities.

Other Events

Another event that could cause sell-offs is when interest rates on government bonds are higher than stock market earning yields. All that would be required at this point is a perceived negative environment for stocks. This could be caused by any number of reasons such as poor corporate earnings, higher inflation rates, higher tax rates, inappropriate government intervention, and global events.

Keep in Mind

Earnings really do matter. If you pay too much for a stock based on potential earnings you could see your share price drop if those future earnings fail to materialize. A helpful tactic is to focus only on stocks that have increased their annual earnings every year over the last five years. You would be well served to search for a company that is consistent from one quarter to the next. Look for stocks that have averaged at least 15 percent increases in earnings each year. Don't fall into the trap of overpaying for those earnings. If a company's stock is priced at over 30 times annual earnings, then you may be left holding the stock after others sell off. Using these rules, you should be able to eliminate many of the stocks available today. This will allow you to focus on the more stable companies.

There are two things to remember about earnings. First, they can change dramatically from one year to the next. If you expect that a stock will increase its earnings almost every year, then you may not mind paying a high price for such a stock. For instance, if a company increases its earnings by 25 percent per year, its earnings could be expected to double in three years. This is why so many stocks are so pricey today. Investors feel that these companies have their best years ahead of them. Many stock buyers will even argue that stocks are cheap today when you consider the possibility of future earnings. They could be right.

The second important factor about earnings is they are not guaranteed; very seldom will companies pass on those earnings to shareholders. If a company were to pass on all of its earnings, chances are it would be out of business because it would probably not be using the money to develop newer products or services. This being the case, competitors could more readily take over their customers. Therefore, most stockholders will see very little of a stock's earnings in their pocket.

The only way most shareholders will receive money is if they sell their shares to another buyer. Therefore, a stock certificate is, essentially, just a piece of paper. The only way you can profit is if there are other investors willing to purchase these shares from you. If these buyers truly understood the importance of earnings, they may be hard-pressed to pay a higher price for your shares. Imagine, even if a company were willing to distribute all of its earnings each and every year, and that company's stock were selling at $100 with annual earnings remaining at only a flat $4 per share, it would take you 25 years to receive back your original investment!

Observe Current Market Trends and Make Changes as Needed

Many retirees react to changing market news by moving out of their current investment positions into other investments that may be perceived as being better suited to their needs. While moving from one investment vehicle to another or from one investment strategy to another may make sense, you should be careful that you are not moving too frequently or too quickly. By the same token, many investors move too slowly from a failing investment strategy thereby endangering their wealth or, at the very least, hampering their overall return.

Investors will generally be rewarded for paying attention to current trends and their relationship to past history. For instance, many times the stock market will favor a certain segment of the market such as larger-size companies. During other time periods, the market pays far more attention to smaller companies. In theory, if you can identify these periods, you could be well suited to take advantage of these trends by shifting your portfolio in that direction.

During certain periods, you will observe that stocks are not moving up in price but moving sideways or, worse, downward. These types of markets can be brought on by many different factors including recessions or poor corporate earnings. Instead of fighting these normal market corrections, you might be better served by increasing your cash positions until you feel the market has bottomed out and then deploying your funds back into the market at that point.

Keep in mind that there will be times when you are better off moving assets out of the stock market. When the yield on 30-year government bonds exceeds the dividend yield of stocks comprising the S&P 500 Index by more than 6 percent, then you may wish to consider bonds as a better asset choice. The problem with these strategies is that very few people can truly determine where the market is going, when it has bottomed out, or when it has hit a peak. If you feel you are in this category, as most investors are, then you may wish to take advantage of a strategy called asset allocation.

Asset allocation is a fancy term for true diversification. The practice of good asset allocation is to spread your investment portfolio among various investment asset classes. These asset classes are typically determined by your risk profile and time frame.

Because stocks typically perform better over time, this asset class will often make up the bulk of an assertive investor's portfolio. Various stock categories will be added to the investment mixture because not all classes and categories of stocks move in the same direction or at the same rate as others. A prudent course of action then, would be to have your stocks diversified among larger-size companies, midsize companies, and smaller companies.

Along with these various stock categories, you many want to consider spreading your stock selections among various investment styles such as growth, blend, and the value approach. International stocks would be advisable as well. This is done in such a manner as to ensure that you will participate overall in the stock market's movements. Not all segments of the stock market move in tandem. This helps prevent the problem of concentrating your entire portfolio in the wrong segment of the market and of missing out on the expected rates of returns that the stock market has delivered over the years.

A truly diversified portfolio will have various asset classes involved that will not participate with the other asset classes, but will move in a negatively correlated manner. This opposite correlation effect has the tendency to cancel out other segments of the portfolio in the short term, yet may add greatly to the value of the portfolio in the long term. For instance, when larger stocks are in favor, the smaller stocks may be falling in value or lagging in appreciation. However, when larger stocks are trending downward, you may see smaller stocks back in favor delivering good returns. This effect has the tendency to reduce overall portfolio volatility while preserving a portfolio's overall long-term return.

Many asset allocation studies illustrate that you would be wise to include real estate stocks and various bonds in your portfolio. This will aid in reducing severe fluctuations and help keep your portfolio in more positive territories over time. It's important to note that asset allocation seldom gives you the best returns in a given year, yet may contribute to an overall above average return over the long term. Some of the reason for this is that a well-diversified portfolio has more staying power.

Having stated the positive points about asset allocation, it is important to note that many asset allocation advocates equate risk as being the same as volatility. The point is that most investors don't agree. Investors only dislike volatility when the market is going down. They are quite pleased with volatility when the markets are heading upward.

In summary, asset allocation models are not perfect. They tend to try to reduce volatility and practitioners operate on the assumption that historical market information will allow them to select the appropriate allocation of investment assets for the future. Because the future is unpredictable, the allocations may not work as planned. These asset allocation programs tend to have a cost associated with them as well, because someone has to determine the proper asset allocation mix and implement the program. When considering a portfolio that will be managed by an asset allocation model, you may want to consider institutional money managers as their management fees and trading costs have a tendency to be much lower than a typical mutual fund.

Keep Investment Fees Low

Many investors focus on performance from their investments while ignoring the fees they are paying. While this may be acceptable while their investments are performing well, they should still be aware of what actual fees they are paying.

FIGURE 7.14 The Difference 2 Percent Can Make over Time

$100,000 at 10% over 20 years = $673,000
$100,000 at 12% over 20 years = $965,000

2% over 20 years can make a difference of 43.5% in your rate of return!

Don't expect all expenses to be explained to you in simple English. You must ask the right questions to ascertain whether you are being taken advantage of. While paying higher fund expenses or higher brokerage fees may not seem serious in the short term, the effects can be very meaningful over the long term. Simply saving 1 to 2 percent per year in fees could translate to a much higher overall portfolio return in the long term, as illustrated in Figure 7.14.

Key Questions to Ask

Questions to ask your investment advisor:

- What are the sales charges for this mutual fund, variable annuity, stock, or bond?
- What are the annual charges associated with the holding of this investment?
- Are there any 12b-1 charges associated with this account?
- What are the brokerage fees associated with the purchase of this stock, bond, unit investment trusts, or other investment?
- What surrender charges, if any, are associated with this investment?

Questions to ask yourself:

- Has your fund group, brokerage firm, investment advisor, insurance agent, or securities representative explained all charges associated with their recommendations? When possible, have them put this information in writing.
- Have you read all prospectuses and fund information given to you?
- Have you sought an educated second opinion before investing?

Keep Taxes Low

Investors who ignore taxes may be investors who are living with a false sense of security. They may feel that they are achieving better rates of returns than they actually are. Always look at your overall return from your portfolio before tax and after tax.

To keep taxes low, you should focus on individual bonds, individual stocks, unit investment trusts, and tax-efficient mutual funds. Many investors find the tax-sheltering ability of qualified plans such as profit sharing plans and retirement plans like individual retirement accounts a real benefit. If you have taken advantage of these plans and still want to defer more investment dollars, then you should check out tax-deferred annuities.

Key questions to keep in mind when reviewing your portfolio:

- Are your investment gains taxed each year or at the end of a certain time period?
- Are your gains taxed as ordinary income or at a more favorable long-term capital gains rate?
- Do you determine when you pay tax on an investment's gain or does someone else make that determination?
- Is there a more tax-favored way of handling your investments?

More information on this topic can be found in Chapter 6.

Select Investments That Offer a Margin of Safety

When creating a portfolio, investors should constantly be on the lookout for investments that offer a margin of safety. This advice is often ignored and can cause great damage to your portfolio's returns. Chapter 2 deals with various risk factors that every investor should look for. In addition to various risk factors, every investor should look for the right investment for themselves. Knowing your time frame for holding an investment as well as how much market volatility you can handle is crucial to you decision-making process. Assuming you have taken all the proper steps and are ready to make an investment decision, you should look to the investment choice that offers the best margin of safety.

For instance, when selecting a bond investment you would look for a bond with the highest credit rating possible or with the most likelihood of returning your money for the risk taken. It simply is not necessary to risk your principal when making an investment. The adage "The greater the risk, the greater your return" is a false one. Far too many investors are taking on risk needlessly.

When looking at a stock investment, you should opt for the stock that offers the most in secure growth potential. In addition, you should look for the stock of a company that has a good management team in place and is following a sound business plan. Make sure that the company you decide to invest in is in the right business and is not up against far better companies that could either take market share away from it or destroy its profit streams.

Never Panic

This is much easier said then done. Assuming you have ascertained what type of investor you are and have done your homework, you should know the following about yourself:

- What your true investment time frame is
- How the class of investments you are investing in have performed over similar market conditions or past time periods
- What your worst-case scenario is
- What your expected returns both positive and negative are

An investor should always perform a fire drill in regard to his or her portfolio. Use a historical perspective to see what the worst years in the stock market would have done to your portfolio. Key questions that should come to mind include:

- During protracted bear markets, how long would your stocks have stayed down?
- How would a diversified portfolio of stocks invested among various size categories and investment strategies have fared?
- Is there anything you could have done to decrease these losses or to mitigate the length of any downturns in the market?
- Are you comfortable with the answers you have come up with?
- Can you create a portfolio you can live with under the most trying of circumstances?

With bonds, you should be asking yourself the following questions:

- Have you selected the highest quality bond?
- Is there something substantial backing the issuer of your bonds?
- Have you selected the proper maturity of bonds to meet your needs?

When looking at risk factors, you would be wise to seek ways of reducing or transferring as much risk as you can to others. For instance, stock investors can reduce financial risk by placing stop loss orders on various individual stocks within a brokerage account. These stop loss instructions will help ensure that your stock positions are sold out during the start of a major market downturn. Typically, investors place stop losses on an individual stock to be executed if the stock issue were to decrease by more than 10 percent. This can help to prevent even larger losses that can affect individual issues at times, regardless of what the broader stock market is doing in general. If you are holding stocks that continue to increase in value, perhaps you will want to move your stop loss instructions up with the rising stock price.

Failure to have stop loss instructions on major stock holdings is a common mistake among novice investors. Make sure you cancel your stop loss instructions on stocks that you have sold. Otherwise you could be placed in a position of having to deliver stocks you no longer own. A competent stockbroker can explain these techniques and others such as hedging.

In addition to using package products such as mutual funds, you may wish to consider using vehicles such as index annuities. They allow you to participate in the appreciations of various stock indexes without taking on the downside risks. These investment vehicles are backed by the financial condition of the insurance company issuing them.

Consider variable annuities if tax benefits or death benefits are a factor. Many variable annuities offer a death benefit, which basically states that your beneficiaries will receive your original investment back, plus a set amount of growth such as 3 percent or 5 percent per year as well, regardless of your account's actual performance. Of course, if your actual account value has grown by more than the guaranteed death benefit amount, then your beneficiaries would get this higher amount. This may be another way to further reduce financial and market risk.

Fixed annuities are excellent substitutes for individual bonds or bond funds. You obtain high yields in most cases without taking on financial risk. This, of course, assumes that you have selected a financially strong company with a competitive product. All of these various strategies can give you tremendous staying power.

Other Books to Assist You in Becoming a Better Investor

- *The Bear Book* by John Rothchild
- *Beating the Dow with Bonds* by Michael B. O'Higgins
- *How to Make Money in Stocks* by William J. O'Neil
- *Stocks for the Long Run* by Jeremy J. Siegel
- *One Up on Wall Street* by Peter Lynch
- *The Warren Buffett Way* by Robert G. Hagstrom, Jr.
- *What Works on Wall Street* by James P. O'Shaughnessy

8

Having the Wrong Type of Life Insurance

Many retirees have done a good job accumulating and investing assets. Hopefully, they have taken measures to protect and preserve their wealth for themselves and their heirs. When the topic turns to life insurance, however, many retirees tune out. They have been conditioned to think of life insurance as death insurance or as just a necessary evil in their portfolio. Unfortunately, this attitude can lead many retirees to skip over this area of their personal and business planning.

Years ago, life insurance policies were peddled door to door by debit life insurance agents. The policies sold were typically either industrial whole life insurance marketed as 20-pay life plans or life insurance policies that were paid-up-at-age-85 programs. Some programs were marketed as endowment plans guaranteeing a policyholder's money waiting for them at the end of their working years and, hopefully, giving them some funds for their retirement years. Most of the benefits of these policies would be considered small compared to the current costs of burial expenses and the annual expenses retirees face today. In their day, these policies served their purpose. However, for the policyholder issued a $500 or $1,000 policy amount, it is easy to see how often these policyholders were underinsured. Today, the average policy size is much larger with greater accumulation features.

Retirees hanging onto old-style industrial policies may want to consult an agent of that company to determine their options. Many of these companies offer much more competitive products that the policyholder may elect to take advantage of. A good Certified Financial Planner can also assist you in evaluating your options. Many policyholders are simply holding on to these types of policies for sentimental reasons.

Current coverage may be completely different than what you are used to seeing. Other programs are still very similar to older types of life insurance. These plans are usually still referred to as whole life insurance. The advantage of these programs is that as long as you make the stated premium, as listed in the schedule of premium payments section of your policy, your policy should last until the day you pass on.

Some of these programs will mature for the face amount of coverage at an age of 90 or beyond. John D. Rockefeller of Standard Oil was the lucky recipient of such a benefit, although he was probably both glad and sad about this event. He was glad because he made it past the age of 90 and probably sad because when a life insurance policy matures or endows it is usually a taxable event. All cash values that are greater than the premiums you paid will in most cases be taxable. Keep in mind that upon your demise, most life insurance benefits are free of federal income tax. The dividends paid on your policy will usually not be taxed. However, any interest paid on the dividends typically is taxed. Whole life policies that pay dividends have proven over time to be some of the best policies for consumers.

It is important to note that policies issued today are much more competitive than policies issued in past years. However, there are some important exceptions and these include many of the small life insurance policies that are offered through television commercials and magazine advertisements aimed at the senior market.

The policies that are offered in magazines and on television are generally non-dividend-paying policies that are under $15,000 in benefits. These policies typically have graded benefits as well. This means that if the insured should pass away during the first three years, the insurance company only has to return the premiums that were paid as a death benefit. Because these policies usually pay no dividends, chances are the senior will end up paying their own death benefits because the premiums being paid in over the years will, in many cases, exceed what is to be paid out.

Many seniors are easy prey for this type of coverage because they don't want to place a burden on loved ones. However, these policies have their place for those seniors who are uninsurable. Whenever possible, every senior should look first to large and highly rated insurance companies to see what is available. The insurance benefits could be greater with lower premiums. Those savings could be used to further the senior's finances. If retirees are sure that they will be considered uninsurable, then they should check with any associations that they have dealings with to see if they offer any type of guaranteed group coverage. Many credit unions will offer small policies as a side benefit to those members who hold accounts with them.

There Are Many Choices

Current plan choices have never been greater. A consumer who is wise and does some comparative shopping or who uses the right life insurance agent may find a large assortment of competitive policies available. Today's policies have many features that were simply not available years ago. Some choices today include policies that offer competitive interest rates as well as mutual fund–type subaccounts.

Newer policies also feature newer mortality tables that often mean lower life insurance costs. These lower insurance costs will often lead to better accumulation values. In essence, today's life insurance policies offer less expensive life insurance costs with better financial returns. Often, critics will state that life insurance is a lousy investment. However, with the advent of today's newer products, the critics may be woefully out of touch with what is available in the marketplace today. Many of today's products offer solutions that cannot be found in other investment products or other investment strategies.

Universal Life Plans

Universal life policies were first offered in the early 1980s and were a revolutionary innovation in their day. Back in the early 1980s, consumers were faced with the common dilemma of rising interest rates coupled with the impact that inflation was having on their portfolios. The universal life policy offered an insurance product that would pay current interest rates that were much higher than traditional rates of return found in the older cash value life policies. Many consumers were delighted by the prospect of earning money market rates of returns within their life insurance programs. The sales of these policies went on to break many companies' sales records.

These universal life policies are still available today and offer consumers competitive rates of return on their accumulation accounts. In order to make a wise policy purchase, you should understand how a universal life policy works and then do your shopping. The most common type of universal life policy will take your annual premiums and place them into a general account. This is the account that typically pays very competitive money market rates of return. The insurance company should have a minimum interest rate payable of at least 3 percent. Check to see what it has paid in past years for any policy you may be considering.

Make sure that you select a company that does not deduct too many charges from your initial deposits. You must give your account the ability to grow. A poor policy design that deducts too much of your premium dollars for sales expenses and other costs of your general account will prove harmful as well. From this general account, the insurance company will deduct the monthly cost of insurance based on the amount of life insurance you have selected. Make sure that you know what its current insurance charges will be and, in a worst-case scenario, what its highest charges will be. Consumers should, therefore, be careful that most of their money goes to work for their benefit and stays working.

Look for policies that have the least amount of up-front charges with the lowest annual operating costs. Avoid contracts that lock your accumulation values up with long surrender charges. Typically, universal life insurance policies will offer lower life insurance costs based on the health of the insured. Discounts are offered for the larger policies that are issued. Therefore, a person applying for a $250,000 policy should expect to pay less per $1,000 of coverage than a person applying for just $25,000 in coverage. Always obtain several quotes from reputable agents or financial advisors before committing your premium dollars.

Many insurance critics say that comparison shopping is too difficult. Instead, they recommend that you keep your investments and insurance separate. The reason for this is twofold. First, you can more easily select your investment accounts to make any needed changes if their performance should prove disappointing. Second, you, the consumer, can more easily shop for the lowest cost life insurance policy. This philosophy is known as "buying term insurance and investing the difference."

Term Life Insurance

Simply put, term life insurance is pure protection. If you pass away while the coverage is in force, the insurance company will be liable to pay benefits. Term insurance represents the cost the insurance company requires to underwrite a policyholder's risk of dying. This, of course, makes comparison shopping much easier. The only problem with comparing policies is that seldom do two insurance companies offer the same policy design.

Insurance companies may offer annual renewable term, which is a policy design that causes your insurance costs to increase each year. While usually very reasonable at younger ages, you may find the premiums too expensive at older ages when the need may be the greatest. Therefore, many insurance companies will offer 10-, 15-, and 20-year level term policies that help steady your premium payments. Typically, you will pay one set of premiums for a period of years, which then goes up for the next time period. Unfortunately, these premiums will usually go up dramatically as you age.

Many insurance companies are offering term insurance policies that closely match certain debt obligations such as mortgage debt. These policies will usually start off at a stated amount of coverage and reduce over a set period of years. The coverage is geared to decrease as your debt obligation decreases. Most policies are issued for the life of your mortgage debt, which is typically 15 to 30 years. One feature of decreasing term coverage is that the premium usually remains steady throughout the life of the policy.

FIGURE 8.1 Annual Ten-Year Term Rate for a Nonsmoker

		Premium Rate	
		Female	Male
Age 55	$100,000 10-year term coverage	$ 490	$ 645
Age 65	$100,000 10-year term coverage	880	1,543
Age 75	$100,000 10-year term coverage	2,659	4,425

Some policies state that the mortgage debt must be paid off upon your demise, while other policies give beneficiaries the option to pay off the mortgage debt or to keep the funds to use as they see fit. Care should be taken to select the right insurance coverage for your needs. Generally, policies that allow you the option to name anyone as your beneficiary will prove more flexible over time. Additionally, you may move or refinance your home and wish to continue your coverage. Generally, this can be easily accomplished with term insurance. Insurance coverage that has been obtained directly through an insurance company should give you these options. Policies sold through mortgage lenders typically do not give you the same flexibility.

Financial Leverage

Probably the greatest benefit that any life insurance plan offers is the benefit of financial leverage. What other product offers the ability to pay back many times what you have placed into it? Life insurance was primarily designed to do this and no insurance program illustrates this better than term life insurance. Because you are only paying for life insurance protection with these policies and not for accumulation within the policy itself, you can see the immediate benefit that a good policy can offer.

Figure 8.1 details the sample term rates using an established life insurance company. These rates assume that you are in good health and are a nonsmoker. The rates reflect the purchase of the company's ten-year term plan and assume you pay your annual premium each year.

Note that taking out a larger policy typically generates lower premium rates overall per base amount of coverage as shown in Figure 8.2. You should also be aware of the fact that not all insurance companies offer ten-year term coverage.

FIGURE 8.2 Annual Ten-Year Term Rate for a Nonsmoker

| | | Premium Rate | |
		Female	Male
Age 55	$250,000 10-year term coverage	$ 530	$ 920
Age 65	$250,000 10-year term coverage	1,800	2,200
Age 75	$250,000 10-year term coverage	3,500	10,600

A Case in Point: Muriel's Daughter

To illustrate how effectively insurance leverage can be used, let's begin with the story of Muriel and her daughter, Laura. Muriel was quite concerned about her daughter and, especially, her daughter's children—Muriel's only grandchildren. If anything should happen to Laura, Muriel knew that she would be in no financial condition to take care of her grandchildren. Muriel's daughter was divorced and working as a waitress to support her children. While the wages were decent, Laura had no life insurance benefits. Furthermore, Laura's abusive ex-husband left the state and was avoiding making child support payments.

The solution to this problem was quite simple. Laura saw a financial consultant who advised her that she should have a proper will and living trust drafted. This would help clarify who should be involved in raising her children in the event of her premature death. Muriel was named as first choice to serve as the children's guardian and custodian. While the ex-husband could claim custody, by funneling any financial assets to Laura's trust they could take away any financial advantage for him to do so.

Muriel had taken out a term life insurance policy on Laura for $250,000 and made sure that her daughter's living trust was named as primary beneficiary. Muriel had herself listed as successor trustee of her daughter's trust so that if Laura passed away prematurely she would have control over the trust funds. This would give Muriel financial control over her daughter's estate assets.

Muriel knew that with the purchase of the term insurance, she would have the financial resources to take care of her grandchildren. Both Muriel and Laura were very happy with this arrangement. Muriel had the peace of mind she was looking for and Laura had a security blanket established for her children. The annual premium of $300 for the term insurance seemed a small price to pay.

A Case in Point: Bill and Jane's Cottage

Like many retirees, Bill and Jane had done well for themselves. While Bill worked steadily for many years, Jane raised four well-rounded children. Add to this the fact that Bill was able to take an early retirement. Together, they found the perfect vacation home complete with lake access. The whole family loved the vacation property. Bill and Jane liked the way it brought the family together. They had continual visits from their children and grandchildren.

Their only real concern was with the mortgage that came with the vacation property. They paid off their home's mortgage and were concerned about taking on a new one. Bill and Jane could probably pay off the vacation property, but felt uneasy about tying up all their liquid funds in a second piece of real estate. Both of them remained uneasy because they knew that if anything happened to Bill, his residual pension that was payable to Jane would be reduced by half. This would mean that Jane could no longer afford the vacation home.

Bill and Jane checked with their mortgage company and were pleased to find that their bank offered a term life insurance policy that would pay off any existing mortgage in the event of Bill's untimely demise. They especially liked the fact that the life insurance premium would be added directly to their monthly mortgage payment. When compared with the peace of mind that the term life policy brought to them, the increase in their monthly mortgage payment was negligible.

Newer Types of Coverage

There are insurance plans available today called variable universal life that offer competitive insurance costs with numerous investment options. The major benefit in having excess investments within your insurance coverage is that those funds will typically be available to pay your life insurance premiums should the need arise. This will help to ensure that the benefits you contracted for will be available when you need them because your premium never goes unpaid.

Several other advantages include the fact that you are allowed to move your funds around inside the policy free of any tax ramifications. This gives you the ability to reallocate your financial resources to take advantage of changing conditions in the marketplace without tax reporting requirements and, more importantly, without taxes being owed. You would be free, for instance, to move from a growth fund to a more conservative growth and income fund without owing taxes on the gain.

A second and even greater benefit is that your funds grow tax-deferred until withdrawn. Your funds could accumulate to a much greater amount inside such a container than if they were taxed every year. These accounts accumulate free from federal income tax and state income taxes. The accumulation values are also not taken into account when computing how much of your Social Security benefits will be taxable.

A third and very important aspect to most insurance policies is that they are designed to offer loan provisions, which basically allow you to access your cash value without paying any current federal income tax on those withdrawals.

Care must be taken that you leave enough cash value within your policy to keep your coverage in force. In the event that your policy lapses before your demise, those amounts withdrawn under loan provisions could end up being taxable. These loan provisions are usually set up to allow you to borrow your funds at a very low cost, if any. This is known as the *wash loan provision* and any policy you are considering should have this important feature in it.

How important is tax-deferred growth and possible tax-free access to your policy cash values? The answer depends on what your marginal tax bracket is during the accumulation period and what your tax bracket is upon withdrawal of your cash value. The higher your tax bracket, in general, the greater the benefit of tax-deferred growth within an insurance policy.

The Benefits of Having a Tax-Free Spigot

Because life insurance is afforded favorable tax treatment, such as tax deferral of gains and possible tax-free withdrawals, consumers can use various life insurance policies not only as a program of protection but as an investment vehicle as well. Many insurance companies downplay this aspect because they fear that Congress will resurrect its attempts to tax the inside buildup of cash values within these policies.

Critics point out that using insurance policies as investment vehicles is improper for several reasons. They feel that, first of all, consumers will have too difficult a time evaluating all of their options. Second, they feel that there is not enough uniformity among the various policies being offered today to allow consumers to comparison shop, thereby leading them into poor choices. Third, they are concerned with the high costs wrapped up in many of these policies.

These critics may have a valid argument because even a seasoned financial professional requires ample time to compare various programs. However, the consumer who takes the time to acquire the right policy could greatly benefit from having the ideal investment vehicle. There are new choices available today that have low insurance costs combined with low sales charges, if any. These may prove a better choice for the consumer. The benefits to consumers are numerous, including:

- Life insurance benefits
- Tax-deferred buildup of cash values
- Possible tax-free withdrawals
- Creditor-resistant vehicle in most states
- Death benefits are usually free from federal income tax.
- Riders can usually be added, such as waiver of premium, that will pay your premiums if you are disabled.

FIGURE 8.3 Tax-Exempt versus Taxable Income

Tax-Exempt Return	Taxable Return Required to Equal a Tax-Exempt Return at Various Top Tax Brackets				
	15%	28%	31%	36%	39.60%
3%	3.53%	4.17%	4.35%	4.69%	4.97%
4	4.71	5.56	5.80	6.25	6.62
5	5.88	6.94	7.25	7.81	8.28
6	7.06	8.33	8.70	9.38	9.93
7	8.24	9.72	10.14	10.94	11.59
8	9.41	11.11	11.59	12.50	13.25
9	10.59	12.50	13.04	14.06	14.90
10	11.76	13.89	14.49	15.63	16.56
11	12.94	15.28	15.94	17.19	18.21
12	14.12	16.67	17.39	18.75	19.87
13	15.29	18.06	18.84	20.31	21.52

Tax laws change often and back in 1988 Congress mandated that life insurance cash values could be accessed tax-free in most cases as long as your contract is not considered a modified endowment contract. The rules are complicated but most insurance companies will notify you if your contract becomes a modified endowment policy so that you can take the necessary steps to correct the situation.

This usually occurs if your policy has so much money placed into it that it causes your policy to take on the characteristics of an investment instead of an insurance policy. The value of tax-free income as compared to taxable income is noted in the chart in Figure 8.3.

The example in Figure 8.4 illustrates the potential of a variable life insurance plan that features both life insurance benefits and investment accumulation potential compared to a regular investment account that has the amount equivalent to life insurance premiums deducted. The rate of return for the regular investment account is net of any brokerage fees or other charges.

The only return reducing factor is ordinary income taxes that are due each year. A federal tax bracket of 28 percent is assumed. Because there are too many different states to illustrate state income taxes, they are not taken into account.

This is an example only. Check with any life insurance company for its actual illustration and make sure to read the prospectus that you are given.

FIGURE 8.4

Male Age 65 with $500,000 of Life Insurance Coverage
(assumes annual deposit of $14,000 at 12%)

Investment Account	Variable Life Program
Year 5 = $ 50,000	Year 5 = $ 51,300
Year 10 = 125,000	Year 10 = 140,000
Year 15 = 240,000	Year 15 = 280,000
Year 20 = 410,000	Year 20 = 525,000

The Purpose of Life Insurance

Obviously, the main purpose of life insurance is to provide financial benefits to the ones we leave behind. Life insurance is one of the finest financial tools available today with which to do this. Simply by taking out a life insurance policy, you can create an instant estate. The scenarios where such an estate would be beneficial are numerous.

A Case in Point: Anne and Her Son, Todd

Anne is a widow who has a severely disabled son to take care of. Her son, Todd, is in his forties and the outlook for his future is not very bright. He is capable of doing menial work at best. Anne has her own financial problems. She is on a fixed income with funds coming in from Social Security and her deceased husband's pension from his former employer, the State of Michigan.

Anne is aware enough to know that she has a potential problem. While she is healthy now and holds some financial assets, she and her son are all right. However, she is concerned about what will happen if she has a protracted and expensive illness and the impact that it could have on the funds that she has set aside for Todd, to be held in trust for his benefit. After meeting with a financial advisor, she was surprised to find out that simply by reallocating some of her financial resources, she could multiply the dollar amount that would be available for her son in the advent of her untimely demise.

Anne committed a portion of her investment assets to a variable life insurance program. These were assets that she had been accumulating for her son's future benefit and were currently being held in stock mutual funds. She was given the choice between a one-time deposit and making annual deposits for a period of years. She

FIGURE 8.5 One-Time Deposit Program

$100,000 Lump-Sum Deposit
(within a single premium life program)

Year	Premiums at 12% in Taxable Fund	vs	Variable Life Account Value	Variable Life Death Benefit
1	$ 108,650		$ 108,650	$ 333,340
5	151,350		151,720	333,340
10	230,000		231,200	333,340
15	346,610		365,090	420,000
20	525,000		580,250	632,470
25	800,000		923,888	979,320
35	1,820,000		2,306,360	2,420,000

chose the one-time deposit program because she did not need to take a health physical and the underwriting guidelines to receive this coverage were much more liberal. The program that she chose is detailed in Figure 8.5.

One advantage is that she only needs to make one deposit to immediately increase the account value that will be available to her son. She also has the benefit of her account accumulating on a tax-deferred basis. The disadvantage is that if she pulls funds out while living, she will cause a taxable event. Any gains that are withdrawn will be taxable. This is because the policy is considered a modified endowment contract. The death benefit will still pass tax-free to her son or to her son's trust.

Exercise caution: Insurance death benefits are included when determining the federal estate tax. Therefore, if you think that your estate will be larger than $675,000 upon your demise, you should consider having an irrevocable life insurance trust as the owner.

How to Pay Estate Taxes Economically

A Case in Point: Paul and Rose Take Action

Paul and Rose had done well for themselves. Paul had managed to accumulate a tidy nest egg that was further augmented by an inheritance that Rose received from her mother. They were both very pleased with their current lifestyle yet remained concerned about the ability to pass on their estate to their children. They decided it was time for a financial checkup.

When Paul and Rose finished their financial planning meeting, they were shocked to find out how much they were really worth. It seemed amazing to them that they should have so much after struggling financially during their early years. Their financial planner calculated that with all their assets including their home, profit sharing plan, investments, and life insurance they were worth in excess of $2 million. The financial planner also advised them of the possibility of federal estate taxes being due upon their demise.

Paul and Rose were able to shelter $1,350,000 of their estate by adopting a revocable living trust with an A-B provision. This would help them take advantage of each of their property exclusion amounts of $675,000. The problem was with the portion of their estate over this amount. Their planner explained that their children or their estate would have to pay a federal estate tax within nine months after the last of them passes away. The amount of the tax was calculated to be over $300,000!

Their financial planner advised them of their options. They could simply plan to have their estate pay the tax. This would require that Paul and Rose make some adjustments in their thinking. If they could come to terms with the thought of the government taking their hard earned savings and thereby leaving less for their children, then they would be required to do no further planning. Their planner informed them that many people took this tack.

Many people, he explained, do not want to think about their estate planning and certainly do not want to take any constructive steps to rectify any possible future problems they may have. This thought rankled Paul and Rose. They wanted a solution to the problem. They also wanted the confidence in knowing in advance that their planning would work.

The other main option explained to Paul and Rose regarded a gifting program. They could each give away $10,000 each year to as many people as they wished. With their three children, their children's spouses, and their grandchildren, the financial planner figured out that they could gift as much as $100,000 per year. This would help reduce their estate size now, while living, and they could see their children enjoying the financial gifts that they had given them. Paul and Rose considered this concept yet were hesitant to gift too many of their assets. What would happen if they required expensive medical care or, worse, a nursing home environment for one or both of them?

Because Paul and Rose were in no hurry to give away too much of their funds, they settled on a limited gifting program. They decided that they were comfortable gifting some of the growth each year from their estate. They decided to gift just $10,000 each year to each of their three children. Their children could use these gifts to pay the premium on a last-to-die life insurance policy. The face amount of this life coverage would easily be enough to pay the estate taxes due on their estate and thereby allow their children to realize the full value of their estate upon inheritance.

Unlike regular life insurance policies that pay benefits on the demise of the insured, last-to-die policies cover two individuals and pay on the demise of the last to die. These policies are also referred to as survivorship life insurance. The advantage of these policies is that the premiums payable are traditionally much lower.

Typically, these policies are much easier to qualify for as well. This stems from the fact that even if one person is not healthy, the life insurance company knows that the other insured may be. Insurance companies also know that the likelihood of one person surviving to an older age is greater when two lives are taken into account instead of just one.

Married couples like this type of life insurance coverage because it allows them peace of mind in advance. Because the individuals in a married couple are typically allowed to leave as much as they want to their spouse under the unlimited marital deduction, they are not usually concerned about estate taxes until the last of them passes away. They like knowing that tax-free funds will be waiting there to help pay any federal estate taxes.

Couples should be careful to make sure that they are not the owners of such policies. That could cause the policies to be included in their estates. Typically, couples will have their children own the policies if they feel that they may need access to a policy's cash value account during their retirement years. Many of these last-to-die policies will build up substantial cash values as the years go by. Knowing that your children can access those values on your behalf can prove a godsend during a financial emergency.

If you have a good relationship with your children and if your children are in good marriages, this method may work just fine. A problem could arise if one of your children should go through a divorce. Your last-to-die policy could be claimed as part of the marital assets by the divorcing in-law.

For larger estates and for those couples who want to make sure the insurance will remain in place unaffected by divorce actions, you may want to consider having your last-to-die policy owned by an irrevocable life insurance trust (ILIT). You then gift the money to your children by giving them notice of the gift. This is known as the notice to trust beneficiary of withdrawal right. They have 60 days to take the funds or they automatically go into your ILIT.

Of course, they are not supposed to take the funds and this will allow enough funds to accumulate within your trust to pay the premiums on your life coverage. Once in your ILIT, the trustee of this trust will pay your life insurance policy premiums. This method of using a small gift of $30,000 each year to pay your life insurance premiums can create a very large insurance estate in most cases, as illustrated in Figure 8.6. It is not unusual to see a magnifying effect that is quite large. See a competent estate-planning professional for guidance on these matters.

FIGURE 8.6

Last-to-Die Policy for Paul and Rose
(assumes both are nonsmokers,
male age 65 / female age 65,
premiums due each year of $28,000)

Year	Face Amount of Coverage	Accumulation Account	
		6% Gross Rate	12% Gross Rate
1	$1,000,000	$ 19,500	$ 20,000
5	1,000,000	87,000	1,050,000
10	1,000,000	230,000	325,000
15	1,000,000	370,000	640,000
20	1,000,000	506,000	1,115,000

Collecting before Your Time

Unfortunately, dying before our time is what gives life insurance its tremendous value. Simply put, you can create a large estate ahead of time in case you are not here to create an estate consisting of real financial assets. Many retirees find it ironic that they have to die to collect from their life insurance policies. However, these are programs that they would like to delay collection from for as long as possible.

Many people become severely ill before they succumb and pass on from various terminal illnesses such as cancer, severe heart disease, and AIDS. These people may need financial assistance more than ever at this juncture of their lives. They may have large amounts of personal life insurance, group life policies, or business life insurance plans. While these programs will be available after they are gone to reimburse medical facilities, the expenses they incurred while ill, or to take care of family members, very little may be available while the insured is living.

In the past, the best many policyholders could do was to access the cash value portion of their life insurance policies. This came in handy for many policyholders. Unfortunately, most of the life insurance policies in force today are term life insurance. Because term life insurance has no cash value, these policyholders have very few options. They can either wait until after their demise to let their family collect or they can hope that a family member or friend will loan them money on the premise that their life insurance plan will pay back the money with interest after they pass away.

Today, there are many more options available for those in need of financial funds while suffering from a terminal illness. Typically, funds may be advanced before you actually pass away if your illness is considered terminal and you are not expected to live longer than two years. Many insurance companies offer what is known as accelerated death benefits. These benefits are typically based on a percentage of the face amount of your life coverage.

Many times, this information will be made available to you after you contact an insurance company regarding such benefits. In the past, these benefits were not added to life policies. However, with the large increase in AIDS cases that were processed during the last decade, the insurance companies realized that policyholders needed assistance. Many insurance companies started adding these benefits to existing policies as well as adding them to newer policies.

Therefore, even if you think you do not have this type of rider on your policy, make sure you check with your insurance company. You may be surprised. Most of these riders will pay up to half of the face amount of life coverage to you while you are living. This, of course, depends on the nature of your illness. Make sure any new policy you are considering has an accelerated death benefit provision. This rider is also known as a living benefit.

If your policy does not contain the above rider, then you may want to consider borrowing funds from a friend or family member. These lenders would be wise to have you assign your policy to them so that they can ensure that your premiums are paid and avoid the possibility of your policy lapsing. This assignment will also help to ensure that they are able to collect the benefits directly from your policy. It is typical to see lenders demand that you name them either as partial beneficiary or as the total beneficiary.

Viatical Settlements

Recently, private individuals and various corporations have appeared that will offer you differing cash amounts based on various factors. These companies will typically buy your policy from you and pay out an amount ranging from 20 percent to 85 percent of the face amount of your coverage.

They base their cash offerings on many factors. They usually look at what type of illness you are suffering from and the financial condition of the life insurance company with which you hold your life insurance coverage. Generally, the worse your illness is, the higher your payout will be. These companies also look at the financial strength of the insurance company that is backing your policy. The higher the insurance company is rated, the greater the potential that you will be offered the highest amount available for your policy.

Be sure to obtain several quotes if you decide to proceed this way. Purchases of life insurance policies by these individuals and companies are known as *viatical settlements.* Different parties offering viatical settlements each have their own list of factors at which they look. Typically, they want a policy that has been in existence for at least two years. This is due to the fact that once a life policy has been in force for a period of two years and one day, it is usually past the contestable period. This is the time period when the insurance company can contest the claim based on any information that may come to light.

Be careful if your policy is a group plan or has lapsed in the last two years and had to be reinstated. This may cause the policy to be open for contesting. Make sure that you obtain sound legal counsel before proceeding with any type of viatical settlement or private loan.

Insurance Company Rating Systems

The financial strength of an insurance company is a very important factor to consider when purchasing life insurance or annuities. Below are the rating systems of three companies that evaluate insurance companies. Note: Some of the classifications listed here are broken down into more levels than illustrated.

A.M. Best

- A++/A+   Superior. Very strong ability to meet obligations.
- A/A−   Excellent. Strong ability to meet obligations.
- B++/B+   Very good. Strong ability to meet obligations.
- B/B−   Good. Adequate ability to meet obligations.
- C++/C+   Fair. Reasonable ability to meet obligations.
- C/C−   Marginal. Currently has the ability to meet obligations.
- D   Below minimum standards.
- E   Under state supervision.
- F   In liquidation.

Standard and Poor's

- FAAA   Superior financial security. Highest safety.
- AA+/AA/AA−   Excellent financial security. Highly safe.
- A+/A/A−   Good financial security. More susceptible to economic change than highly-rated companies.
- BBB+/BBB/BBB−   Adequate financial security. More vulnerable to economic changes than highly-rated companies.
- BB+/BB/BB−   Adequate financial security. Ability to meet obligations may not be adequate for long-term policies.

- B+/B/B−   Currently able to meet obligations. Highly vulnerable to adverse economic conditions.
- CCC   Questionable ability to meet obligations due to high vulnerability to adverse economic conditions.
- R   Regulatory action. Under supervision of insurance negotiators.

Weiss Research, Inc.

- A+/A/A−   Excellent financial security. Strong ability to deal with economic adversity.
- B+/B/B−   Good financial security. Severe economic conditions may affect this company.
- C+/C/C−   Fair financial security. Susceptible to downturns in the economy.
- D+/D/D−   Weak financial security. Could impact policyholders.
- E+/E   Very weak financial security. Significant risk, even in a stable economy.
- F   Failed. Under supervision of state insurance commissioners.
- +   Indication of a possible upgrade.
- −   Indication of a possible downgrade.

Glossary

A trust The surviving spouse's portion of an A-B trust. Also called marital trust or survivor's trust.

A-B trust A living trust with a provision that lets you provide for your surviving spouse, keep control over who will receive your assets after your spouse dies, and leave up to $1.35 million (in 2000) to your beneficiaries, free of estate taxes. (This amount should increase over the next several years as the federal estate tax exemption increases. By the year 2006, an A-B living trust may let you and your spouse leave your beneficiaries up to $2 million free of estate taxes, with no probate.)

administrator Person named by the court to represent a probate estate when there is no will or when the will does not name an executor. A female is an administratix.

asset Basically, anything you own, including your home and other real estate, bank accounts, savings bonds, life insurance, investments, furniture, jewelry, art, clothing, and collectibles.

B trust The deceased spouse's portion of an A-B trust. Also called credit shelter, bypass trust, or family trust.

basis What you paid for an asset or, if gifted to you, what the donor paid for it. The value that is used to determine gain or loss for income tax purposes.

bear market A market environment where prices of stocks or bonds reduce in price. Sometimes this will last for only a short period, while other times it may endure for quite a few years. The average bear market lasts for 15 months. A major bear market can last for ten years or longer. Although such long-term bear markets are rare, they have taken place.

bond A debt note or security issued by a corporation, local government, municipality, state government, federal agency, or federal government. It typically is an

IOU backed by the issuers. It pays interest to you for the use of your money. The interest income typically is paid semiannually.

certificate of deposit (CD)   A debt instrument issued by banks and savings and loan institutions. Deemed safer than most investments because it guarantees principal plus interest. You should make sure that the account and the amount invested will be protected according to current banking regulations covered under FDIC regulations or an equivalent federal organization.

children's trust   A trust included in your living trust. If, when you die, a beneficiary is not of legal age, the child's inheritance will go into this trust. The inheritance will be managed by the trustee you have named until the child reaches the age at which you want him or her to inherit or receive distributions.

codicil   A written change or amendment to a will.

cotrustees   Two or more individuals who have been named to act together in managing a trust's assets. A corporate trustee can also be a cotrustee.

common stock   Evidence of ownership in a corporation. A common stock represents an equity interest in the corporation that issued such certificate. You usually purchase this type of share from a brokerage or on a stock exchange. Investors usually acquire these shares when they are first offered to the public in a process called an initial public offering (IPO) or by placing a purchase through a broker-dealer and buying the shares in the secondary market. It is possible to purchase these shares through a private investor. Shareholders typically have rights such as voting rights and the right to receive dividends in proportion to the shares owned.

conservator   One who is legally responsible for the care and well-being of another person. If appointed by a court, the conservator is under the court's supervision. May also be called a guardian.

conservatorship   A court-controlled program for persons who are unable to manage their own affairs due to mental or physical incapacity. May also be called a guardianship.

consumer price index (CPI)   The measure of price changes in certain consumer items. The U.S. Bureau of Labor Statistics calculates it monthly. Newspapers and economists constantly refer to this indicator as it closely tracks inflation in the economy. When the CPI moves up, it generally indicates an inflationary period in our economy. Likewise, when the CPI goes down, it could indicate a deflationary trend. Many government benefit programs and many private pension benefits are tied to this indicator. When this indicator goes up a certain amount, it may trigger an increase in a retiree's pension benefits such as Social Security.

convertible security   A corporate bond or preferred stock that may be exchanged at the holder's option for a set amount of the issuer's common stock shares. Not only can the convertible security holder obtain a set amount of shares, but the price to be paid has been predetermined as well. A convertible security generally yields a significant dividend (preferred stock) or interest (bonds). It also tracks the underlying common stock in most cases. This tends to make it more of a conservative investment than owning the company's common stock. You must be careful when purchasing these securities because many are callable by the company. This means the company can request that you redeem your shares at an agreed upon price.

corporate trustee An institution, like a bank or trust company, that specializes in managing trusts.

credit shelter trust Another name for the B trust in an A-B living trust because this trust shelters or preserves the federal estate tax credit of the deceased spouse.

credit rating A report on the strength of the entity issuing a corporate bond, municipal bond, and other securities. Common rating agencies are Standard & Poor's Rating Services and Moody's Investors Service. Insurance companies may be rated by these agencies, but investors usually will check with A.M. Best for more detailed information. Rating services provide information on an issuer's strength that would not be otherwise available to ordinary investors. Read their reports very carefully. Only experienced investors should be involved in purchasing investments that are not rated.

custodian Person named to manage assets left to a minor under the Uniform Transfer to Minors Act. In most states, the minor receives the assets at legal age.

deceased One who has died.

deed A document that lets you transfer title of your real estate to another person(s). Also see warranty deed and quitclaim deed.

default Failure of a company or entity to make good on its bond interest payments or principal payments as they come due.

disclaim To refuse to accept a gift or inheritance so it can be passed to the recipient next in line.

distribution Payment in cash or asset(s) to one who is entitled to receive it.

dividend Distribution of earnings to shareholders. A dividend usually is paid in cash or in shares. A dividend is not guaranteed. A company could choose to decrease or suspend dividends if the board of directors feels the company would be better served by doing so. Mutual funds must pass on their dividends each year as they are earned by the fund. These may be paid out monthly, quarterly, semi-annually or annually. This greatly depends on what type of mutual fund you own. Income funds usually pay out more often. Growth funds typically only pay out dividends toward year-end. An investor should be fully informed of the underlying company's strength and ability to pay consistent dividends. A company's or mutual fund's past track records should be fully investigated. In regard to purchasing mutual funds, be careful of purchasing these funds in taxable accounts toward year-end. You may end up receiving a large dividend or capital gains distribution, which may be fully taxable.

estate Assets and debts left by an individual at death.

estate taxes A federal or state tax on the value of assets left at death. Also called inheritance tax or death tax.

fiduciary   Person having the legal duty to act primarily for another's benefit. Implies great confidence, trust, and a high degree of good faith. Usually associated with a trustee.

funding   The process of transferring assets to your living trust.

generation-skipping transfer tax   A steep tax (55 percent) on assets that skip a generation and are left directly to grandchildren and younger generations.

gift   A transfer from one individual to another without fair compensation.

grantor   The person who sets up or creates a trust. The person whose trust it is. Also called creator, settler, trustor, or donor.

growth stock   A company that is reporting above-average growth of earnings and can be expected to continue this trend.

heir   One who is entitled by law to receive part of your estate.

incapacitated/incompetent   Unable to manage one's own affairs, either temporarily or permanently.

income stock   A company that manages to produce steady income via dividend distributions. It historically follows this strategy to maintain shareholders interest, especially conservative investors.

inheritance   The assets received from someone who has died.

intestate   Without a will.

joint ownership   When two or more persons own the same asset.

joint tenants with right of survivorship (JTWROS)   A form of joint ownership in which the deceased owner's share automatically and immediately transfers to the surviving joint tenant(s).

living probate   The court-supervised process of managing the assets of one who is incapacitated.

living trust   A written legal document that creates an entity to which you transfer ownership of your assets. Contains your instructions for managing your assets during your lifetime and for their distribution upon your incapacity or death. Avoids probate at death and court control of assets at incapacity. Also called a revocable inter vivos trust. A trust created during one's lifetime.

living will   A written document that states your wishes when or when not to be kept alive by artificial means when an illness or injury is terminal.

marital deduction   A deduction on the federal estate tax return allowing the first spouse who dies to leave an unlimited amount of assets to the surviving spouse free of estate taxes. However, if no other tax planning is used and the surviving spouse's estate is more than the amount of the federal estate tax exemption in effect at the time of his or her death, estate taxes will be due at that time.

money market mutual fund   An investment in corporate paper, bank certificates of deposit, Treasury bills, and other notes usually deemed more conservative than general securities. While individual money market securities can have high initial minimums, a money market mutual fund does not. In general, a money market mutual fund is very liquid and safe. It is not, however, guaranteed, as many investors think. To ensure that your funds are not unduly at risk, consider investing in a money market mutual fund that specializes in government securities.

mutual fund   A fund that offers diversification, recordkeeping, and active management. An open-end fund raises funds from its shareholders and manages those assets for a nominal fee, which usually ranges from 1 to 3 percent per year. In an open fund the fund stands ready to redeem shares from its shareholders. This fund will state what its investment objective is in a document called the prospectus. Read your prospectus very carefully as it will contain information on expenses, risk factors, investment objective, management of the fund, and track record. Most investors fail to read the prospectus and this leads to unhappy results. A smaller number of funds are closed end funds, which after initially being offered will be found on regular stock exchanges such as the NYSE.

per capita   A way of distributing your estate so that your surviving descendents will share equally, regardless of their generation.

per stirpes   A way of distributing your estate so that your surviving descendents will receive only what their immediate ancestor would have received if he or she had been living at your death.

personal representative   Another name for an executor or administrator.

pour over will   A short will often used with a living trust. It states that any assets left outside of your living trust will become part of (*pour over* into) your living trust upon your death.

probate   The legal process of validating a will, paying debts, and distributing assets after death.

probate fee   A legal, executor, or appraisal fee, or court costs collected from an estate as it goes through probate. Probate fees are paid from assets in the estate before the assets are fully distributed to the heirs.

prospectus   An official document which must be given to a potential investor before he or she invests in a newly offered security or mutual fund. This document will cover important details such as risk factors and expenses.

quitclaim deed   Document allowing transfer of title to real estate. The party signing the quitclaim deed makes no guarantees regarding any encumbrances on said property.

real estate investment trust (REIT)   A vehicle that holds various real estate properties. It typically is a high-yielding investment vehicle and most are publicly traded. It can be either quite narrow in focus such as only investing in shopping centers, hotels, or other properties, or broadly diversified by investing into several segments of the real estate market.

required beginning date (RBD)   The date you must begin taking required minimum distributions from your tax-deferred plan. Usually, it is April 1 of the calendar year following the calendar year in which you turn age 70½. If your money is in a company-sponsored plan, you may be able to delay your RBD beyond this date if you continue working (providing you are not a 5 percent or greater owner of the company).

required minimum distribution (RMD) The amount you are required to withdraw each year from your tax-deferred plan after you reach your required beginning date. It is determined by dividing the value of your tax-deferred account by the life expectancy of you and your beneficiary. The intent is that by the time you and your beneficiary are both expected to die, your tax-deferred savings will be fully withdrawn.

successor trustee Person or institution named in the trust document who will take over should the first trustee die, resign, or otherwise become unable to act.

testamentary trust A trust in a will. Can only go into effect at death. Does not avoid probate.

title Document proving ownership of an asset.

total return The interest, dividends, capital gains, and price changes of an investment. This is important to understand because most investments return more in the form of price changes than dividend income.

trustee Person or institution who manages and distributes another's assets according to the instructions in the trust document.

unfunded Not having assets. Your living trust is unfunded if you have not transferred assets into it.

warranty deed Document allowing transfer of title to real estate. The party signing the warranty deed is making a guarantee that the title is free of any encumbrances.

will A written document with instructions for the disposing of assets after death. A will can only be enforced through the probate court.

yield The amount of dividend or interest paid on any investment.

Index

A

Accelerated death benefit, 211
Accumulation account, 199–200
Advice, 29
Aetna Life Insurance Co., 176
Airborne Express, 188
Alzheimer's disease, 67
American Century Funds, 14
American Funds, 12, 14
American Skandia, 175
Amortization method, 141
Anchor National, 175
Annuitization, 173, 176, 177
Annuity
    contract, 5, 7
    factor method, 141
    fixed, 131–32, 133
    index, 72, 132–33
    systematic withdrawal program,
       73
    tax-deferred, 72, 131–35
    variable, 72, 132–33, 173–82
Arbitrage bond, 128
Assets
    allocation, 190–91
    collection of, 78
    distribution of, 79
    gifting, 102–3
    of minor, 85–86
    trust provisions, 86
Assignor, 88

B

Bank account
    estate planning, 84
    taxation, 120
Beneficiary, 77
    children as, 111–13
    estate planning, 84–85
    IRA, 109–15
    trust provisions, 86–87, 88,
       109–10
Benefit restoration, 69
Bills, 5, 9
Blended fund, 154
Bond, 3, 5, 169
    call provision, 172
    inflation–protection, 8–9
    maturity date, 170–71
    safety margin, 193
    speculators, 171
Broker-dealer, 168
Business entity, 29
Bypass trust, 98–100, 111, 144

C

Call provision, 172
Capital gain, 122–25, 145
    deferral, 122–23
    excess, 122–23
    long-term, 178
    mutual fund, 125–27
    primary residence, 124–25
    short-term, 125–26, 178
    table, 124
    timing of, 122
Cash value, 210
Centarians, 2
Certificates of deposit, 3, 5, 9, 120,
    184
Certified Financial Planner, 184, 197
Charitable organizations, 117
Charitable remainder annuity trust
    (CRAT), 107–8
Chronic illness, 65
Closed-end mutual funds, 157–64
Common disaster, 77, 110–11
Common stock mutual fund, 151–54
Company size, 151–53, 190
Compound interest, 27
Conservator, 43
Consumer price index, 4
Corporate bonds, 172–73
Cost basis, 142–43, 145
Coverage coordination, 67
CRAT. *See* Charitable remainder
    annuity trust
Creditor-resistant vehicles, 30
Credit risk, 22
Credit shelter trust provision, 144
*Cruzan v. Dir. MO Dept. of Health
    1990,* 36
Current income, 3
Custodial care, 59
Custodian, 43, 77, 85, 86, 90
Customs, 121

D

Davis New York Venture Fund, 12
Death benefit
    accelerated, 211
    life insurance, 198, 207
    long-term care coverage, 69–70
    variable annuity, 72, 174–76, 195
Debt instruments, 3, 5, 7
Debt payment, 78
Deferred sales charges, 156
Dependent exemptions, 120
Dignity planning, 34
    disability insurance, 53–54
    financial affairs, 37, 43–52
    medical decisions, 35–37, 38–42
    power of attorney, 44–52
Direct rollover transaction, 139
Disability, 141
Disability insurance, 53–54
Diversification, 22–23, 30, 190–91
Diversified investment company, 149
Dividend-and-interest method, 9
Dividend income, 125
Dividends, 10–11, 30, 198
Do not resuscitate situations, 36
Dollar, 5, 6
Domestic trust, 101
Donor, 88
Durable power of attorney, 44
    drawbacks of, 52
    effective on disability, 50–51
    effective on execution, 48–49
    exempted powers, 52
    general, 44–45
    for health care, 35, 39–42
    nontax powers, 45–46
    special powers, 47
    springing, 45
    tax-related powers, 45–46

E

Earnings, 189
Earnings-per-share (EPS) ratio, 167
Economic Growth and Tax Relief
    Reconciliation Act of 2001, 119–20
Economic Recovery Tax Act, 92, 101
Elimination period, 60
Employer stock, 142–43
EPS. See Earnings-per-share ratio
Equity investments, 3, 4–5
Estate
    accounting of, 78
    closing of, 79
    large, 91
Estate planning, 31, 75–76
    bypass trust, 98–100
    common disaster, 110–11

foreign spouse, 100–101
generation-skipping, 101–2
gifting program, 102–3
gift to minors, 85–86
IRA, 109–15
joint tenants with rights of
    survivorship, 81–83
life insurance, 103–5
living trust, 86–91
married couples, 84–85
step-up basis, 83
tax laws, 91–96
unified credit, 98–100
will, 77–81, 96–97
Exchange, 182
Executor. See Personal representative
Executrix. See Personal representative

F

Family trust, 98–100
Fannie Mae's Home Keeper, 17
Federal estate and gift tax, 76, 92–93,
    94
    income in respect to decedent,
        139–40
    insurance death benefit, 207
    on life insurance, 104
    reduction strategies, 106–8
    unified credit amount, 94–96,
        98–100, 103, 110, 144
    unlimited marital deduction, 92,
        97–101, 209
Federal Home Loan Mortgage
    Corporation (FHLMC), 7
Fidelity Funds, 14
Financial leverage, 201–3
Financial risk
    definition of, 7, 21
    diversification and, 22
    example of, 24–25
    investment questions, 23–24
    market risk and, 26, 171
    personal protection from, 29–30
    politics and, 23
    reduction strategies, 22, 23, 29,
        194, 195
    risk-return pyramid, 32
    written agreements, 23, 29
First Trust Investments, 157, 160
5/5 power, 99
Fixed annuity, 131–32, 181, 195
Fixed investment
    age rule, 4–5, 7, 8
    choices, 5, 7
    government offerings, 7–9
    income-producing, 9
    interest rates, 3
    portfolio percentage, 4–5, 7, 8

risks, 7
Fraud, 68
Freddie Mac, 7
Frivolous withdrawal privilege, 99
Fundamental analysis, 166–67

G

General durable power of attorney,
    44–45
Generation-skipping, 101–2
Generation-Skipping Transfer Tax
    (GSTT), 102, 144
Gifting program, 101, 102–3, 208
GNMA. See Government National
    Mortgage Association
Government agency offerings, 7
Government debt obligations, 172–73
Government National Mortgage
    Association (GNMA), 172–73
Government policies, 121
Government securities, 7–9
Grantor, 88, 89
Growth fund, 154
GSTT. See Generation-Skipping
    Transfer Tax
Guardian, 43, 77, 80, 85, 90

H

Hartford, 175
Health care directives, 35–37, 38–42
Health care proxy, 35, 39–42
Health Insurance Portability and
    Accountability Act of 1996, 64
Health status, 70
Heirs
    declaration of, 78
    intestacy laws and, 79–80
    release/disclosure, 79
Holder, 44
Home Equity Conversion Mortgage,
    17, 18
Home health care, 59, 67, 70

I

ILIT. See Irrevocable life insurance
    trust
Illiquid investments, 30
Immediate annuity, 174
Income
    dividend-and-interest method, 9
    dividends, 10–11
    in respect to a decedent, 139–40,
        181
    reverse mortgage, 15–19

systematic withdrawal program, 10, 11–14
Income-producing investments, 9
Indemnity plans, 61–62
Index annuity, 132–33, 195
  inflation risk and, 31
  insurance premium funding and, 72
  market risk and, 30
Index fund, 12
Indigent, 57, 58
Individual retirement account (IRA)
  beneficiary, 84, 109–15
  common disaster and, 110–11
  penalty-free withdrawals, 141
  plan document, 115
  required minimum distribution, 111–13, 115, 143
  rollover, 138–39, 142–43
  self-directed, 114
  stretching, 111
  withdrawal penalty, 140–41
Inflation
  cause of, 5
  consumer price index, 4
  effect on dollar, 6
  erosion power of, 2–3
  fixed investments and, 3
  protection provision, 67
  purchasing power, 5
  rider, 70
  risk, 27, 30–31
Inflation-protection bonds, 8–9
ING Insurance, 176
Institutional fund managers, 157
Insurance
  annuity sales, 173
  company rating, 68, 74, 212–13
  rating of, 68, 212–13
  disability, 53–54
  indemnity plan, 61–62
  liability coverage, 29
  life, 103–5
  long-term care, 59–61
  reimbursement plan, 61–62
Interest rate, 3
Interest rate risk, 27–28, 31, 170
Intermediate care, 59
Internal Revenue Service
  income in respect to decedent, 139–40
  on municipal securities, 128
  Publication 590, mortality table, 1–2, 3
  72t distribution rules, 140–41
  substantial equal payments, 140–41
International markets, 152
Intestacy laws, 79–80
Inventory, 78

Investment
  backing the, 29
  capital gains treatment, 121–25
  cost-basis rules, 145
  definition, 148
  fees, 191–92
  firm, 29
  objective, 182–84
  powers, 47
  questions, 192
  short-term, 185
  spill out effect, 188
  step-up basis, 83
  style, 154, 190–91
  tax-deferred, 128–35
  tax-exempt, 127–28, 129
Investment portfolio
  diversification, 190–91
  failure to accumulate, 14–15
  fixed investment portion, 5, 7–9
  income from, 9–19
  joint tenants with rights of survivorship, 81
  laddering, 31
  maturity dates, 28, 31
  past advice, 3–4
  performance, 188
  safety margin, 193
  tax issues, 120–22, 192–93
  time horizon, 4–5, 30
Investment strategy
  accumulation, 147–48
  asset allocation, 190–91
  bonds, 169–71
  company earnings, 189
  company size, 190
  individual stocks, 164–69
  knowledge profile, 185–88
  market trends and, 190–91
  mutual funds, 148–57
  risk profile, 185
  time horizon, 184–85
  unit investment trust, 157–64
Investor resources, 195
Investor's Business Daily, 167
IRA. *See* Individual retirement account
Irrevocable life insurance trust (ILIT), 104–5, 209
Irrevocable trust, 58
  charitable remainder trust, 107–8
  as tax reduction strategy, 106–8
  wealth replacement trust, 108

J

Jackson National, 175
Joint bank account, 84
Joint ownership, 76, 84–85

Joint revocable living trust, 89, 99–100
Joint tenants with rights of survivorship (JTWROS), 76, 81–83, 96

K

Knowledge profile, 185–88

L

Large-cap company, 153
Last-to-die life insurance, 208–10
Legal agreements, 29
Legal reserve system, 132
Letters testamentary, 78
Liability insurance, 29
Life expectancy, 1–3, 111–13, 141, 143
Life insurance
  beneficiary, 85
  death benefit, 207
  estate planning, 103–5
  financial leverage, 201–3
  graded benefits, 198
  guaranteed group coverage, 198
  last-to-die policy, 208–10
  loan provisions, 203–4
  policy assignment, 211
  purpose of, 206–7
  single-premium, 181, 206–7
  tax issues, 198, 204–5
  term policy, 200–201, 202–3, 210
  universal life policy, 199–200
  variable universal life policy, 203
  viatical settlement, 211–12
Lifestyle, 1–2, 3
Lifetime benefits, 67
Liquidity, 149–50
Living benefits, 176–77, 211
Living probate, 43
Living trust, 47, 52, 86–91, 202
Living will, 35, 38
Load mutual fund, 154–56
Loans, 203–4
Long-term care, 55–57
  costs, 57
    Medicaid coverage, 57–58
    Medicare coverage, 57, 60
    nursing home costs, 62–63
Long-term care insurance, 59–60
  benefits, 60–61
  contract provisions, 66–71
  deductibility limitations, 64
  elimination period, 60
  indemnity plan, 61–62
  nonqualified policy, 65, 70
  obtaining coverage, 71
  policy exclusions, 63

premiums, 69–74
reimbursement plan, 61–62
riders, 70
tax-qualified policy, 64–65, 70
Loss, 123
Lump-sum payouts, 138–39

M

Managed money accounts, 156–57
Management fees, 151, 158
Marginal tax system, 118
Marital trust, 98–100
Marketability, 149–50
Market capitalization, 152–53, 160
Market conditions, 188
Market risk, 30
    definition of, 26
    example of, 25–26
    financial risk and, 171
    reduction strategy, 195
Market trends, 167, 190–91
Marriage, 30
Married persons
    estate planning, 84–85
    primary residence, 124–25
    revocable living trust, 89
Maturity date, 28, 31, 129–30, 170–71
Medicaid, 57–58, 59, 73
Medicaid trust, 58, 73
Medical decisions, 35–37, 38–42
Medicare, 57, 60
Medigap, 57, 60
Midcap company, 153
Minor
    assets of, 85–86
    custodian of, 77
    gifts to, 85–86
    guardian of, 77
    intestacy laws and, 79
Money market mutual fund, 5, 9, 121, 150–51
Morningstar, 127
Mortality table, 1–2, 3, 199
Municipal bonds, 172–73
Municipal securities, 127–28
Mutual fund, 148–49
    bond accounts, 31
    capital gain, 125–27
    categories, 151–54
    charges, 154–57
    common stock fund, 151–54
    diversified, 149
    estate planning, 84
    investment style, 154
    liquidity, 149–50
    load/no–load, 154–57
    management fees, 151
    marketability, 149–50

money market account, 150–51
multiple manager approach, 12, 14
municipal, 128
nondiversified, 149
performance, 178
safety of, 151
single manager approach, 12
systematic withdrawal program, 11–14
tax issues, 121, 125–27, 165, 178–79
turnover rate, 178
12b-1 fees, 154, 155–56
variable annuity comparison, 179–80

N

Nasdaq 100 Index, 162
Nasdaq Target 15 strategy, 162, 163, 164
National Center for Home Equity Conversion (NCHEC), 17
Net unrealized appreciation (NUA), 142
New York Life, 176
News media, 183
Nike Securities LP, 157, 160
No load mutual fund, 154–57
Nondiversified investment company, 149
Nonforfeiture option, 69
Nonqualified insurance policy, 65, 70
Nonqualified tax-deferred annuity, 85
Nonrecalculation method, 143
Nonrecourse loan, 19
Nontax powers, 46
Notes, 5, 9
Notice of probate, 78
Notice to trust beneficiary of withdrawal right, 209
NUA. *See* Net realized appreciation
Nursing home, 62–63
Nuveen Investments, 157

O

Offshore accounts, 29
Omnibus Budget Reconciliation Act of 1993 (OBRA '93), 58
Open-end investment company, 148
Opposite correlation effect, 191

P

Pacific Life, 175
Patient advocate, 37, 42
Payable upon death instruction, 84

PE. *See* Price-earnings ratio
Pension plans, 84, 174
Personal exemptions, 119–20
Personal representative, 77, 78–79, 90
Pharmaceutical companies, 160
Pharmaceutical sector, 159–60
Political risk, 23
Politics, 121
Pooled funds, 62
Pour over will, 90
Power of attorney, 44. *See also* Durable power of attorney
Power to disclaim, 110
Preexisting condition, 68
Premium
    cost reduction strategy, 73–74
    funding, 72–73
    joint-life annual, 73
    rate guarantees, 68
    rates, 70–71, 72, 73
    refund, 69–70
    single-life annual, 72
    waivers, 69
Price appreciation, 161
Price-earnings (PE) ratio, 167
Price-to-sales ratio, 160
Primary residence, 123–25
Principal, 44
Private annuity, 15–16
Probate, 43, 80
    definition of, 78
    notice of, 78
    process, 78–79
    property transfer through, 87–88
Profit sharing programs, 84
Progressive tax, 118
Prospectus, 148
Provisional income, 134–35
Purchasing power, 5

Q

Qualified domestic relations order (QDRO), 141
Qualified plan, 83
    distributions, 138–39, 143
    early withdrawals, 140–41
    mandatory withholding, 138–39

R

Real estate
    cost-basis rules, 145
    investment, 31
    joint tenants with rights of survivorship, 81, 82
    step-up basis, 83
Recalculation method, 143
Redistribution of wealth doctrine, 91–92

Reimbursement plan, 61–62
Releasor, 88
Renewability, 66
Required minimum distributions (RMD), 111–13, 115, 143, 146
Retirement accounts, 84
Reverse mortgage, 15–19
    collateral, 16
    definition of, 15
    programs, 17
    repayment, 19
    requirements, 16, 18
Revocable living trust, 47, 52
    with A-B provision, 97–100, 208
    advantages, 86–87
    control, 90–91
    foreign spouse, 101
    language, 88–89
    large estates, 91
    married persons, 89
    objections to, 87–88
    pour over will, 90
Riders, 70, 175, 176, 211
Risk
    credit, 22
    factors, 21–32, 194
    financial. *See* Financial risk
    inflation, 27, 30–31
    interest rate, 27–28, 31
    market, 25–26, 30
    political, 23
    profile, 185
    transfer, 30
Risk-return pyramid, 32
Rolling stock strategy, 186
Roth IRA, 143, 145–46
RMD. *See* Required minimum distribution

S

Safety margin, 193
Sales charges, 156, 158
Savings program, 147–48
Second opinion, 29
Sector funds, 153–54
Sector investment, 158–60
Securities Investor Protection Act, 168
Securities Investor Protection Corporation (SIPC), 168
Segregation, 111
Self-doubt, 183
Sense of self, 33–34
Separation of service, 140–41
Series EE savings bonds, 129–31
Series HH savings bonds, 129–30
Series I savings bonds, 129, 130
Settler, 88
72t distribution rules, 140–41
Short-term capital gain, 125–26

Single-premium variable life (SPVL), 181
Single-premium life insurance, 206–7
SIPC. *See* Securities Investor Protection Corporation
Skilled care, 59
Small-cap company, 153
Social Security, 46, 121, 134–38, 145–46
Specialized funds, 153–54
Spill out effect, 188
Spouse
    as beneficiary, 113–14
    bypass trust, 98–100
    consent, 84
    discounts, 67
    estate tax, 144
    noncitizen, 100–101
    unlimited marital deduction, 92, 97–99
Springing durable power of attorney, 45
S&P Target 10 strategy, 160–62
SPVL. *See* Single-premium variable life
Standard deduction, 120
State death tax, 95
State guaranty funds, 132
State residency, 80–81
Step-up basis
    capital gain investments, 122
    estate planning, 83
    gifts, 103
    loss of, 144–45
    real property, 180
    stocks, 166
    trust provisions, 87
Stock, 3, 164–69
    certificate, 167–68
    dividends, 10–11
    earnings, 189
    employer, 142–43
    performance comparisons, 10–11
    safety margin, 193
    stop-loss order, 194–95
Substantial equal payments, 140–41
Successor trustee, 52, 89
Surrender charges, 182, 200
Surrender period, 156
Survivorship, rights of, 76, 81–83
Survivorship life insurance, 209
Systematic withdrawal program, 10, 11–14, 73

T

Taxable income, 118
Tax-deferred annuity, 72, 131–35
Tax-deferred investments, 128–35
Tax-exempt investments, 127–28, 129

Tax-free municipal securities, 173
Tax issues
    awareness, 118
    credit, 94–95, 96, 121
    deferral, blended method, 181
    estate planning and, 91–96
    exemptions, 119–20
    income in respect to decedent, 139–40, 181
    individual stock, 166
    investment, 192–93
    life insurance, 198, 204–5
    mandatory withholding, 138–39
    mutual fund, 125–27, 165, 178–79
    Social Security benefits, 134–38
    variable annuity, 178–82
Tax law changes, 28
Taxpayer Relief Act of 1997, 124
Tax payment, 78
Tax-qualified policy, 64–65, 70
Tax Reform Act of 1976, 91
Tax-related powers, 46
Tax-sheltered annuity plans, 84
Tax subsidy, 121
Tax table, 119
Tax trust, 98–100
Technical analysis, 166–67
Telecommunication companies, 159
Telecommunications sector, 159
Ten pay programs, 68–69
Term life insurance, 200–203, 210
Terminal illness, 210–11
Testamentary property, 145
Testamentary trust, 77, 87
Thirdparty notification, 69
Time horizon, 4–5, 30, 184–85
Totten Trust Provision, 84
Transferor, 88
Transfer upon death instruction, 84
Treasury, Department of. *See* United States Treasury
Treasury bills, 7
Treasury bonds, 7–9
Treasury notes, 7
Trust, 77
    A-B provision, 97–100, 144, 208
    as beneficiary, 109–10
    bypass, 98–100, 111, 144
    declaration of, 89
    domestic, 101
    family, 98–100
    flexibility of, 89
    irrevocable. *See* Irrevocable trust
    living, 47, 52, 86–91, 202
    marital, 98–100
    Medicaid, 58, 73
    property transfer through, 86
    step-up basis, 87
    testamentary, 87
    wealth replacement, 108

Trustee, 88
Trustor, 88
Turnover rate, 178
12b-1 distribution fees, 154, 155–56

U

Umbrella policy, 29
Unified estate and gift tax, 91
Unified tax credit, 94–95, 96
    failure to use, 144
    life insurance and, 103
    power to disclaim, 110
    preservation of, 98–100
Uniform Gift to Minors Act, 85–86
Uniform Transfer to Minors Act, 77,
    85–86
United Parcel Service, 188
United States Treasury, 7–9, 130, 173
Unit investment trust, 157–64
Universal life plans, 199–200

Unlimited marital deduction, 92,
    97–101, 209
Up-front costs, 30
Up-front sales charges, 156

V

Value fund, 154
Value Line target strategy, 162–63,
    165, 166
Variable annuity, 72, 132–33
    annuitization value, 176, 177
    death benefit, 174–76, 195
    early withdrawals, 181
    exchanges, 182
    living benefits, 176–77
    mutual fund comparison, 179–80
    performance, 177–78
    subaccount, 177–78
    surrender charge, 182
    tax-deferred, 173–74
    tax issues, 178–82

Variable life insurance, 205
Variable universal life policy, 203
Viatical settlement, 211–12
Volatility, 191

W

Waivers, 69
Wash loan provision, 204
Wealth, redistribution of, 91–92
Wealth replacement trust, 108
Whole life insurance, 197, 198
Will, 43, 96–97, 202
    death without, 79–80
    pour over, 90
    probate process, 78–79
    state residency, 80–81
    substitutes, 81
Withdrawal penalties, 29, 30, 140–41
Wrap accounts, 156
Written agreements, 23, 29

The 8 Biggest Mistakes People Make with Their Finances Before and After Retirement

For special discounts on 20 or more copies of *The 8 Biggest Mistakes People Make with Their Finances Before and After Retirement*, please call Dearborn Trade Special Sales at 800-621-9621, ext. 4364.

Dearborn™
Trade Publishing
A **Kaplan Professional** Company